# Travels in The North of Germany.

# Part 2

## Updated and annotated version

# Travels in The North of Germany.
## Part 2

Being Volume Four
of The Collected Works of
**Thomas Hodgskin**

Edited and Annotated by

Dr. Fred Day[1]

---

# Praescientia Press

## "For Science and for Art"

This paperback edition first published in 2019
by Praescientia Press
© Frederick George Day 2019
The moral right of the author has been asserted.
All right reserved. Without limiting the rights under copyright reserved
above, no part of this publication may be reproduced, stored or introduced
into a retrieval system, or transmitted, in any form or by any means
(electronic, mechanical, photocopying, recording, or otherwise) without the
prior written permission of both the copyright owner and the above
publisher of this book.
ISBN: 9781073316779

# The Collected Works of Thomas Hodgskin

# Table of Contents.

# Editor's Notes on the Textual Content

Early 19th century writing, if Hodgskin is an example, suffered from a number of structural complications. The sentences were very long by modern standards, often with many sub-clauses. These convoluted sentence structures necessitated the copious use of commas, as well as semi and full colons. Semi-colons often got used where we would use commas today, and full colons were sometimes, albeit rarely, used as full stops (periods). These extensive structures could lead to sentences of up to 200 words. Such long sentences inevitably resulted in lengthy paragraphs that could, in extreme cases, last for a number of pages.

Where it has been felt appropriate, these issues have been addressed editorially, in favour of a more modern eye.

In addition to these difficulties, there are not only spelling differences with modern wordage, but also inconsistencies of spelling. For example, in Hodgskin's day, "show" and "shown" were "shew" and "shewn"; "control" was "controul". Words that today appear suffixed with "thing", e.g. "everything" were often shown as two separate words, i.e. "Every thing". Such variances as these are merely presentational, and have been according addressed herein.

Hodgskin's original footnotes have been reproduced, suitably identified. Additional editorial (explanatory) footnotes have also been added where necessary and hopefully useful. References, sometimes lacking from the original sources have been provided where possible, to enhance readers' understanding and experience of the material. It is hoped, that these editorial enhancements do not prove too distracting for literal purists.

It is also intended that the content and natural of the material covered in this volume will illustrate for its reader, the character of the concerns that not only preoccupied Hodgskin but also the wider literary classes, during the formative years preceding his main economic writings.

The original errata from the 1820 edition has not been reproduced as the necessary corrections have been made within the corrected text. Footnotes appropriately mark where such changes have been made.

Errors in the original Index have been corrected.

# Travels in Germany.

## Chapter I.

## Courts for the Administration of Justice.

Property the foundation of the right to administer justice. – Patrimonial courts. – Justice chanceries. – Appointments of judges. – Salaries. – Chief court of appeal. – An example of tolerance. – Curious distinction. – High reputation of this court. – Advocates. – Regulations concerning. – Effect of public pleading on their importance.

The French introduced the code Napoleon, and their own forms of procedure, into Hannover. They swept away the whole of the ancient institutions for the administration of justice, but they did not possess the country long enough to conquer the habits of the people, and, with some few amendments, the ancient methods are again fully established. The present tribunals may be conveniently described as patrimonial courts, justice chanceries, and the court of appeal.

Both the administration of justice, and the power of declaring what justice ought to be, or the whole of the legislative and judicial functions, were in most European countries, at a period antecedent to the present, considered as the attribute of property. Many of the regulations now imposed on us as the will of the society, were originally the regulations of lords for their slaves; and in their origin some of the highly honoured laws of Europe may be compared to the slave-codes of the West Indies.

This state of things still in some measure exists in Hannover. The possessors of certain properties have the power of administering justice within their limits, and they appoint all the persons connected with the administration of justice. Courts constituted by their authority are called patrimonial courts. It is by virtue of the right of property that the monarch appoints his amtmen, who being officers for the administration of justice, amts[2] are

---

[2] [**Editor's F/N:-** Amtmen were officials in Germany that acted within an

considered as patrimonial courts. The jurisdiction of town magistrates was confined to the land which belonged to the town, or which was under its immediate protection, and they possessed this jurisdiction by virtue of the right of property. Towns, therefore, are also patrimonial courts. Hannover itself presents an illustration of this truth. It is divided into two parts, the land on which one is built belongs to the town magistracy, and is under its jurisdiction; the land on which the other is built belongs to the sovereign, and is placed under a person appointed by him. I do not know the number of patrimonial courts belonging to individual noblemen which yet remain in Hannover, but at present the number is not considerable. The royal amts amount to at least 160.

Patrimonial courts are distinguished by some of them having jurisdiction in civil suits only, while others have both civil and criminal jurisdiction. This difference is not a consequence of these courts belonging to individuals, or to the monarch; it seems to have been introduced by chance, and to have been established by custom. There are at least twenty towns with tribunals possessing full powers, and there are at least two courts belonging to noblemen, those of Hardenberg and Adelepsen, which also possess them. A committee of the states which was appointed to inquire into the administration of justice, recommended the separation of all criminal jurisdiction from the patrimonial courts, which are the property of individuals; but owing, I believe, to the power of the individuals, this recommendation has not yet been complied with.

The magistracy of the towns has been described in the chapter on Government. The members of patrimonial tribunals are appointed by the proprietors. They must be persons properly educated, and, in general, they must be approved of by the Crown. Each of these tribunals consists at least of a judge, with two assistants, who bear the title of secretaries, or assessors. Many of them employ several more assistants. Formerly these judges presided in some instances over two courts, which afforded them an opportunity, by multiplying the acts of both courts, to increase their emoluments at the expence of the unhappy suitors. They were sometimes also advocates by other tribunals; and on the borders of two countries, they sometimes, till they were forbid, served two different masters.

There are at least three educated jurisconsults, distinguished as amtmen, assessors, and secretaries, at each of the one hundred and sixty amts mentioned, so that the persons of this profession

---

Amt (an administrative area) in a manner similar to a modern bailiff.]

employed in the minor tribunals may be considered as extremely numerous. The amtman frequently unites a great deal of power in his own hands by being at the same time the tenant of the royal property within his district. In this the tithes, and a right to a certain portion of the labour of the peasants, is frequently included. He has also the superintendence of roads and bridges, in short, all the powers of the proprietor, of government, of the administration of justice, and of the police within his district. The persons living under him may certainly apply to superior courts if he oppress them, but, as far as the peasantry are concerned, this must be out of their power from poverty, and over them he is completely the lord. The amtmen sometimes live very splendidly, and when they happen to dwell in some old monastery, or ancient baron's castle, they seem not imperfectly to represent the feudal nobility. They possess all their consequence without their pride, independence, or ferocity. Among their other duties, I must not forget to enumerate, that they are ordered frequently to visit the inns, in order to see if the guests have good food and drink provided for them. They have also to see that no more of the land occupied by the peasant is ploughed than he is allowed to plough by his contract.[3] This is surely, therefore, a most benevolent government, which takes such care of its subjects' palates and health, and which so carefully limits their exertions.

The union of the administration of the royal property with the administration of justice, has long been a matter of complaint, and probably of serious inconvenience. It is, however, common in Germany, though, in some of the countries, in Brunswick for example, the two are separated. Absurd as the union appears, if the separation is to make two offices where one only now exists, it must rather be considered as an evil than as a good. The whole of these functionaries are said to have borne their power so meekly, that it is doubtful if the evil of multiplying offices should be incurred for the advantages of the separation. The best way to affect it would be, to sell or let the domains as if they were private property.

All these minor officers of justice are principally paid by fees, which are regulated according to law. Magistrates of towns have also salaries. But it is unwisely made the interest of all these gentlemen to increase law-suits, and thus increase their emoluments.

Since the restoration of Hannover to its former masters, many minor patrimonial courts have been abolished. The French had also

---

[3] **Hodgkin's F/N:-** Amts Ordnung.
[**Editor's F/N:-** Ordnung is a German word for "order".]

abolished them, but it is only now that it can be said that they are abolished never again to be revived. It is curious to read of courts whose power was confined to single houses, or by the marks made by the water as it dropped from their roofs. There were many other similar ones, with uncouth untranslatable names, and they prove completely how utterly ignorant our ancestors were of what we call order and good police. In all the alterations which have been made, it is evident that power is leaving the nobles, and concentrating itself in the hands of the sovereign.

In all the former practices, a state of society may be traced, in which power and government were founded on no views of general good, but on individual strength. He who was stronger than his neighbours usurped authority over them, and he established his power for the gratification of his own lusts. The general good of a former period could only mean the good of a part of those inhabitants who now form the different kingdoms of Europe. As conquest and usurpation went forward, − as the ambition of governing was more extensively gratified − the terms general good were extended from the castle of the noble to the neighbouring villages and towns, and at length they were applied to provinces and nations. The powers of modern governments were originally ill-acquired, and, from being concentrated in the hands of few sovereigns, they have now become an enormous evil. Its very enormity, however, makes it more visible, and we may hope for its limitation from the doubts and alarm it will excite.

Most of the patrimonial courts possessing jurisdiction in criminal cases have a curious method of examining or trying prisoners, without passing sentence on them. Many of the magistrates of the minor courts are ordered to send all the acts, as the papers relative to processes are called, to some superior court, for its judgment. And the magistrates of the towns, who are not obliged, very frequently send the acts both of civil and criminal processes to some superior tribunal, or to the members of the faculty of jurisprudence, at some university, who pronounce the judgment. The examinator and the judge are, in such cases, different persons, and none of those passions which are so likely to be occasioned in the examining judge, by the obstinacy, impertinence, or independence, of the persons examined, can have any influence on the judge who pronounces the sentence. He may be deceived by the reports of the examining judge, but he has the power, if he suspects anything wrong, to send the acts back to be revised. The examiner may give to the evidence the colour of his own kindness or malignity, but the operation of either of these dispositions is easily detected.

The judge, therefore, pronounces according to the facts presented to him, independent of all other sympathies than those occasioned by his preformed moral opinions, and so far as these facts are correctly stated, his judgment is likely to be correct. By the acts of one tribunal being thus exposed to the inspection of another, a sort of publicity, though far from the best sort of publicity, is given to the proceedings of courts, which produces, in a small degree, motives for honesty. On the other hand, as distant judges share with the examiner the responsibility of ordering the punishment, he may sometimes be tempted to be careless or unjust.

I am not quite sure that it is right to condemn a man to punishment after an examination of a written statement of facts, and without being guided by sympathy or antipathy. In a personal examination there are many little circumstances of voice and manner, which have a powerful effect on determining our opinions as to guilt or innocence. These are part of the materials of an accurate judgment, and of all these the distant judge must be entirely ignorant. There is a consciousness of innocence or of guilt, which lives in the eye or speaks in the voice of every man; there is a nobility of thought, whose simple utterance commands belief; and there is a baseness of mind which deprives all words of any power of conviction. These the sentencing judge should see and hear, for it is on his conscience the weight of a conviction, or the joy of an acquittal, rests. A man may be capable of convincing his judge by one emphatic word; but this power is denied to every prisoner who is sentenced by judges whom he never saw.

The law also hurls its vengeance against certain specified actions, the guilt of which was determined, perhaps, by the sympathies of law-makers who lived some ages ago. But guilt or innocence is something different from a visible or tangible action. A rifleman of an army coolly selects his victim, and kills him, but he does not commit murder. An individual who shoots his deadliest foe, the despoiler of his fortunes, or the defiler of his bed, though he have been ten thousand times more injured than the rifleman, commits murder. The law, that is, the sympathies and opinions of perhaps barbarous legislators, condemns him to expiate with his life the act which he has committed.

I shall not decide if he or the man who kills his fellow-men for sixpence per day be most guilty; but from this example, it is clear that guilt is perfectly independent of any visible action. And a judge who pronounces on mere facts, who condemns any man because he has done a certain action, inflicts on that action all the pain which the antipathy of the legislator appropriated to guilt.

There are seven superior tribunals, called Royal Justice Chanceries; one is situated in the town of Hannover; one at Celle; one at Göttingen; one at Stade; one at Osnabrück; one at Hildesheim; and one at Aurich, in East Friezland. Each one of these chanceries has a director, and six or seven persons called justice-councillors, who are the judges, with a proportionate quantity of auditors, secretaries, assessors, taxators, clerks, and persons bearing other titles, to the amount of thirty persons for the worst provided, and fifty for the best provided court.

The jurisdiction of each of these courts extends over several provinces, but it does not extend equally to all persons. Thus, the magistracy of the town of Hannover, with the exception of the bürgermeisters, are amenable only to the town tribunals. The members of the chief court of appeal at Celle, with their domestics, children, wives, and widows, so long as they remain at Celle, are amenable only to this tribunal, with sundry other similar exceptions.

These courts are, of the first instance, for certain persons, such as all their own members, of whatever rank, for noblemen, for clergymen, for both the actual and titular servants of the crown, and also for some persons who, being under the jurisdiction of some inferior court, have obtained the special privilege of having these as courts of first instance. They are courts of second instance, or of appeal, to persons to whom the amts towns and private patrimonial courts are courts of first instance. Such distinctions are very strange. They appear to suppose that the inferior tribunals are only capable of administering justice to inferior persons. By the members of the various courts being subjected to these courts only, and by the jurisdiction of certain courts being obtained as a favour, it seems as if partiality, or something more than justice, were to be obtained for particular persons.

There are some reasons, however, to believe, though this practice may now be perverted, that it had its origin in a principle which was once common to all Germany, and somewhat analogous to that great axiom of the English law, that every man should be tried by his peers; at least, that no man should be tried by persons of rank inferior to his own.[4]

---

[4] **Hodgskin's F/N:-** See Pütter, Vol. I. 210, 211, for a proof that this principle was general, and that something analogous to juries were known in all parts of Germany.
[**Editor's F/N:-** From notes in part 1 of TNG we can presume Hodgskin is here referring to: Johann Stephan Pütter (1725 − 1807) − Historical Development (1787). Full title = Historische Entwickelung der heutigen Staatsverfassung des Deutschen Reichs (Historical Development of the

From the great many tribunals which there are in the kingdom, and from this difference in their jurisdiction, there is great uncertainty to which court a person must apply. In the town of Göttingen, for example, which contains 12,000 in habitants, there are eight different tribunals, including those of the university as one. The jurisdiction of each of these tribunals is not only limited by place, but also by the condition of the parties, and the nature of the offence committed, or the value of the thing in dispute. All these distinctions must be accurately known, before an action can be brought, or a prosecution commenced; or the court will declare its incompetence; or, being incompetent, if it gives judgment, its incompetence is a reason for appeal, which will be sure to render the judgment invalid.

The director and all the councillors of the justice chanceries are nominated by the ministry and confirmed by the king. Advocates do not rise to these situations. The councillors or judges are taken, in general, according to seniority, from what are called the auditors, who are young men of good or noble families, who study jurisprudence expressly to fill these situations, and who have little else to do till they receive the place of judge, but to attend to what is done by the judges. The auditors also are nominated by the ministers and confirmed by the king. They are examined by the director and the whole of the bench, both when they are made auditors and when they are made judges.

The college or chancery in general divides itself into two parts, for the quicker dispatch of business; and from this circumstance, and the number of courts, the auditors and the judges have very little to do. Instead of being grave men, dignified by great wigs and silken gowns, they are some of the gayest young men of the whole country. The director of the justice chancery of Hannover, who may be considered as one of the dignitaries of the law, dined regularly every day at a tavern, where the price of dinner was about 1s. 8d. without wine, and 2s. 9d. with. He went regularly to some public garden to drink his afternoon's coffee, and passed his evenings at a public place, playing ombre[5] or whist. There is a great difference between such a person and an English judge. If the latter have more wealth, more stately vigour of mind, and a greater dignity than the former, he has fewer of the light and amiable pleasures of life.

---

present state constitution of the German Reich).]
[5] **Editors F/N:-** Ombre was a three-handed trick taking card game in which a single player (known as Ombre or l'Hombre (the man), played against his two opponents. The game was originally played with a Spanish style forty-card deck with suits of coins and cups (round) and swords and clubs (long).

An Hannoverian judge has in truth so little to do with professional duties, and so much with the amusements of society, that he has every appearance of being a perfect man of the world. He bears no distinctive professional marks.

The settled salaries of the directors and of the councillors of justice are said to amount to 1,200 or 1,500 Thalers per year, – from £200 to £500. They have also fees, the amount of which cannot be known. They are generally considered as holding their places for life, unless they are promoted. One instance has been mentioned of a judge being removed at the will of the sovereign. Several of the judges enjoy other situations under the government. Some of them, indeed, such as superintendent of a theatre, seem to be incompatible with the dignity of a judge. From this circumstance it is correct to assert, that the judges are dependent on the crown. If the country be to have political liberty, the perfect independence of these gentlemen should be one of the first things insisted on.

The chief court of appeal, situated at Celle in the province of Lüneburg, was first established in 1713. Till August 1818, it was composed of a president and fourteen chief councillors of appeal, as judges. At that time four more councillors or judges were added, and two vice-presidents. It now, therefore, consists of one president, two vice-presidents, and eighteen judges, with a proportionate quantity of secretaries, clerks, procurors, and other subordinate persons. The reason as signed for the addition to the number of judges, was the increase of business which the court was likely to have, from the territories of Hannover being so much increased. One of the additional councillors was said to be for Friezland, one for Hildesheim, one for Osnabrück, and one for the other little spots which have lately rounded the territories of Hannover.

The greater part of the inhabitants of Hilde sheim and Osnabrück are Catholics, and those of Friezland are Calvinists. It was therefore wisely declared, with regard to religious toleration, that these new members might be Catholics or Calvinists. And as the right of presentation to the new places was at the same time conceded to the states of these provinces, the declaration would not remain a dead letter. It was not mere words which the sovereign could follow or not as he pleased. The king of Hannover has no spiritual councillors with large revenues. Neither bishops nor archbishops have access to the royal ear, and influence on the royal conscience; and he is much more tolerant than the king of Great Britain. Though he be a Protestant monarch, and his subjects chiefly Protestants, he admits Catholics to be members of the highest court of appeal in his kingdom; and he sets an example of treating his subjects equally, without any regard to their religious persuasion, which is worthy of the imitation of the monarch of England.

The tenderness of the royal conscience has often been made the excuse for withholding from the Catholics of Great Britain some of their rights as subjects of the empire. But the same tenderness is not felt in the much more beloved kingdom of Hannover. This, therefore, must be considered as the mere excuse which interested men have made to cover their own bigotry.

A portion of the members of this court, six, with the three presidents, are appointed by the sovereign ; the other twelve are appointed by the states. This practice was once general in Germany. For example, the members of the celebrated Cammer Gericht, which was a court for the whole empire, were partly appointed by the emperor, and partly by the states of the empire, who were, however, in this case the electors, and other sovereign princes. The reason assigned for this was, that members might be named out of every province, who were acquainted with the local laws. Another feature common to all the courts of justice in Germany may be traced in the former constitution of this one. -

It is composed of two distinct banks of judges, a bank of nobles, and a bank of learned men; and formerly the youngest noble member preceded in rank the oldest learned member. When a part of them met in a committee, without the presence of the usual president or vice-president, the youngest noble member assumed the temporary presidency before the eldest of the learned members. It is an evidence of improvement, that by the regulations of August 1818, this superiority of the nobles, which has been long complained of, was abolished. In all matters of business, the eldest learned member now follows the eldest noble member, and in committees, the eldest member present, whether noble or learned, is the president.

Notwithstanding this distinction of noble and learned members, the nobles are also learned; that is, they study jurisprudence; and when they are appointed councillors of this court, they are examined by the other members, and are obliged to give a proof of their ability to fill the office, by drawing up a legal argument on some particular case. These judges are, both from situation and birth, men of distinction in society. Even the learned members are generally men of privileged families, and they often possess sufficient influence to bequeath their office to one of their sons. The judges from the minor tribunals, and the auditors of this court, are the persons from amongst whom the judges of the chief court are selected.

Its title explains most of its duties. It is the last court of appeal for causes sent from the other courts. It is a court of the first instance for all the members of the court, for parties that live, and for properties that lie in different provinces, which are subject to different jurisdictions, and it is a court of first instance in all cases where a jurisdiction is doubtful. It is a court of appeal both in civil and criminal causes, and it has a criminal jurisdiction over the persons to whom it is a court of first instance. It has the inspection of all the minor tribunals of the kingdom, and the examination of persons who, after a due course of study, wish to practise as advocates. It is necessary for all the advocates to undergo this examination, and to have the permission of this or some other court before they can practise. On questions of great importance, the whole court are called on for their opinion. Generally, however, it carries on business by means of three committees, each of which has a president. Some particular member is appointed to examine the written acts of every case, and report on them. In fact, with all the multitude of judges, the judgment is more generally the result of the investigations carried on by one person, than by several.

The salaries of the members are said to be 1,500 to 1,800 Thalers, or from £250 to £300 per year, exclusive of fees, whose amount is totally unknown, but everyone is regulated by laws. The persons connected with the law, who are said to make most money, are called cancellisten, and their duty consists chiefly in clerkship.

The reputation of this court for impartiality is very great. George the Second expressed his surprise to one of his friends, that he lost all his causes in this court. "Sire," was the reply, "the reason is obvious;- your Majesty is always in the wrong." Nor is its reputation now diminished. There was a dispute between the government of Hannover and some of its subjects, relative to some domanial property which had been sold during the French government. They recently petitioned the diet at Frankfort, that the question might be decided by a court of law ; and if their petition were granted, they declared they selected his Majesty's court of appeal at Celle, as the one to which they wished the question might be referred. The members are bound, in cases in which the crown is concerned, to do justice with impartiality, without regard to anybody but God; and they have generally so well preserved their character, that the court has obtained the honourable name of the *Doomsday Court*. The expression is more applicable in the German than in the English language, because *our day* of judgment is expressed in that language by words signifying the last court, *Dasjungste Gericht*.[6] And it is this name which is given to the court of appeal.

Such are the courts, and such the judges appointed in Hannover to administer justice. They may be taken as a model of the courts of other parts of Germany. Each country has its subordinate courts and its court of appeal, each of which is composed of many members. In all a due regard to subordination may be traced, and in all, the same form, that of a college, as a body of judges are called, exists. This is a distinctive mark of the institutions of Germany. It is a sign of the influence of a sect, and of the want of influence on the part of the people.

The college form of the different courts is very much praised, as leading to more accurate judgments. The matter in all its "bearings," it is said, "is discussed by the different members, and the opinions or judgments of a majority, which are so much better than the opinions of one person, decide." The maxim is true, but it is not clear that it is followed in these courts. To me it appears, that the reporter is the only judge; and all the ends here proposed are much better obtained by public examinations, public pleadings, and trial by jury. When the administration of justice in our own country is compared with that of other countries, it seems as if one excellence of the trial by jury is its natural tendency to make justice cheap to the community.

That justice is not cheap in Great Britain, arises from other causes than the institution of juries; and certainly, this evil would not be remedied by the appointment of a multitude of judges with fees, when it is because a *few* at present have *fees*, that justice is so extravagant.

The whole of the sittings of the judges are held in such secrecy, that even persons having business with them, such as advocates, are not allowed to enter their room without being previously announced, and without having obtained permission. No more of their proceedings than the judgments which they deliver, and the executions which they order, are known to the public. With this permission to do wrong, there is, perhaps, no land where the character of all the superior functionaries employed in administering justice is more unsullied than in this. I have suggested to persons who were in many particulars hostile to these functionaries, that it would be easy to bribe them. "True," was the reply, "but they are all too honest to allow themselves to be bribed." A similar opinion of their virtue is generally entertained. This sort of union between

---

[6] **Editor's F/N:-** *Dasjungste Gericht* translates as *The Last Judgement.*

permission to do ill, and abstaining from doing it, is a very anomalous feature in the character of persons enjoying power, and it does vast honour to the individuals. Its causes may probably be discovered in the general good education and manners, and in the peaceful enjoyment of superiority which the members derive from their situation, without being eternally goaded by a desire to obtain the distinction which is in other countries more exclusively given to wealth.

The advocates, who are generally at the same time notaries, are obliged to study jurisprudence at some university, for three years; but this term, provided they have before studied any other branch of science, and have afterwards diligently devoted themselves to jurisprudence, may be shortened to them. With certificates of three years' attendance and industry, the young man announces himself to some one of the tribunals, generally to the chief court of appeal at Celle, which examines him, and allows him to matriculate, and practise as an advocate, if he be found qualified. Advocates are directed to be conscientious men; and to make them so, they are threatened in all cases of bad behaviour with punishment. They are commanded to begin no suit of whose justice they are not convinced, and to cease the pleadings at any time in the course of it, if they discover that the cause is unjust. They may be fined at the discretion of the judges, for contravening these rules, or for bringing frivolous appeals. They are commanded to promote the settlement of disputes, by arbitration, to speak of the magistrates with respect, and to treat their opponents with politeness.

They are very moderately paid, though the regulations which fix the amount of their fees are not rigidly attended to. One or two of them in Hannover are, comparatively, opulent men; but as a body, the advocates of Germany do not possess the same rank, and the same political influence, as the advocates of Britain. The influence of the sect arises from the number of educated lawyers who are magistrates, and who fill situations under government, but to which the professional advocate rarely aspires, and which he rarely obtains.

Their want of political influence may be in some measure owing to their numbers, which may have made the whole too cheap. There are fifty for the little town of Hannover, and a proportionate number for all the other towns in which a justice chancery is situated. A quantity also are scattered through the country, sometimes pleading before the amtman, sometimes filling, as magistrates of some of the smaller towns, the two offices of advocate and judge. Another reason probably is, that there are very few higher situations open to them. They may become secretaries to the magistracy of the larger towns; they may even become bürgermeisters, but this is rare; and all the higher places are possessed and almost hereditarily enjoyed by families, no member of which ever engages in the business of an advocate.

There can be no doubt that much of the importance of the counsellors or advocates in our country arises from public pleading, by which they embody themselves with the interests of the people, and make themselves so well known, that they are afterwards selected to fill offices of political importance. The advocates of France, like the advocates of Germany, were also an insignificant race of people till the Revolution and public pleadings brought them into notice, and gave them political importance. We cannot hesitate, therefore, to ascribe the want of importance of the professional advocates of Germany chiefly to the want in that country of all public pleading.

The order which has been mentioned above for the advocates of Hannover, to treat each other in their writings with politeness and respect, and the want of public pleading, do not allow that brow beating of witnesses, – that scandalous aspersion of private character; and that vile abuse which the gentlemen of the English bar sometimes heap on their unfortunate victims, and which is very often urged by foreigners as a great national reproach to us. In speaking with a German gentleman, who had been long in England, on the value of the two different modes of procedure, the secret one of Germany or the public one of England, most of his objections to our mode rested on the vituperation our barristers allow themselves to use. Noman's character, he said, was safe from their attacks if it were for the interest of their clients to traduce it. A virtuous and a retired man might be dragged as an evidence to a court of law, or be compelled to appear as a prosecutor, and must submit to that mental torture which may be there inflicted, and which is possibly not inferior to the thumb-screws or the parchment boot of more arbitrary tribunals. If these gentlemen have any regard for their own interest, they should be careful how they bring discredit on their own profession, and how they bring the practice of public pleading into disrepute; for they may be assured, when they lose the countenance of the public, they will sink into that same degree of dependant insignificance which is common to advocates in other parts of Europe.

# Chapter II.

## Hannover – Civil - Laws and Processes.

*No civil code. – Different laws. – Dissimilarity between civil and criminal process. – Civil process described. – Great length. – Difference of opinion as to codes of law. – Opinions of Savigny and Thibaut.*

In Hannover, so well as in England, there is no regular code of civil law, and its place is in some measure supplied, in both countries, by similar expedients. In the former country there are, and have been for many years, sorts of statuary laws made by the sovereign and the states conjointly; and, although the rescripts of the sovereign bear not the name of laws, yet, in their actual effects, they may be so considered. Some property is still held by feudal tenures; some by a tenure corresponding to our copy-hold; and some land is absolutely free. Because at one time each province was an independent power, each one has different statuary laws; and because the greater part of the towns were in like manner independent, because, in fact, each nobleman was a sovereign, the provinces, the towns, the villages, and even separate properties, are all subjected to different laws and customs. When neither these, nor the statuary laws, nor the customs of the province, dictate what is to be done in matters of dispute, the jurisconsults apply to the law of Rome, and regulate their decisions by its precepts.

It will be easy for the reader to conceive the perplexity, complication, and confusion, which must necessarily ensue by mixing such dissimilar institutions as the ancient laws and customs of the almost barbarous, yet free inhabitants of the north of Germany, with the regulations of the polished, effeminate, and degraded inhabitants of the south of Italy. It will be easily conceived, also, what a quantity of power it must give the interpreters of the laws, that those by which they endeavour to regulate all the others, are written in a language which is not the language of the people.

Laws, instead of being what Judge Blackstone has defined them, "a rule of conduct," a beacon to direct us, are everywhere a trap for the unwary, an instrument employed by a particular class to enrich themselves at the expence of other men. It is impossible to describe these laws accurately without describing them minutely, and therefore nothing further will here be said of them.[7]

In England civil and criminal processes are both very much alike. In both it is required to establish a fact, and in both it is done by an examination of such evidence as each party can bring to support his plea. The names and the first steps of the process are different, but whatever has any influence on the finding of the jury, is in both substantially the same. In Germany they are different from one another, and the manner of conducting both is different in the different countries, and even in the different provinces of Hannover. Causes of small value, that is, not exceeding £2, brought before the minor tribunals, and having nothing very intricate in them, may be pleaded by speaking. Then, however, no persons are admitted but the advocates and the parties, so that publicity of judicial proceedings, except that sort of publicity before mentioned, is unknown.

When a person thinks he has a just cause of complaint against any other person, he applies to a regular advocate, and makes his complaint known to him. The advocate sifts, or ought to sift, the complaint to the bottom, – ought to hear what the man has to say, and what his witnesses have to say. When he has done this and ascertained to what court the jurisdiction of the particular case belongs, he writes a petition to this court to grant him what he supposes just. In this petition, a duplicate of which must be given into court, the facts of the case are to be stated, the nature of the proof to be brought hinted at, the instruments which relate to the claims, either in the original or copies of them, must be subjoined, and the remedy prayed for must be distinctly stated.

Some courts have ordered, – for judges are allowed, in Germany as in England, to prescribe the conditions on which they will administer justice, – that each of these petitions shall relate to one point only. Consequently, when there are more points than one in dispute, either of law or of fact, a different petition must be written on each one.

---

[7] **Editor's F/N:-** Here we have a prime example of Hodgskin's early connection of Law with Power and with Class relations.

Judge Blackstone is a reference to William Blackstone (1723-1780), whose *Commentaries on the Laws of England* (1765-70) was influential in 18th century Law but was subject to later criticism by Bentham (in his *A Fragment on Government* (1776)) and James Mill; both of whom Hodgskin eventually came to opposed in terms of legal and political theory. It would seem here that Hodgskin siding with Blackstone against Bentham.

Other courts, again, – and this is now the general rule, – allow more points than one when the things litigated are not of great value, and the parties concerned are the same, to be mentioned in one petition. When the petitions also are made by conjoined persons, and when more than one person are complained of, they are now allowed to compress their complaint in one paper. The order to make more than one petition, shows the influence which jurisconsults have had, and the manner they have been disposed to employ it. Such an order could only have been made for the purpose of increasing their emoluments.

The judges privately examine this first petition, if it contains nothing reprehensible, they note the day on which it was given in, communicate it to the other party, and invite him to reply to it by a certain day. The chief court of appeal allows four weeks, the justice chanceries fourteen days; at the end of which time the answer must be given in. The first reply, called the Exceptions paper, contains the reasons the opposite party has to urge either as to forms, or as to the jurisdiction of the court, why he ought not directly to reply to the accusation.

In general, it prays further time. There are some cases in which the exceptions are thought to make further pleading unnecessary. When this is thought not to be the case, the reply contains some bye-blows at the complaint. The advocate hints at his opponent's inaccuracy, boasts the means he has of shaming him, and skirmishes and makes sham fight with him. The history of the cause may be told, and if victory is certain, the point in dispute may be fairly and clearly stated. The judge has the power of sending back for revisal, or of refusing all petitions which are not dressed according to forms; and if they send one twice back, the point in dispute is taken against the party who fails in form or in elegance of phrase.

In this stage of the process, either party can require the judge to make his opponent find bail to answer the complaint, or to carry on the process. Bonds are required when the parties have no landed property in the province, or they are required to deposit a sum of money, or give such other security as the judges suppose will secure their attendance.

In this stage the judges have a curious power of terminating the cause, they examine it to the bottom, and calling the parties before them, recommend them to compromise it in the manner which seems fit to the judges. If their advice be not followed, and the thing in litigation will not pay the expence of the process, they are allowed to refuse further to hear the cause, and they decide it as they please. This is called suchen die Güte[8], and seems to be complained of by the lawyers as unsystematic. It does not allow them to chase one another through all the labyrinths of a process till they reach a formal decision.

Should the cause not be concluded in this manner, the Exceptions paper is communicated to the complainant, who replies in fourteen days, or a month, according as the cause is before the court of appeal, or one of the justice chanceries. The judge decides on the exceptions, or he communicates the reply to the opponent, who again rejoins in the prescribed time of fourteen days or a month. From these four papers the first judgment may be given. The judge, however, may allow the parties, or call on them, to make further explanations, but no cause is decided from less than these four papers. No others are necessary for a decision, there is no cross-examination of witnesses, no appealing to evidence, and the unhappy clients lose or gain their suit without the pleasure of knowing what is said in their behalf. Every man who raises a process is ignorant why he loses or gains an estate, except he learns it from the favour of his lawyer.

All the papers are written after a regular prescribed manner, and they are all subjected to stamp duties. Ours is not, therefore, the only country in which justice is taxed, and in the same proportion injustice protected.[9]

When the preparatory steps are considered which are necessary to engage a lawyer, to collect evidence, and to write out the complaint; when the time which is allowed an adversary to reply, and the time again demanded before the reply is replied to, and when the time which the judge takes in examining these papers before he can decide, is recollected, it is clear that the shortest possible time in which any process can be completed in Germany is more than two months. And the courts are here always sitting. There are no assizes twice a year in Germany. It is not, however, unusual for the judges, who are subjected to no control, to delay giving their judgment for several weeks or months. A cause is, therefore, seldom terminated with the least possible delay, and with the power of appealing from a first decision, it may last for many years.

---

[8] **Editor's F/N:-** *Suchen die Güte* translates as *Look for the goodness.*

[9] **Hodgskin's F/N:-** See on this subject the masterly and unanswerable work of Jeremy Bentham, Esq., entitled, *A Protest against Law Taxes* [1793].
[**Editor's F/N:-** here we see an example of Hodgskin's initial alignment with some aspects of Bentham's legal ideals.]

The first judgment, also, may be interlocutory or definitive. In the former case, there is some point which requires further elucidation, more documents are necessary, or more evidence is demanded, and the further hearing of the cause is then postponed for many months. When the judgment is definitive, it may then be appealed against, and when at length, after months and years of tedious waiting, a judgment is pronounced, from which there is no appeal, the law allows the execution to be staid in several ways. So tenacious have the judges been of doing everything deliberately, and so fearful of not doing right, that a whole life is not thought too long to keep one case under consideration.

Law suits, when not absolutely endless, can yet be so protracted, when there are any funds to pay the lawyers, as to last the life of man; indeed, more than one process is known, which have lasted more than two or three generations. The interference of society, or rather of a few jurisconsults prostituting its name for their own selfish interest, is in such cases carried to the very climax of absurdity and injustice. They attempt to regulate the disputes of individuals, and points of litigation, that, if men listened only to the voice of right, might be thoroughly sifted and decided in a few hours or days, and that would be so decided but for them, they keep undecided for many years.

The justice of lawyers is but another name for litigation and injustice. et men are told, and what is still more absurd, they can believe, that such practices are for the good of society. What a cumbrous means have legislators here devised for ascertaining what is right. But we may trace in this, as in all their regulations, the influence of a particular class, who have never sought anything beyond their own interest, which they have called the good of society.

On this point, probably, Britain has no model to offer to Germany. Ours, as it has been aptly called, superstitious process, when not positively so bad as that of the Germans, is most wretched, and is much more-worthy of being amended or destroyed than of being imitated. There is a blind faith in other doctrines than the doctrines of religion. Men have long had such a faith in the assertions of lawyers, and they will assuredly continue to suffer under their dominion while they place so much confidence in them.

All the means by which a process can be lengthened, and all the law chicanery which men can invent, are regularly taught at German universities. There are professors who instruct in the art of conducting processes, and who are particular in dwelling on the means of gaining a victory for a bad cause, or of so lengthening it as at least to perplex and ruin an opponent. This is a perversion of the mind, and a teaching of injustice, yet it is denominated science and wisdom. We ought not to wonder that a love of falsehood and chicanery should be common amongst men, while it is thus openly taught and praised.

There is one practice common throughout Germany which deserves mentioning, because it is a substitute, though possibly a bad one, and certainly an expensive one, for that publicity which all honest men should wish to give their transactions. The best security for both parties in all bargains of great value, in extensive contracts, and in mortgages, is to conduct them openly, and in the face of the world; then few men will cheat or be cheated.

In countries where everything is regulated, buying and selling, particularly buying and selling land, must be under the direction of the magistrate. In the towns no house can be sold without his permission, and in the country no land can be disposed of without his knowledge. Buying and selling is, in fact, regulated by laws, and under the direction of the magistrates. At every magistracy, and at every amt, a book is kept, in which every person who possesses landed property within the jurisdiction of the particular magistrate has a leaf to himself, in which his name is written, and his property described; or every person has his own separate book, which is deposited in the custody of the magistrate, and then the name of the person, where he resides, and a description of his property, are inscribed in his book.

According to law, no mortgages on land, and no sales of fixed property are valid, unless they are mentioned either on the leaf or in the books. No person, therefore, can make either a mortgage or a sale without the knowledge of the magistrate, nor without inscribing it here. Before money is lent on mortgage, recourse is always had to these books, or to a certificate signed by the magistrate, of the amount of the incumbrances on the estate. It costs something either to inspect the books, or to procure the certificate. This practice may possibly prevent fraud, which publicity would do equally well, without the expence of feeing the magistrate; but it is another means by which the interference of the government is extended to every concern of individuals. These books are called mortgage books, Hypotheken Bücher, and they are often the subject of regulations and ordinances. Indeed, they are thought one of the most important and wisest parts of the civil policy of Germany.

The evils naturally resulting from such mixed institutions, and from such confused codes of laws as exist in Germany, are acknowledged to be very great; and it may be worthwhile to state, that our intelligent neighbours are making great progress in this arduous field of human inquiries. Austria, Prussia, and Bavaria, have each a new code both of civil and criminal laws; and, during the usurpation of the French, the code Napoleon was introduced into the kingdom of Westphalia.

A whole code of laws, or rather five codes, making together a complete code both of laws and procedure, and written in a language that so many persons could read and understand, made a powerful impression on the Germans. Many of those who could compare it with the unintelligible, voluminous, and mixed laws of their own country, loudly demanded, when circumstances again restored Germany to its former governors, that one code for the whole of the country should be digested and introduced. Some wished for the code Napoleon, with such improvements as were necessary; others, that the most celebrated civilians of Germany should meet together in council, and frame a new code for their country. There arose, however, another party, composed, or at least led, by some of the most celebrated civilians themselves, who, after pointing out a great many errors in all the new codes, came to the conclusion, that there ought to be no codes of civil law.

This party was chiefly led by a Mr. Savigny, professor of law in Berlin, whose work, entitled, Beruf unsrer Zeit für[10] Gesetzgebung,[11] written with a view of supporting the opinion, that there ought to be no written civil code, excited much attention; and by Mr. Hugo, professor at Göttingen,[12] who, in several papers in the Göttingesche gelehrte Anzeigen, supported the same side with much vigour and ingenuity. These gentlemen are two of the most celebrated professors of Germany, and it appears that their writings have had a considerable influence in checking the rage which did exist in Germany for making new and simple codes of laws.

I can give but a faint view of the principal arguments used by this party. They were, that the rights of the different classes of society were never stationary, and that the knowledge of these rights, or the science of right, Rechtswissenchaft, grew with the people

---

[10] **Editor's F/N:-** The word *unsrer* corrected inn accordance with an erratum, from unsere, and likewise *für* for *zur*.

[11] **Editor's F/N:-** Hodgskin was referring to the 1814 pamphlet *Vom Beruf Unserer Zeit Für Gesetzgebung und Rechtswissenschaft* (which literally translates as *From the Profession of our Time for Legislation and Jurisprudence*) which was written by Friedrich Carl von Savigny (1779–1861): a German historian and jurist.

[12] **Editor's F/N:-** Presumably Gustav Hugo (1764-1844), who eventually founded the German Historical School of Jurisprudence.

themselves, and with their progress in civilization. That it was, therefore, wrong to make that a positive law to-day which an improvement in knowledge might hereafter shew to be unjust. That because the opinions of the people as

to right were constantly changing, it was not possible for any written precepts constantly to express those opinions. That as the rights of men in society became more complicated, they required a particular study, and that the persons who made those rights their study, acquired more knowledge on the subject than other individuals, and they might be considered as the legal depositaries of the laws, the representatives of the opinions, and, in truth, the living codes of the society.

Medicine and mathematics, they said, were constantly improving, and so was the science of right, and that it was equally absurd to make codes of medicine and mathematics as to make codes of rights or laws. That, as the former was left to the doctors, the latter should be left to the jurisconsults, who, constantly studying what was right, and constantly improving their decisions, were more to be relied on than codes of laws which only contain the legal knowledge of the age in which they were made.

This was the main principle of their objections, and they supported their arguments by referring to the common law of England, which was rather decisions of judges than a written code. And also, by referring to our acts of parliament, which were described to be decrees suitable to the knowledge of the times, and which constantly improved our laws.

They still further affirmed, that the code, if it were made by several civilians, would assuredly be unequal in its parts, if it were made by one alone, it would assuredly want wisdom, and would fail in giving satisfaction to all parties. They affirmed, that it was impossible men should make a perfect code of laws, and that, therefore, it was better the power of constantly amending the practice of law should remain in the hands of the civilians.

They were perfectly sensible of the great advantages which would result from one set of rules being followed throughout Germany; but they affirmed, that, owing to one system of teaching being followed in most of the universities, owing to the education of all the civilians being the same, to law books being common to the whole country, and owing to the great bases of laws being in all the different countries of Germany the same, this benefit was already in a great measure attained, and would be perfectly attained as the society increased in knowledge of what was right.

There is probably much truth in the arguments which apply to the unfitness of men to make codes of laws, and there is certainly much cunning, or much wisdom, in the civilians claiming, from their studies, a power of deciding on the rights of all men. They openly claim to be the depositaries of the legal knowledge, and the representatives of the opinions of society. The jurisconsults of Germany have long been the possessors of the Roman law, and according to it they have decided questions concerning the property of the Germans. They have studied the quibbles of this law, and with them they have perverted the sense of right among the people. They have been the legal priests, but most assuredly have never been the representatives of the people.

The chiefs of the opposite party were a Mr. Thibaud,[13] professor of civil law in the university at Heidelberg, and a Mr. Feuerbach,[14] who lives, I believe, at Munich, and was employed in making the code for Bavaria. The arguments they principally urged were the uncertainty of the present civil law, from being written in a language that was no longer in common use; that there was no perfect copy of all the Roman laws; and that criticism was unable to supply the defects: they pointed out the possibility of different professors interpreting these codes differently; they expatiated on the confusion which existed; and they enforced the fitness of the season, when all Germany was re-united, to form one code for the whole empire. They did not despair of making a code much better than any which at present exists, and they demanded one as the only security for the rights and property of individuals.

Without pretending to give an opinion on the great point here disputed, whether a written code of civil laws is of itself good or bad, I may be permitted to remark, that the dispute itself is an evidence of the rapid improvement which the Germans are making. Such questions involve the best interests of society, and it can only be from fully discussing them, that these interests can be well protected. Accustomed as we are to hear it constantly held up as a matter of first necessity, that every society should be regulated by laws, our faith is somewhat staggered by the learned disputing on the utility of laws. For unwritten laws can only be considered as vague traditions, and somewhat like no laws at all. To dispute the utility of a written code is assuredly to dispute the utility of laws

---

[13] **Editor's F/N:-** Anton Friedrich Justus Thibaut (1772–1840): a German Jurist and musician.
[14] **Editor's F/N:-** Paul Johann Anselm Ritter von Feuerbach (1775–1833). He was the father of Ludwig Andreas von Feuerbach (1803-1872), whose fame often rests upon Friedrich Engel's *Ludwig Feuerbach and the End of Classical German Philosophy* (1876).

altogether. Yet this is now disputed by some of the most celebrated men in Germany.

Although many individuals who are not professional men have felt interested in this dispute, and although many a wish has been expressed for a new code; for the want of uniformity and simplicity in the present codes is what the great mass of the people complain of ; yet I do not know an instance of any person taking part in it who was not a professional man. Unfortunately, all such questions are decided by what are called learned men; by men intimately acquainted with the pandects and the institutes; by men accustomed to pry after quirks and detect trifling discrepancies, but who are not men of enlarged views, nor much acquainted with the business of life. They are too much educated not to be full of the prejudices of education; and there would be a greater certainty of improvement, if such questions as the one here mentioned were to be decided by men, and not by civilians.

# Chapter III.

## Criminal Laws – Processes and Punishments.

*Criminal code of Hannover – Remarks on it. – Unfitness of the code. – Is not followed in decisions. – What the judges do follow. – Torture abolished. – When last inflicted. – Criminal process secret – Is regulated by the convenience of the judge – Great length of processes. – Fail to instruct the people. – Tribunals formerly public. – Number of persons punished in Hannover in a year – Proportion of females. – Proportion of thefts.-Cruelty of punishments. – Are more humane than formerly. – Few persons punished in Hannover for coining or forgery. – Punishments of the police. – Comparative statement of the number of persons punished in Great Britain and Hannover.*

The only code of criminal laws which exists in Hannover, – if it deserve the name of a code, – is the celebrated Carolina, or Hals, or Peinliche Gerichts Ordnung of the Emperor Charles V. This was formerly the penal code for all Germany. Austria, Prussia, and Bavaria,[15]" have now adopted new codes. As it has long been the chief and only criminal code of the country, it must have had a considerable influence on the manners of the people. It is eminently worthy of remark, however, because it shows clearly how perfectly unfit men formerly were to legislate for the present time. And we may infer from this how perfectly unfit the laws, which the present race of legislators are so eager to make, will be for posterity. There was no monarch of his time who was superior in talents to Charles V. and in making this code he was aided by all the learning and wisdom which Germany then possessed.

In this code crimes are not classified, they are set down as chance has directed. Enchantment is ordered to be punished as

---

[15] **Hodgskin's F/N:-** Weimar and Oldenburg have recently adopted the code of Bavaria.

severely as murder. Minor offences are punished by cutting out the tongue, or cutting off the ears or the fingers, or by some other cruelties. But its chief abominable principle is, that it recommends and recognizes no other means for the discovery of truth but the infliction of the torture. It says, at page 17, as a general rule:

"In cases where it is certain crimes have been committed, if the accused deny his guilt, he shall be compelled to confess the truth by torture, in order that for all well-known crimes the final judgment may be given, and punishment may be executed with the least delay and expence possible."

The torture was not only used when it was certain a crime had been committed, but also when it was only suspected. At p.68, this code says, for one of its particular rules:

"When a female who, on such grounds, – as having been seen with an enlarged body, and having secretly delivered herself – shall be suspected of child-murder, and she shall deny it, she shall be brought to confession by torture, in order that she may be finally judged to death."

We here see distinctly that connection which former legislators supposed to exist between crime and punishment. The former had been committed, and they thought, without any reference to the good of society, it was necessary to inflict the latter. People were to be tortured that their confessions might justify the judges in inflicting punishment. There seems to have been no principle whatever followed, more than a vague motion of some conformity between guilt and burning to death.

The death which was to be inflicted for child murder was drowning, and this was a step towards improvement, for a former custom is mentioned of flaying and burying the criminal alive. That these legislators might not, however, be too humane, it is stated in the same article, that if child-murder is frequent, burying alive and flaying may be used; and, further, that, "with the advice of men knowing in the law, the flesh may be torn from the criminal with burning pincers." Such is the humanity of this law.

We shall, however, be more thoroughly sensible how unfit these men were to legislate, if we at tend for one moment to the nature of that crime which they employed torture to discover, and which they punished with death. At present it is no longer doubted, that society is rather injured than benefited by a number of children being thrown upon it. So far, therefore, as the increase of the society is concerned, it is not injured by infanticide. Though an infant be born alive, a few moments of misery can give it no connection with the world; it can have no knowledge of enjoyment: and if its being be extinguished before it have well existed, it may be doubted if it suffer any injury. How common is the exclamation, that the poor child was well rid of a troublesome world? Neither the child, therefore, nor the society, can be said to suffer by the crime of the mother. But the child is in fact a part of the mother, and might be as great a source of enjoyment to her as the faculty of vision. To deprive herself of a mother's love, and her child of life, is synonymous with doing herself a serious injury.

The state of misery to which a woman in European society must be reduced before she can bring herself to do so foul a deed, gives her a claim to our pity; and it is most cruel to add to her misery, by torturing her to confess what she had done herself so much injury to conceal. Infanticide is a terrible crime, inasmuch as it is a terrible injury to the unhappy mother who commits it; but while it is concealed, it can do the society no injury whatever.

By the very terms of the law in question – by its directing an examination by midwives, and to force a confession by torture, it supposes the crime not to be known, but only suspected. Being unknown, it could have no effect as an example; and the more perfectly it was concealed, the more exclusively did the whole evil belonging to it fall on the unhappy mother. By lawgivers endeavouring to discover such a crime, and by making it known, they spread that horror which men so naturally feel on such an occasion, through a greater number of bosoms, and they inform all those from whom it was most desirable such information should be for ever concealed, that it is possible to commit such a crime, and yet escape punishment.

An idea that they never could have formed, but for the trouble the lawmakers took to discover and inflict punishment on the crime. In this case it is the law itself, it is the meddling of legislators, which in reality causes all the evil which may fall on the society from the conduct of the female. And if the evil which any action causes to the society be the measure of the guilt of that action, legislators are, in such cases as this, far more guilty than the unhappy mothers. From the terms of this law it seems as if legislators delighted in discovering crimes; and they ordered the most horrible torments, to produce a confession that might in their opinions justify the infliction of death.

It must be clear, from the specimens which have been given of this code, and from this one case being so contrary to our present feelings and our modes of thinking, that the legislators of that period were perfectly unfit to dictate the laws which ought at present to govern the world. And surely such an example should teach us, that many of the boasted codes of the present time will appear equally cruel and absurd to posterity. With such specimens of ignorance and failure before us, and how many might be added? it is most strange that we should yet be taught, that legislators are the greatest of human beings, and that to obey and reverence them is one of the greatest virtues.

The Carolina is not only very unsuitable to the present time, but it is also very imperfect; in many cases, therefore, it is not followed; and many others occur for which it prescribes no punishment. In all these cases the judges follow their own good sense. They moderate the punishments which the code orders; they punish many actions not mentioned by it; and in all their judgments they appear to act more according to the present state of knowledge in the society, than according to any fixed rules.

One advantage which has resulted from this is, that infanticide, which the code orders to be so cruelly punished, is punished with imprisonment for a few years. When the crime is only suspected, the torture is no longer employed to force a confession, and the pain of concealing delivery is only further enhanced by confinement for some months. On this point our neighbours are superior in humanity to us. They regard the anguish of the mother as a severe punishment, and no longer imbrue their hands in the blood of the unhappy and guilty wretch who already suffers the penalty which nature inflicts on her crime.

What the judges are taught while they study at the university, and the books which have been written by celebrated professors on criminal jurisprudence, serve to make the judgments of different judges alike; and all of them are therefore guided by some common rules. The professors who lecture at the universities on criminal jurisprudence, explain the present state of knowledge on this subject. They give their own opinions, and the opinions which they have collected from other writers; and these, with the sentences previously pronounced, form that body of knowledge on which the judges act when they condemn any man to punishment.

This is, in fact, a sort of code; but as it has no other authority than that of reason, it is always modified by the private opinions of the professors and of the judges. Hence it is gradually and constantly amended as the society improves in knowledge. The principal work which is at present used as a guide is, "The Principles of Criminal Jurisprudence, by Professor Meister of Göttingen."

There is one evil, however, belonging to this practice, which is perfectly evident. The judges having it in their power to institute investigations not only into acknowledged crimes, but into such actions as they think criminal; having this discretionary power to punish; not being exposed to public censure; and anxious, like all such persons, to prove the value and utility of their ministry, they punish a great number of actions which are regarded in other countries as out of the common jurisdiction of tribunals.

Thus, for example, "a midwife neglecting her duties," " quarrelling with a land-dragoon," "insolence," muthwilligheit, "drunkenness," "not profiting by example," are all crimes pregnant with mischief, but utterly beyond the proper jurisdiction of any tribunal. Much, undoubtedly, of this interference is caused by the judges seeing no other power but their own to check and restrain the conduct of men. The ill health of the drunkard, the loss of practice by the negligent midwife, the constant enmity and quarrels occasioned by insolence, are nothing visible to the judge; and he must see something, or he will not believe any punishment is felt.

From the specimen of improvement which has been mentioned above, however, it seems on the whole to be good that laws should in their execution be thus left to the magistrates, and should thus be constantly modified by the opinions of the day. Possibly these opinions alone would be a better guide than any code which should remain unalterable. It is no bad thing that the writings of clever men are allowed to have all that influence which in Germany is allowed to the instructions of the professors; and this system would be worthy of all praise, provided the trials were all carried on in public, and the judges were more subjected to public opinion. But almost the only point in which civil and criminal processes agree is, that they are both secret.

A great improvement has recently been made in the criminal process of Hannover, by abolishing the torture. The French abolished it, but it was again introduced on the return of the country under the present government. It has since then been several times practised. In the town of Hannover, a man was tortured so late as the month of March 1818. His crime was stealing a cow, and the judges were anxious to make him confess. In 1817, two other persons were tortured in the same place; and in 1818, three other men were tortured in various parts of the kingdom. It was in the month of December 1818 that torture was finally abolished.

The first-mentioned instance of torture excited a great deal of attention in Germany; and there can be no doubt that the reprobation with which it was treated in many public journals was the chief cause why it was afterwards abolished. It may be reckoned as one benefit which has been gained for humanity by men devoting their attention to political subjects. If no others were to follow, this will remain a lasting memorial of the improvement of the Germans in political knowledge. It may be quoted also as proof of the falsity of that perhaps general opinion, that mankind are depraved. The voice of the multitude is generally on the side of humanity.

At the same time that the torture was abolished, some alterations were also said to have been made in the mode of conducting criminal processes; but what they precisely were, is not known. I shall therefore here endeavour to describe the former criminal process, and the reader will be enabled to form some estimate of the effect it has had on the character of the people.

It has before been mentioned what courts have a criminal jurisdiction. One of the first regulations concerning criminal processes is, that the examinations shall never be carried on by one person alone. If there are not two judges belonging to the court, or if from any circumstances one only is able to attend, he must take with him a notary, or an auditor from some other court, or some qualified person, to attend the examination. In cities, and under the chanceries, where the magistracy is numerous, the examining judge must not only be attended by an actuary, but also by two persons called Schoffen or Schoppen.

At present these persons are some of the officers of justice, but originally, they were impartial persons taken to witness that all things were conducted properly. And prior to the introduction of the Roman law, and of secret trials, they seem to have had a vote in the judgment. This is a point in which the forms for the administration of justice have very much deteriorated. The whole of the examination, the questions put, and the answers given, the names and characters of the persons present, and every incident which during the examination may help to prove either the guilt or innocence of the prisoner, must be written by the actuary in a clear legible hand.

Finally, it is ordered, that the person who conducts the examination shall never of his own authority order the torture, or punishment of any kind, to be inflicted. The written examination must first be submitted to other magistrates, who alone can order either punishment or torture. There is reason, however, to believe this latter rule was not always attended to, and that the whip was frequently employed by the examinators of the minor tribunals, as a convenient mode to make the accused give consistent answers.

In case any person is accused by another of having committed a particular crime, the judge examines the life and general conduct of both parties, and the probable motives of the accuser; and he must have reason to believe that the accusation is just, before he subjects the accused to a particular examination.  In cases, however, of public and notorious crimes, the judges in whose district they may have been committed are not to wait till some person is accused, but they are immediately to proceed in what is called a general inquisition.  They examine all the circumstances, visit the spot where the crime was committed, inspect the body, if a person has been murdered, open their ears to any reports against the probable criminal; and when they are satisfied on good grounds that any person is guilty, they subject that person to what is called a special inquisition.

The only protection which the community has in this case against the power of the magistrates is, that they are warned to be cautious in their proceedings, and that if they do any wrong, they  may be punished by a superior court.  One instance of a judge being punished for improper official conduct is known.  But when the committing is also the examining judge, he has such a power to give a colour of probability to the accusation, he can make such a multitude of excuses in his zeal, and the esprit d'corps is so strong in the profession, that the possibility of punishing him if he do wrong is so remote, that it can  afford to the ignorant and poorer classes of the community no protection whatever against his power.  It is at all times of great importance to any community to have a protection against its own servants; but it must now be doubly important to the Germans, when they are beginning to struggle for political freedom, and the judges are the dependant servants of the government. To render the judicial independent of the executive power, to provide some security against the power of the judges, and to have open courts, should be some of the first reforms demanded by the patriots of Germany.

All the circumstances which justify special inquisition justify the arrest of the suspected person.  It is ordered that all the tribunals shall be provided with two prisons – one for security, another for punishment.  It has been expressly forbidden that any one hardship whatever shall be inflicted on the prisoner, which is not necessary to secure him.  If the suspected person be loaded with irons, be shut up in a damp unwholesome dungeon, as he is in England, if he have not "full light and full liberty to read, and pray, and sing," it must be in defiance of very precise orders which have been given on the subject.  Where circumstances allow of kind mess, prisoners intended for trial are not, in fact, subjected to any hardships not necessary for their security,

The liberty of the subject is also protected by the law allowing bail to be put in for the appearance of the person accused, when the crime is not liable to be punished by death, or imprisonment for life. He may either be bailed by people being bound for him, or by his delivering up such a quantity of property as may be thought necessary to ensure his attendance. Even in cases which involve the severest punishment, the Chanceries – have the power, if they think fit, of admitting the accused person to bail. This law is not a dead letter, it is in daily use, though its operation does not extend to persons whom the government might think fit to punish. Allowing bail, however, also depends very much on the will of the magistrate. Though the law prescribes it, he allows it or not as he thinks fit. This custom of bailing is, I believe, confined at present to the north of Germany.

So soon as possible after a person is apprehended on suspicion, the judge is to examine him, to warn him to speak the truth, to threaten him with the torture or horse-whipping, and to ask him if he will confess to have committed the crime of which he is accused. On the first examination nothing further is done. If the accused can bring forward proof of an alibi, or that the accusation is founded in malice, he is allowed to do it in writing, before the expiration of fourteen days. After this period the judges consult their own convenience as to proceeding in the examination. If any circumstances whatever induce them either to delay or to hurry the trial, it is perfectly at their option to choose the time for its further prosecution. The superior courts may be applied to, and may sometimes be prevailed on to order the inferior courts to proceed or stop a trial; but with this exception, the prisoner is entirely at the mercy of his judge.

Prior to further examination, the judge writes out all the questions he means to ask the prisoner; to him, however, they are not communicated, till the judge requires him without his advocate being present to answer them. The apparent aim of most of the questions is, to induce the prisoner to confess his guilt.

The judge has the power of examining such witnesses as he pleases; and before he examines them, the questions he means to ask them are communicated to the prisoner, who has the privilege of suggesting to the judge those questions he may wish asked of the witness. Witnesses may be examined in presence of the accused; and when, from any circumstances, they cannot be brought to the place where he is confined, he may empower some person to attend their examination in his name. When he does not do this, the judge does it for him.

No advocate employed by the prisoner is allowed to suggest to the judge what questions to ask; nor does any other cross-examination of witnesses take place at this time, other than what the judge thinks necessary for the discovery of the truth. If the witnesses have deposed to something denied by the accused, the judge may confront them, and the accused may then remark on all the absurdities, falsities, and other imperfections which he may discover in the testimony of the witnesses. This confrontation, however, is not a necessary duty towards the prisoner, it is a part left to the discretion of the judge. Of course, the judge has equally the power of confronting the witnesses and accomplices one with another.

At this stage, the justice chanceries, or, if the examination is conducted by some minor court, that university faculty or superior court to which the acts of the examination have been sent, may order, if it think it right, the torture to be inflicted. This order is not to be immediately made known to the accused, but he is first to be more strongly exhorted to tell the truth. If he persist in denying his guilt, he is to be threatened; but one or two days are to be allowed him to deliberate. He may now affirm, on oath, that he believes he can yet produce something more in his defence, for which a few days may be allowed him. His further defence is judged of by the court to which the acts were before sent, and if it confirms its former judgment, the torture is then to be applied.

The judges collect in the court; the prisoner is again questioned, and his answers registered. If he still denies, he is introduced into the torture chamber. The executioner is informed to what degree the torture is to be carried. The eyes of the prisoner are bound, and this degree is to be applied for half an hour, or more than an hour, unless the prisoner in the meantime confesses. The instruments employed are various, but the principal one is the whip, while the man is fastened to the wall with iron cramps, and a judge and a surgeon direct the pain to be augmented or diminished, in proportion as the criminal is obstinate, as he relaxes, or suffers.

In a pamphlet which was published anonymously, but which was evidently written by some person filling a subordinate situation in the courts, this is called a wholesome method for the discovery of truth, and the author appeared extremely indignant that it was then no longer allowed to be practised by the minor tribunals. He compares it to opium, which may be sometimes misemployed, but which is, in the hands of a skilful practitioner, of sovereign usefulness. A solution of the celebrated ironical proposition of the Marquis Beccaria, "The force of the muscles, and the sensibility of the nerves being given, it is required to find the degree of pain necessary to make an accused person confess himself guilty of a given crime,"[16] appears to have been sometimes actually aimed at. It is commanded, "that when the tortured man confesses his guilt, the degree of torture at which he does this shall be accurately marked," in order, possibly, to know at what degree to begin with the next similarly circumstanced criminal.

The accused person is allowed, in all cases that involve a greater degree of punishment than confinement for two years, to select one of the advocates received by the court, to defend him. If he be too poor to pay a defender, the court appoints one, and the advocates fulfil this duty in turns. The court orders such a reward as it thinks the advocate employed merits. The advocate is allowed to see all the acts of the process, and, if necessary, to take copies of them. He is allowed to speak to the person he defends in presence of one of the judges. Should the prisoner wish to see the acts after an order has been given to inflict torture, he is only to be allowed to see them when the judge is fully convinced it is not intended to use them as a means of bringing a suit against the person denouncing the accused, but that they are only sought by the prisoner as a means to defend himself better.

After this the final judgment is formally announced to the criminal, who may still demand further time for his defence, and this, too, is at the option of his judges. In the whole of the proceeding, everything is left to the examining judges, who seek for evidence, examine so far as they please, and so often as they please. It is something in which no man but the sufferers and the judges has any concern.

There are some conspicuous faults in this manner of trial. First, there is no time fixed during which the process is to be proceeded in. All this is left entirely to the discretion of the judges, and the

---

[16] **Editor's F/N:-** This is an oft quoted section from the famous opponent of judicial torture and the death penalty, Cesare Bonesana di Beccaria, Marquis of Gualdrasco and Villareggio (1738-1794). For example, T.B. Howells (*A Complete Collection of State Trials and Proceedings for High Treason and Other Crimes and Misdemeanours from the Earliest Period to the Year 1783, with Notes and Other Illustrations*, Volume 30 1822) cites this from Blackstone's use, as being from chapter 16 of Beccaria *On Crimes and Punishments* (1764).

There appears to be much that aligns the attitudes of Hodgskin and Beccaria on the use of judicial violence.

consequence is that criminal processes last, in doubtful and difficult cases, for some years. There are instances in which the value of the property stolen would have been more than compensated by the labour of the accused skilfully directed during the time he was shut up for trial. Criminal processes for stealing things of no great value last sometimes more than two years.

Throughout Germany, even in those countries in which new codes of laws have been introduced, the forms of procedure are nearly the same, and in 1817, a trial was concluded at Vienna that had lasted twenty-six months, and had cost the public 90,000 florins, or, according to the value of an Austrian paper florin at that period, about £2,600 Sterling. And this was the trial of a murderer who expiated many crimes at the gallows. It was not enough that he was convicted of one, but his whole life was tried, and he was questioned as to every year of his existence. In no case, however complete may be the proof, can the process in any degree be ever assimilated to a summary, or, as it has been better named, a rational process. Delay is so great, that the criminal, when he is to be punished, may forget, and certainly the man injured must long have forgotten, what was the crime committed. One of the good effects attributed to punishments must by this mode be absolutely lost. They follow the offences at so great a distance of time, that no man can connect one with the other, and they can never operate as an example.

The trial is in a manner secret. The judges, the advocate, and the criminal, are the only public. It is for the interest of society that men are tried and condemned. Trials, as well as punishments, are instructive to the world. They are intended not only to prove the guilt to the judges, but to demonstrate to mankind the justice of the sentence, which can never be known unless all the proceedings are known. Between the accusation and the punishment, how many proofs may be imagined of innocence? Till these are known, punishments decreed by secret tribunals can never deter from crimes, because no man can be convinced that they are the consequences of guilt. They are the consequences of something unseen and unknown, of the opinions, prejudices, and passions of the judges; they may, and they do, reduce other men to a dependence on the administrators of the law, but they bring home to no man a conviction of the evil of crime, and can, therefore, correct no man's immorality.

What a different idea do men form of justice, as its proceedings are open or secret. In the former case, when it is at all administered as it ought to be, its punishments may be distinctly traced to be the consequences of guilt. In the latter, it is for the mass of society a dreadful power that strikes like lightning, and like the tempest. Their causes are unknown, and they are only seen and felt by the fear, and pain, and destruction they occasion. When justice is publicly administered, it is known to be an establishment of men which men may inquire into and improve. When it is privately administered, men regard it as something above them, and they submit to it with all its accumulated horrors, as they would to a superior being, whom it is impossible to resist or control. Its rules are even above its ministers, and thus the absurd institutions of ignorant men are made fetters to their better-informed posterity.

It is said in favour of secret proceedings, that they can reach man in his most private doings, and only stigmatize him with punishment when he is really found to be guilty. That they are like the powers of conscience, always and only felt when wrong has been committed. But, to prove their efficacy as a means of preventing crimes, they should be equally directed, like the silent penalties of nature, against all the actions which produce evil to man. The heartless inactivity which slumbers through life, the turbulent restlessness which permits no peace, the makers of bad laws, so well as law-breakers, should all have proportion ate penalties inflicted on them by secret tribunals. Till they extend their power to every evil caused by man to which man is subject, and this is impossible, they can only be regarded as an inefficient means of preventing crimes. Men also console themselves when they are punished by asserting they do not deserve punishment. Secrecy of trial must always aid this, because it affords the criminal a chance of being believed.

The proceedings of the tribunals were public during the usurpation of the French, they are now public in a part of Germany, their publicity has been demanded in some of the writings of the day, and as they were public at a period long past, that they should now again be so may not only be claimed as a formerly existing right, but as a great probable benefit.

While it is cheerfully admitted that the spirit of criminal justice is improved, that the cruelty of punishments is fast diminishing, that probably none of the judges deliberately commit injustice, it cannot be denied that, in form, the tribunals are much worse, than formerly. They have been entirely regulated by jurisconsults, whose thoughts have in no country ever gone beyond the consideration of their own sect, and whose present influence is one of the worst evils under which Germany, and perhaps Europe and America, suffer. But Germany appears particularly cursed by them, because they have there introduced the laws and usages of a foreign and enslaved people.

The following passages will both show the former state of the tribunals of Hannover, and that the opinion here enunciated of jurisconsults is not singular:

"How honourable and simple was everything before this new class of men, learned doctors of the law, was known. The prince held a court in the open air, attended by his nobility, some few times in the year, either in the Baumgarten at Hannover, by Lauenrode, or on the Leineberge by Göttingen. He gave justice to those who came before him, and many came without support, and without any person to speak for them; because they who had been injured could best explain in what manner, and why they believed they had been injured. So soon as the news were spread that the prince and his nobility were again assembled, people came quickly together from all the neighbouring country. As the delay of his coming had made many people forget why they would complain, and as the manner of proceeding in each dispute terminated it quickly, in a few days' quietness was restored to the whole district. In disputes between nobles, or when nobles, clergymen, or the officers of the prince, were accused, justice was seldom delayed to these periodical times, but the accuser sought the prince, followed him far and near, and always found a hearing when elderly experienced nobles were with him, whom he could use as witnesses or jury men, Schoppen, to assist him in pronouncing judgment."

"All the relations, however, that sprang out of the whole circumstances of the society, were without foresight, unsparingly destroyed, as the doctors of the Roman law gathered about the courts. They not only introduced new principles of decision but gave to the whole of the proceedings a finer form, which, in a short time, necessarily made the whole of the business their property."[17]

---

[17] **Hodgskin's F/N:-** Spittler, *Geschichte des Fürstenthums*, Vol. I. p.127–129.

**[Editor's F/N:-** Ludwig Timotheus Spittler (1752 – 1810) – Full title = *Geschichte des Fürstenthums Hannover seit der Reformation* [*History of the Hanover Principality since the Reformation*] Splitter, 1786).

This work was referred to in Part 1 of Hodgskin's *Travels in the North of*

Laws in Germany are still called the property of a sect of men, Ein casten Güt.[18] At a former period, therefore, courts of justice were held in the open air, and justice was not then a mystery known only to a few adepts. It was rude, perhaps, but it was something which every man knew, which was then equal to the wants and knowledge of the society, and which has only been kept below the level of our wants and knowledge, by having been monopolized to trade with by the learned doctors of the law.

In the whole of the kingdom of Hannover, between the 1st of May 1817, and the 1st of May 1818, there were punished by the different tribunals, for the crimes of:

| | | | |
|---|---|---|---|
| Stealing, | 402 | Brought forward, | 499 |
| Cheating, | 29 | Neglecting light and causing fire | 2 |
| Murder, | 7 | | |
| Concealing delivery, | 7 | Bigamy, | 1 |
| Infanticide, | 3 | Arson, | 4 |
| Ill-treating parents and other people, also drunkenness, | 29 | Highway robbery and attempt at murder, | 4 |
| Hunting excesses, | 2 | Perjury, | 1 |
| Simple adultery, and adultery with incest and with thieving, | 12 | Embezzlement, | 6 |
| Manslaughter, | 4 | Midwife neglecting her duties, | 1 |
| Beastly crimes, | 2 | Coining and uttering false money,[19] | 5 |
| Procuring abortion, | 1 | Breaking an oath, | 1 |
| Child-dropping, | 1 | Exporting forbidden rags, | 1 |
| Carry over, | 499 | | 525 |

Of these 525 persons 106 were females, consequently rather more than one-fifth only of the persons punished belong to the other sex. Similar, or rather greater, proportions in favour of women are found in other countries, and if punishments be at all an index to

---

Germany.]

[18] **Editor's F/N:-** *Ein casten Güt* translates as *A caste Goodness*.

[19] **Editor's F/N:-** the crime of uttering amounts to putting into circulation counterfeit money (or other *false instrument*). In modern terms it would be knowingly using or passing off counterfeit money, rather than the act of creating it.

crimes, this proves the females to be much more virtuous than the males. .

Here also, as in all other European countries, notwithstanding more severe laws have been in constant existence for the punishment of theft than for any other crime, the greater part of the punishments are inflicted for some violations of that right of property which all men allow to be, as it at present exists, the mere creation of social institutions.

Without setting myself to find out whether any better system might be introduced or not, it is clear that the greater part of the crimes now punished by the laws of Europe are occasioned by the social institutions of Europe. Whether other and greater crimes would not exist without these institutions, is not at present a matter of inquiry; but it is a certain fact, that somewhat more than four-fifths of all the crimes punished by the laws of Europe are violations of the artificial right of property.[20] In vindication of nature and of mankind from the aspersion of legislators, it must always be remembered, that the great part of the existing crimes of men are not crimes of the heart, or of natural passions, but of ignorance, and of the systems of these legislators themselves.

Among the thefts are a very few burglaries; they are mostly stealing in houses and gardens, or stealing of horses, sheep, or linen. Some persons have been punished for stealing game. Many of them have been repeatedly punished. In Hannover, therefore, as in England, the punishments of the laws do not deter from committing crimes. Another curious fact concerning this land, – the females of which, common report says, and I believe says true, are not so chaste as in our country, is, that adultery is punished. The same crime was punished in France before the Revolution, and is still occasionally punished in that country, which seems also to substantiate the assertion, that the punishments of laws do not deter from committing crimes.

---

[20] **Editor's F/N:-** It thus seems obvious that this issue of the artificial right of property was somewhat of a theme throughout Hodgskin's writings.

It can be seen as the major theme of his *Natural and Artificial Right of Property Contrasted* (1832)

Similar issues with crime's relationship with property can also be found in his *Economist* articles. For example, in *Population – Wealth – Criminality* (12th January 1856) Hodgskin noted that "Nine-tenths of the crimes which torment society are violations of the rights of property," (Hodgskin, 12th Jan. 1856, p.32).

Out of the 525, 35 were punished with death. Some were strangled, some were hung, some were beheaded, some were broken on the wheel, and some were dragged to the place of execution on a cow's hide, stretched over a hurdle, and were beat to death with iron clubs, beginning, as the sentence says, at the head. Such barbarities are disgraceful and were it not that they have never been made a matter of public examination, it would be extraordinary how they should be continued by the mild, kind, amiable, and enlightened Germans. The sentiments of men are formed by their gradual progress in knowledge, while the punishments inflicted by the laws are the remnants of times of ignorance and barbarity. Though in situations do not stop, they impede our progress; and nothing but the native goodness of the heart, and the common interest of men, enable them to triumph over the obstacles which the vain meddling of a few legislators have laid in their paths.

Cruel as the present punishments appear, they are now much more humane than formerly. Those ordered by the code of Charles V. to be inflicted have been mentioned, and, in the beginning of the eighteenth century, it was customary to make the punishment of death so painful as possible. The criminal was frequently tortured in public, and every fine feeling was destroyed by frequent and barbarous executions.

> "The robbers of the gold table at Lüneburg were suspended from a gallows; on the following day when they were not dead, they were taken down, their tongues were cut out and burnt, and the mangled body was again hung up by the heels, and dogs were tied up near it."[21]

The principal crimes punished with death are murder, arson, highway robbery, with attempt to murder, and repeated stealing. The other punishments inflicted are confinement, barrow-wheeling, and public labour, called "Karren schieben," for the men, and confinement in a penitentiary, Zucht-house, for the women. Some are confined for life, and some for the short space of three months. All the intervening degrees are inflicted. These are the punishments which are generally in use. It is, however, sometimes customary to punish people for minor offences by making them stand against a wall, or against a post, with an iron collar round their necks. There are such posts, with collars, or collars chained to the churches, in

---

[21] **Hodgskin's F/N:-**, Venturini, p. 659, Vol. III.
**[Editor's F/N:-** presumably *Handbuch der Väterlandischen Geschichte*, von Dr. Karl Venturini, Vol. III, as mentioned in Part 1.]

most of the parishes, and the offences which they are employed to punish may be known by the inscriptions sometimes painted on them,-" For disobedient servants." The custom which Selwyn, or some other wit, facetiously denominated a proof of a civilized country, exposing the bodies of men suspended from a gallows, for the purpose of terrifying others, is still continued in Hannover.

One that I saw had been a robber and a murderer, but appeared to have committed no crime so great as refusing to confess when tortured. Other persons had in their agonies accused him, but his sturdy nerves, or his consciousness of innocence, refused obedience to the rack, and his tongue uttered not, at the command of his judges, the mechanical acknowledgments of his guilt. He was perhaps guilty, but his honour was piqued, as a superior thief, not to confess, and, after having been rack ed, he died protesting his innocence.

Few persons are punished in Hannover compared to the number punished in England, for uttering or coining base money, and the crime of forgery is almost unknown. These facts appear to prove certainly one, perhaps two things. They certainly prove that the number of forgeries in England are the effect of our paper money, and paper money has been created by a regulation of the society, and they make it probable that punishments, forgeries being very severely and very generally punished in England, absolutely cause an increase of the crimes punished. This is probably an effect of all the punishments inflicted by laws.

To have a correct view of the mass of misery which is directly inflicted by the laws of Hannover under the name of punishments, those which are inflicted by the police, which, though trifling as to severity, are of importance as to numbers, must be added to those which have been already mention ed. It inflicts a few days' imprisonment, or it punishes with fines, for what often appeared to be very trifling offences. The police of the town of Hannover alone punishes on an average 180 persons monthly and lists of the persons punished are regularly published to serve as an example to others, and to prove that the police is an active useful institution.

To establish a body of men to keep order and punish crimes, is like establishing a legislative body. This is encouraged to make laws, and that to inflict pain. The members must show that they are useful. The number of persons they punish is the index of this utility, and it is their object to shock us with the number of crimes which are committed, rather than to prevent them.

To establish such a body of men argues in the society an avarice of blood and pain, which it is their business to gratify. A disposition to gratify it, even unjustly, is known to belong to the police of France and Germany, to the constables of England, and to the darogahs of India;[22] and the fact ought to caution us not to empower and set apart a particular body of men to detect crimes and to punish them.

Taking the population of Hannover at 1,314,124, and that of England and Wales at 10,000,000, the number of people punished in the former country, in one year, without, including those punished by the police, is 525. The proportion which this number bears to the population of the country should make the number, punished in one year, in such a population as is stated to be in England and Wales, 3,995, but in the same year there were 13,982 actually committed to prison, and 9050 punished. The police punishments of our country are also not included in this amount. In Hannover, one person out of 2503 is punished; in Britain, one out of 719 is committed, and one out of 1104 is punished. It may be fairly stated, therefore, that there are proportionately twice as many persons punished in England and in Wales as in Hannover; and it must be further remarked, that many of those persons punished in Hamnover are punished for trifling crimes, such as never enter our gaol calendars.

This is a frightful picture of the comparative morality of England. At the same time, it is pleasing to record, that the number of executions were comparatively less; – in Hannover, one out of 17 of the whole number of persons punished was executed; in England and Wales only one out of 78. We have, therefore, more punishments, but a less number of persons are punished with death.

Unhappily for the cause of freedom, this part of the character of our country is too well known on the Continent. Much of the evil which disfigures other countries is hidden from the view of the world, but there is not a speck on our illuminated land that is not seen and known. She is bespattered, too, with much imagined dirt, and she may well say, with Schiller's Maria Stuart,

> "Das Aergste weiss die welt von mir, und ich
> Kann sagen, ich bin besser als mein Ruf." "[23]

---

[22] **Hodgskin's F/N:-** See *History of British India* [1817] by James Mill, Esq. Vol. III. p. 321.

[23] **Hodgskin's F/N:-** "The world knows the worst of me, and I can say, I am better than my fame."

[**Editor's F/N:-** Schiller's *Maria Stuart* (1800) is a play by Friedrich Schiller about the last days of Mary Queen of Scots.]

To us this sort of exposure is a consolation, for it must bring amendment after it, but it is pernicious to the reputation of freedom. All its adversaries, and many of its friends, attribute the crimes of our country to its political freedom. I have met many sensible men in Germany who entertained such an opinion as this, and who preferred their own all-directing governments to ours, because they thought a less degree of interference on the part of government would bring on Germany the same atrocity of crime of which they read in English newspapers. In this opinion there are probably few of our countrymen who will join. The multitude of crimes in Great Britain is much more to be attributed to the increase of taxation, and to the many temptations held forth by our high duties to break through the principles of virtue, and then fall into the deepest abyss of vice. We have been fleeced to build up the old despotisms of the world, which has degraded our people, and half destroyed their morality. The wars in which we have been engaged for the last thirty years, in the name of liberty, have brought her into disrepute by corrupting a people who still profess to admire her.

There is no set of opinions which are more likely to influence the happiness of a nation than those which it may entertain relative to criminal justice. It is, therefore, a pleasure to observe, that all the nations of Europe are now, for the first time, beginning to regard this subject with that philosophic attention which it merits. The improvement which has taken place in the humanity of the Germans has been mentioned, and the whole of that mild people are averse from the cruelties of their former bloody and barbarous codes. Many of their literary men busy themselves with discussions on laws and tribunals.

Knowledge is rapidly advancing. New codes of laws, both criminal and civil, have been talked of for all Germany, and whatever defects they may have in the eyes of our posterity, they will assuredly possess the wisdom and the humanity of this generation.

It is right to add, that all new laws and regulations are carefully published by being affixed near church doors, and in other public places; and the whole of those of Hannover are regularly printed in quarto, under the name of Gesetz Sammlung, Collection of Laws.

# Chapter IV.

## Hannover. – Appropriation of Landed Property.

*Different sorts of proprietors. – The sovereign. – Nobles. – Corporations. – Free property. – Large farms – Minute division. – Meyer tenure described. – Leibeigen tenure described. – Consequences. – An example – Discussion and improvement. – Economists. – Farmers.-Bauers. – Middling class increasing. – Regulations influencing the number of poor. – One forbidding marriage without permission considered. – Manner of providing for poor – A custom of exposing them. – Institution at Hersberg. – Benevolence and charity.*

The land of Hannover is divided amongst persons who may be conveniently classed thus: – The sovereign, the nobles, town and religious corporations, persons not noble. In what proportions it may be so divided is not known. One-sixth at least belongs to the sovereign, and possibly more than three-sixths may belong to the nobles, one sixth to the corporations, and less than one-sixth to persons not noble. That which belongs to the sovereign is again divided in general into large portions, which have once been noble or ecclesiastical properties, and are now let by the crown in their entire state. They may contain from 500 to 3,000 acres, or in the unfruitful provinces even more, with rights of pasturage over large districts, and in some cases, with a right to the services of the peasants. The tithes also are sometimes united to them. They are let to the amtmen, to individuals, or to noblemen filling the office of amtmen; but it is always considered as a favour to have them, and they are let only to those persons whom the government wishes to gratify or reward.

Although the individuals in general pay a certain rent, they are rather considered as administrators of the royal property than as tenants making a bargain and dealing with landlords. The duties of the amtmen as magistrates are generally combined with this administration. These large portions are sometimes cultivated entirely by the first tenant, sometimes they are again divided into many small portions, which are held by the bauers according to some ancient tenures and some certain conditions, called either Meyer or Leibeigen, and to be afterwards described. Sometimes also the property of the sovereign is divided into small farms held immediately of him on such conditions; and then the amtmen are the collectors of the revenues from the farms of this sort which lie in their districts.

The whole of this property, whether divided into large or small portions, is never put up to auction, nor is the letting subject to competition; consequently, the rent is never high. Some portions are in fact held for almost nothing, as a large farm which was formerly the property of a monastery, at Wehnde near Göttingen; for others a very moderate rent is paid. They are let sometimes for the life of the tenant, sometimes for a term of years, and sometimes during pleasure; yet, as the persons who hold them are generally respectable magistrates, they are never subjected to lose their farms without some gross impropriety of conduct. The sovereign has more or less property in all the provinces, but comparatively little in the marsh lands and in Friezland.

There are 644 noble properties in the kingdom, several of which are united in the hands of one person; but there is no one nobleman whose income amounts to more than 80,000 Thalers, or £5,000 per year. Counts Hardenberg and Platen are amongst the most opulent of the nobility. I have met with three instances which have been mentioned, of nobles cultivating their own estates; but in general, there are no houses on the properties of the nobles, other than the houses of the farmers; and few of the nobles ever live in the country. Those who retain their property in their own hands generally live in towns. Some exceptions have been met with ; but for a nobleman to live in the country without being a magistrate, or without holding some office, is looked on as degrading. Such persons are rather treated with contempt and are designated by the odious name of "Land Junker."

Some of the nobles have full power over their properties, and can let them all to one person, and on what terms they please; in which case they make respectable farms and may contain from 100 to 500 acres. Such are the farms belonging to the family Von Lenthe, situated at Lenthe, near the town of Hannover. But more generally the nobles have not full power over their property. It is divided into small portions of 5, 10, 20, 30, or 80 acres, which are held on certain conditions, either of doing service, or of paying rents which have been long ago established, and which the landlord has no power whatever to alter. It may be from this cause that so few nobles reside in the country. They have in truth no land but what is occupied by other people. The use of these small portions of land on certain conditions, is the property of the occupier, which he can sell; as the stipulated rent and services are the property of the landlord. The bauer has a hereditary right to the use, the landlord a hereditary right to be paid for that use.

The land belonging in name to religious corporations, in reality to the crown, is again divided like other crown lands, into large and small portions, held on similar conditions to those by which they are held. That which belongs to towns is sometimes divided into farms of from 60 to 100 acres; but it is much more generally divided into very small lots of 1, or 2, or 10 acres, which are hired by the tradesmen, and other inhabitants of the towns, who use them as gardens, or to grow corn for their family consumption.

Instances have been met with also of the amtmen dividing a portion of their hired land into smaller portions, which they let to the peasantry. In fact, almost every family of the middling and poorer classes, whether living in town or country, and whatever may be its other occupations, has a small portion of land, at least large enough to grow the fresh vegetables necessary for its own consumption, and very often large enough to grow both the potatoes and the corn it requires. This minute division is in some measure convenient but carried too far it becomes pernicious; and may be remarked as an example of an imperfect division of labour. For example, bakers, butchers, shopkeepers, and others, are also farmers of 10 or 12 acres of land. They are too poor to keep horses, and they are obliged to hire them and agricultural instruments from other persons. They have no time to look after the people they hire to do their work; mutual discontent ensues, and the ground is never more than half tilled. I might wish every mechanic and artisan to have so much ground as he can cultivate himself in his spare time, but for him to have more is wrong.

Most of the towns and villages have large commons also, on which the inhabitants have a right to keep one or two cows. The milk, and what can be made of it, very often forms a great part of the nourishment of the poor, and the delicacies of the rich.

The occupiers of small portions of land, whether held under the crown, under nobles, or corporations, may be conveniently divided into two classes, distinguished by the conditions of their tenure. There are a great many different tenures, so many, indeed, that, even rich as the German language is, it hardly contains terms for them all. I have enumerated more than twenty, but the division here adopted may serve to give a general idea of their nature. The first class are called *Meyers*, half *Meyers*, or quarter *Meyers*, according to the size of their farm. It is, however, very rare for a whole meyer, in any of the fertile districts, to possess so much as one hundred

*Morgen* of land,[24] about eighty acres; from thirty to forty acres is the more usual size of their farms, while the half and quarter *meyers* have much less. The other class are called *Leibeigeners*. The German words are here used, because farmer would most inadequately represent meyer, and so different an idea is connected with the term slave, or bondman, when it is applied to the slaves of the West Indies, from what it ought to signify when applied to the German leibeigener, that I shall use neither of them, though one or other is the translation usually given in dictionaries. The term leibeigener signifies strictly a person who owns his own body, and nothing more.

The conditions by which the meyers have the use of their land, consist in paying to the landlord a certain fixed yearly sum, or yearly quantity of corn, for rent. The landlord cannot alter these conditions, neither can he refuse, except when the heir is an idiot, or the rent has not been paid, to renew the lease on the death of the occupier. I never found the rent, in the fertile districts, to exceed twelve shillings per acre; generally, it was between this sum and seven shillings. I have heard that it has been so high in Hildesheim as thirty shillings. It amounts to this sum in the marsh lands for free land, but throughout Kalenberg, and the provinces moderately fertile, it may be roughly stated as between seven and twelve shillings per acre, or from two to three and a half Thalers per Morgen.

In Lüneburg, Bremen, and the other desolate provinces, much land which is occupied pays no rent, but it all pays tithes, and is burdened with small services. The meyers have also to give the landlord a certain sum when, from death or from sale, the occupier is changed. I met one instance of a much higher rent. The people in the neighbourhood of Göttingen hired small portions of land for a season to grow tobacco, on which the landlord laid a certain quantity of dung, and for this land they paid at the rate of thirty-five shillings per acre. The rent is sometimes paid in corn, sometimes in money, sometimes in both. When paid in corn, it seems to give endless trouble. The corn is thought not good, or fault is found with it, and the parties are sure to disagree. With rent sometimes, though rarely, trifling services are also combined, such as supplying the landlord with a pair of horses when he wants to go to town, but all these services are fixed, not to be altered at the will of the lord,

---

[24] **Editor's F/N:-** Morgen is the German word for morning, and as such the German unit of land known as a morgen was traditionally the about of land that a man could normally be expected to plough within a morning. As such its exact size tends to vary in time and location.

and an exemption from them may be, and has been, very generally purchased. A progress is making, particularly on the lands held from the crown, in abolishing them. All the buildings, stock, instruments, belong to the meyer, to the landlord nothing belongs but the rent.

The conditions by which the leibeigener holds his land are also fixed, they are not the arbitrary will of his lord, and it descends with these to his children; but they are conditions of service so onerous, that they reduce him almost to slavery. He is obliged to cultivate the land of his lord a certain number of days in the year, to neglect his own harvest while he is carrying in that of his lord, to employ his horses to bring home his lord's wood, to supply his lord with coach-horses when he demands them ; in short, to do him all sorts of feudal services. This relation of the two parties to one another is equally prejudicial to both. If the landlord had to hire labourers, he might have his work tolerably well performed, but it is now shamefully performed, because the people who have it to do have no interest whatever in doing it well, and no other wish but to perform so little as possible within the prescribed time. The people acquire from this sort of labour habits of slothfulness and neglect, which they never lay aside, even when performing their own work. This relation of the peasant to the landlord has been properly named "a school to teach idleness," and both parties are now injured by their adherence to the absurd regulations of people whose very names are forgotten.

It is remarked, that the inhabitants of Hoya and Diepholz, where the tenures approach most to leibeigen, are much worse in their manners, and more stupid than the inhabitants of Kalenberg, whose land is all held by the meyer tenure; but these again are as much inferior to the perfectly free farmers of Hadeln or Friezland as they are superior to the people of Hoya.

The following quotation from a periodical work, but which is no longer published, points out some of the evils of this practice, and the good of abolishing it.

"We know," the editors speak, "a property in Mecklenburg whose owner was obliged, according to the laws of that country, to supply the leibeigener with whatever was necessary for his subsistence, which the heavens had denied him. So long as this practice lasted, nothing was preserved to supply a harvest that failed, and the proprietor was not only obliged to suffer all the losses which were occasioned by bad harvests on his own land, but he was also obliged to support his leibeigeners."

"On changing their tenure into free property, their manner of living changed also. Eggs, butter, fowls, calves, and other products, which before were unnecessarily consumed, were now made into gold. The rent was punctually paid, the proprietor improved his revenue, and the tenants elevated themselves from the deepest poverty to a state of comfort."[25]

A few years ago, such a tenure existed in a great part of Germany and has undoubtedly been a great cause for that slowness with which the Germans are reproached by more active people. From this fact we may learn, that men are only improvident in proportion as their wants are supplied by other persons, and that the simple means of making the race frugal, is to supply the wants of no man, and to leave every man the produce of his own labour. This would be the best Agrarian law which could possibly be made. And to legitimate without diminishing luxury, every man should be honest enough not to take to himself the natural share of another.

The meyer ordinance, as the law is called, which secures the rights of the tenants, and regulates all the relations which they have to their landlords, might possibly have been when it was made extremely beneficial. It prevented the landlords from making arbitrary exactions, it hindered individuals from accumulating large properties, and it secured the cultivator from violence. But the day of violence is now fortunately passed, general competition, if left free, will render large accumulation not possible, and long continued customs exclude arbitrary exactions. Contracts of all kinds must and will, from the interest of both parties, be fairly made, and generally observed, and this law, therefore, which continues to prescribe the conditions on which land shall be used is now decidedly injurious. Neither the landlord nor the occupier is completely the owner of the land.

It is the law. He who, by his industry, can unite the farm of an extravagant neighbour with his own, and cultivate it, ought not by law to be hindered from doing it. But the meyer law does not allow of two farms being united in the possession of one person. The landlord who can get a greater rent for his land ought also to be at liberty to take it. The rights of the occupant are equally good, or perhaps better than the rights of the landlord, and no possible means can be taken to reconcile one with the other but by permitting either to buy the rights of the other, and thus to make the

---

[25] **Hodgskin's F/N:-** *Annals for the Electorate of Brunswick-Lüneburg*, year 1788. Part I. p. 30.

land, however minutely it may be divided, the perfect free property of either one or the other.

Prussia, it has been mentioned, has attempted to effect it by a law. This is the very greediness of legislation. The customs of men are with their governors only a sort of air bubbles, that they can puff up and burst at their pleasure. But nature will not be hurried ; ages of bad laws have degraded the bauer, and he can neither be made industrious nor energetic by a decree. And the decrees of Prussia, which were to make all property free, have not accomplished it.[26] *

The quotation above made, and the instances adduced of alteration, must have shown the reader that this important subject has already occupied the attention of the writers and the governments of Germany. The restrictions on a free use of property have long been regarded by all the intelligent people of Germany as great evils; and I am happy to say that a progress has been made not only in Hannover, but in many other places, in acquiring accurate notions of their nature, and in abolishing them. The situation of the peasants is, in truth, everywhere a great deal better than it was a century ago.

From the increasing freedom of discussion, there can be little doubt but that the whole of these restrictions are in a fair way of being totally abolished. The French abolished them during their occupation. They have since been partially restored. For example, all land formerly held by a feudal tenure in Hannover was restored to this tenure on the restoration of the present government, but that abolition was violence, and what is now going on is the effect of an improvement in knowledge. That was but momentary, this will be permanent. It is only to be wished that it may be rather left to the people than accomplished by the laws.

The landed property which is entirely free is confined principally to Friezland and the marsh lands and is divided into farms of from 40 to 100 acres; some few farms are larger. Much of that belonging to the towns, which is divided into small parcels, may also be classed as free; that is, the magistracy of these towns have power to let it in what sized parcels, and on what terms they please.

---

[26] **Hodgskin's F/N:-** Bavaria, and indeed most of the other powers of Germany, are also making some attempts at what is called *Güter Arrondirung*. These sort of alterations which give freedom to property, and give importance to the bauer, take place almost in secret, but they are the alterations which will have the most permanent influence on the welfare of Europe.

From the manner in which land is divided, there are three distinct classes of cultivators, each of which follows in some measure methods of cultivation peculiar to itself.

First, those who have large farms, whether hired of the crown or of nobles. They are called economists,[27] have tolerably large capitals, and when they have a very large amt-farm, keep one or more bailiffs to superintend the management, and have establishments that are regulated with all the nicety of military subordination. There is first a head bailiff, or steward, then there are two or three under-bailiffs to look after particular divisions of the farm; clerks to keep accounts; a chief shepherd, who has the management of the sheep, and the superintendence of the other shepherds; a chief wagoner, who has the same office with the teams, and a chief workman, who in like manner looks after the thrashers, weeders, and other labourers. Many of the actual tenants are jurisconsults, and have not received an agricultural education; of course, their stewards are the managers. The stewards consult their employer on any great alterations, show him their accounts, and pay into his hands the profits, but they have all the management themselves. Formerly, the stewards were mere practical farmers, who were taken from cultivating their own ten or twenty acres to look after such an establishment. They were admitted to the table of their principal once or twice in a year and were highly honoured by such a notice. Some such are yet found, but, in general, they are persons who have been regularly educated as agriculturists at some one of those academies or in situations for teaching agriculture which are at present numerous in Germany. They are not only farmers, but they are men of a liberal education, who live with their employers. They are said to receive from 300 to 180 Thalers, £50 to £30 per year.[28]

The second class of cultivators are the owners of free property. These persons direct the labours on their farms, have some considerable capital, own or hire the land, and own the stock. They hire labourers to do the work of their farms, and they resemble very much English farmers.

The third are the occupiers of small farms, whether leibeigeners or meyers, for these in their manner of cultivating and living only differ as to more or less of knowledge and activity. They have this

---

[27] **Editor's F/N:-** This seems to be an archaic use of the term *Economists* perhaps unique to German agriculture. It would seem to be Hodgskin's English translation of the actual German term.

[28] **Editor's F/N:-** by comparison, Hodgskin's Navy pension, at this time, amounted to £66 per year (Stack, 1998, p.43).

in common, that neither of them have, in general, much more capital than their necessary implements, two or four horses, and money to support themselves and families. When they have servants, they are generally the junior members of their own families; but they think of what is to be done, and they themselves are the persons who do it. This is by far the most numerous class of cultivators, and they are what we call peasants; in German they are bauers. Probably four-fifths of the country is cultivated by them.

A class of men, resembling strictly our agricultural labourers, that is, who work merely for hire, are in no part of Germany very numerous. They are found in the marsh lands; some are met with at all large farms, but at both these places they have, in general, also some little property of their own. By far the greater part of the agricultural labourers are the bauers, who are at the same time the occupiers of the land, and the owners of the stock.

The large farmers are the people who are theoretically acquainted with agriculture, and who introduce improvements, till they slowly make their way through all parts of the country. They bear some analogy to our country gentlemen, and the consequence of having such a class of men seems to have been, that the agriculture is in no part of Germany so wretched as it is in some parts of France and Italy. I never saw in the former country, though I have in both the latter, women breaking the clods with wooden mallets, instead of its being done by horses dragging a roller, nor did I ever see them carrying manure to the field on their heads.

The middling classes of farmers are, however, confined to particular spots, and between the great farmers and the bauers there is so great a difference in point of wealth, and so great a dissimilarity of education, and of habits, that the knowledge of the former descends but slowly to the latter, and when it reaches them is scarcely of any service.

The large farmers are gentlemen of education, but the bauers are so occupied by the labour of routine, that they are excluded from all theoretical knowledge, and can make no other improvements than those which they may see practised by the larger farmers. They are too often objects of ridicule not to make their children, when they have acquired wealth by parsimony, eager to leave the occupation of their parents. Every man would rather be one of the inferior servants of the government than a bauer.

Another class of men is wanted between these two to promote the improvement of all; and it appears to be growing up. Agriculture on a large scale is no longer dishonoured, and several instances are known of intelligent men practising it. None of them have given up a residence in towns, and become mere farmers, but tradesmen, medical men, and others, bought or hired portions of land when the French occupied the country, some of which they still retain. And they have neither all the advantages of the great agriculturists, nor the disadvantages of the peasants.

The clergymen are also very often intelligent farmers, and spread by their influence, more knowledge, and better habits, among the people. The sale of the domanial lands would be one of the most important improvements that could be adopted for Hannover. It would effectually create such a class of men. I know no single act which, without offending the prejudices, or injuring in any way the interest of any one person, would so much tend to improve the agriculture, and to increase the industry and wealth of the people of Hannover, as the sale of all the domanial land by public auction. It should be divided in good sized farms, as the individuals who have now an interest in it die, and then be sold. Prussia has done this in all her newly-acquired provinces.

I may here state the conditions under which landed property is held in other parts of Germany. Most of the sovereigns, like the sovereign of Hannover, have large domains. The King of Prussia has sold or given away much of his. The Elector of Hesse Cassel is supposed proportionately to possess the most. Leibeignshaft exists generally in all the eastern parts of Prussia. In the greater part of Brandenburg, and in Saxony, the cultivators hold their land on a tenure resembling the meyer tenure, and sometimes even more free. In Mecklenburg and Holstein most of the property is free. In south-eastern Germany Leibeignshaft is predominant, and in the neighbourhood of the Rhine hardly known. From the manner in which the land is appropriated in Germany generally, and from the effects of that different mode of appropriation which is the rule of the marsh lands, and which resembles the mode followed in England, it seems that much of the prosperity of Great Britain has been owing to property in land being entirely free. The owner has been at liberty to dispose of it as he thought fit, and, instead of its being neglected, it is certainly one of the most highly improved countries of Europe. This same fact is true of Holstein and Mecklenburg, where the land is in general not subjected to any restriction, and where the agriculture is well known to be better than in the other parts of Germany. Private interest has, therefore, in this instance, effected a great public good, without any limitations or directions by a legislator.

Where he has interfered, as in the meyer law, he seems to have done mischief on the whole. While I mention the advantage of our system, it would be unjust totally to pass over the advantages of the other. The minute division of landed property in Germany, the regulations which have forbid an augmentation of rent, or a union of farms, and which have secured to the bauer the full enjoyment of the use of the land, have prevented any person, except the sovereign, from amassing an enormous quantity, and have preserved among the inhabitants a species of equality as to property.

There are, comparatively, few absolutely destitute labourers. The mass of the people do not live in such affluence as Englishmen, but this is more than compensated to them by all being in some measure alike. In civilized society, it is not destitution, but the craving wants which the splendour of other persons excites, which are the true evils of poverty.

The meyer regulations have hindered improvement, but they have also hindered absolute destitution and enormous accumulation. I would not be understood to affirm, that these evils, so far as they exist in our country, have in the slightest manner been occasioned by property being free. They have been occasioned by other causes, totally distinct from this freedom, which also exist in Germany, but which have been there partly counter-acted by those restrictions on property which have prevented accumulation.

There is, on the whole, therefore, a great difference between the agricultural labourer of Germany and the agricultural labourer of Britain. The bauer must give one portion of his produce to the state, another as tithes, and a third to his landlord, but the remainder, though small, is his own. He tills his own field, and the reward of his industry depends, in some measure, on nature. Our labourer has to give portions of his labour to the state, to the landlord, and as tithes, and he has also to give a large portion to his employer. He tills the ground that is appropriated to another, and his reward depends so little on the seasons, or on his own exertions, that, whether the heavens give or withhold their bounties, whether he is idle or laborious, he has usually enough, with parish support, barely to subsist. The bauer depends on himself, and so long as he can labour, he is never degraded by being told he is subsisted by the state, or by his landlord. There is but one country in which the productive labourers, who are the most industrious men of the world, are said to be maintained by the charities and bounties of persons who produce nothing.

The landlord and the capitalist produce nothing. Capital is the produce of labour, and profit is nothing but a portion of that produce, uncharitably exacted for permitting the labourer to consume a part of what he has himself produced.[29]

When this is given to him as charity, if he be not oppressed, he is at least insulted. Those who imagine themselves to be very benevolent people, while they dole out to the labourer a pittance of what they have exacted, delude themselves with a hypocritical cant, that, however it may be sanctioned by laws, and however it may accord with the customs of society, was never surpassed by any of the cant of the most absurd religion. By your labour shall ye eat bread is holy wisdom, and he who does not gain what he consumes by his own industry, assuredly eats the bread which nature made the property of another. The poor are the terror of the rich, and the scourges of society. But the affluent have little right to complain when their repose is disturbed, for it is they who inflict poverty on their fellows, and at the same time teach them to desire wealth. The evils of society cannot be remedied by acts of parliament. Individuals must reform themselves. Avarice must exact less, and it will have more security and enjoyment. Generally, it seems to be supposed, because the rich make laws, that the poor only need restraints, and to be reformed. This is a mistake. It is the class of society which has long ruled that most needs reformation, and that deserves most of the blame for the social evils which exist.

I may here add the little I learnt relative to the support and management of the poor. It seems consistent with the regulations concerning landed property in Germany, that there should not be so many paupers there as in our country. Some other regulations are known, which have probably assisted in protecting Germany from the evil of pauperism to the same extent in which it exists with us. There is no legal provision for paupers. A law of the guilds, which extended to most trades, forbad, and still forbids, where guilds are not abolished, journeymen mechanics from marrying, and, in most countries of Germany, people are obliged to have the permission of the civil magistrate before it is legal for the clergyman to celebrate a marriage. The permission seems to be given or withheld as the parties soliciting it are thought by the magistrates to be capable of maintaining a family. At least, it is to prevent the land from being overrun with paupers that the law on this subject has been made. There are so many persons who are ready to impose restrictive

---

[29] **Editor's F/N:-** This is Hodgskin's earliest printed expression of the economic themes that were to dominate his economics, on Capital and the exploitation derived from it.

laws on their fellow men, and such an undue value seems to be set on the good they can effect, that it is necessary to observe that the whole good of this last restrictive law seems not equal to the evil resulting from it. It is hoped, therefore, nobody in our country will be fond of extending the power of the magistrate to give or with hold a permission to marry.

This regulation substitutes the permission of the magistrate for the natural reasons why people should or should not marry. These latter are the proper motives for conduct; and of them the parties can be the only judges. The magistrate may give his permission from caprice, and, from the reverence with which he is regarded, they who can obtain it, imagine nothing more is required to justify their union, and make it full of happiness. A union that is sanctioned by both priest and magistrate is regarded as doubly sacred, and all the evils which may follow from it as decreed by nature. Thus, the people on the Harz, who marry young, are said to have looked on the small pox as a blessing, because it relieved them from the super-abundance of their children. They refused for a long time to allow inoculation, saying, they would not interfere with the will of the Lord. "He hath given and He hath taken away, blessed be His name." They seem to have regarded marriage as a duty, and the misery consequent on it as an infliction they were bound patiently to suffer. The misery which may follow from a marriage, is the natural reason why it should not take place. This important fact the magistrate prevents the parties from knowing, by substituting his permission for the natural reason.

From the quantity of children born out of marriage in these countries,[30] it is also probable that this regulation, though it may prevent hasty marriages, does not much diminish the number of births. It drives men and women to live together without the permission either of the magistrate or the priest. Their passions are stronger than their respect for the law, and they violate their own principles of religion because they cannot obtain the permission of the magistrate. When once principles are violated, no man can tell where the violation will stop. It is, therefore, of paramount necessity, that no laws should ever be made which supply a strong temptation to violate them. On this principle we ought to be careful not to lay any impediments in the way of reasonable gratifications, and not to make a law which tempts men to reject the authority of the magistrate, and at the same time violate their own principles of religion.

---

[30] **Hodgskin's F/N:-** See Table, Appendix, No. I.

There is no legal provision in Hannover for the poor. The Vorstehers of the villages, and some of the citizens of the towns, call on the inhabitants, generally of a Sunday, for some little contribution for the relief of the distressed, which, from the publicity of the thing, they are under a sort of necessity to give, and if they do not, the collector is ordered to notify it to the clergyman. The collectors bring with them a book, in which the sum given by each person is inscribed, and they, in some cases, receive a small recompense for their labour. The funds so obtained are distributed by the collectors, by the clergymen, and by the magistrates of the towns, according to the wants of each person soliciting relief.

When this money is collected, the inhabitants are warned by the collectors not to give alms, and they seem to expect, that, for what they give on this occasion, they ought never to be tormented by beggars. With the exception of some wandering journeymen, I saw, in fact, very few beggars. In the town of Hannover itself I scarcely saw one. In some of the marsh lands the practice is to allow the poor to beg for themselves on a Sunday. They then go regularly from house to house, and the inhabitants as regularly bestow their mite on the afflicted. I met a similar custom in France, where the old ladies lay by a certain portion of sous ready to bestow on every Sunday. In both these cases the quantity of beggars seemed so regular, that each inhabitant knew pretty accurately how many would call for relief.

In the town of Hannover, which contains 20,000 inhabitants, about 800 persons, including children, may receive occasional relief from the funds collected as above mentioned. They are under the inspection of the police, and are employed by it to sweep the streets, &c. Most of them were women, and, till I inquired the reason, I was astonished to see a number of debilitated old females occupied as scavengers in the midst of winter. Nor did the assertions that they were idle, worthless characters, justify the practice. There is something about women, something in the honour which is due to the sex of our mothers, which forbids us giving them so nauseous and disgusting an employment. Twice a-year all the persons receiving this sort of alms are led in procession about the streets, in order that they may be known, and their idleness exposed to contempt. The children sang, and the men and women followed, accompanied by police officers. Some of them hid their faces, but most of them seemed totally to disregard this public exposure. If it were always true that poverty was a consequence of neglect, idleness, or dissipation, to expose it publicly might merit praise; but, in the present state of the world, it may be brought on men by misfortune; they may be born to it as their inheritance; it may be inflicted on them by the rapaciousness of their rulers; and, in such cases, it is cruel to steep the bread of charity in the bitter waters of public infamy. This is the proper reward of crimes, not of misfortune.

Exclusively of the persons so relieved, there is in Hannover a work-house, in which were 13 children and 80 grown up persons. Some of the latter were sent here as a punishment. All were employed. The children were taught reading, writing, and arithmetic. Formerly the funds of the establishment were greater than at present, and then the children were further instructed. The master still shows some of the first essays at drawing of a man who has since enjoyed a little reputation as a sculptor. There are also in Hannover two establishments for orphans.

In Celle, a town containing between 8,000 and 9,000 inhabitants, some funds bequeathed to an orphan-house, and what is collected from the people, are both appropriated, under the inspection of the master of the work and orphan house, to support the poor and orphans. The children are sent into families to be nursed, and distressed persons are relieved at their own houses, chiefly by giving everyone who is able to work something to do and paying for it. About 80 imbecile and aged persons lived in the house; about 200 orphan children were brought up by the funds; and about 200 persons were occasionally relieved.

In Linden, a village close to Hannover, containing between 800 and 900 inhabitants, who were chiefly working people, there were between 40 and 50 persons who occasionally received relief. In one other, or rather several villages united into one parish, Eingepfarred, containing nearly as many people, but removed from any town, there were only four persons who received relief, and one of these was a blind woman. In the marsh lands the numbers were greater.

From these few facts there is reason to believe that neither the number of paupers nor of beggars is so great in Hannover as in Britain. In no country has so many regulations been made concerning the poor as in our's, and nowhere are they so numerous. Is this not another proof of the inefficiency or folly of legislating so much? It is most strange, that, with an ingenuity surpassing that of all the world, with all the great branches of productive industry united in our own hands, that a greater portion of our people than of any other should be found subsisting on the charities, either ordered or spontaneous, of the rest of their countrymen. Though paupers be few in Hannover, there, as in other parts of Europe, it has been found necessary to found alms houses and form societies for their relief. Amongst these, one resembling, in its spirit and form, the plan adopted in Hamburg, deserves to be mentioned. It was carried into execution in the little town of Herzberg, in 1800, by the present Hofrath Arenhold, when he filled the situation there of chief magistrate. I was assured it had been attended with the most beneficial effects, and that his benevolence and praise-worthy exertions were still gratefully remembered by the inhabitants. Wherever the power of the magistrate is efficaciously exerted, begging may undoubtedly be prevented, but comparative poverty is a constitutional evil of European societies, which no outward and local remedies can cure. From several other establishments of this kind, I know the Hannoverians are not behind in the race of benevolence. It may, however, be doubted if benevolence does not sometimes extend to interference, and if the error of our present systems is not a ridiculous desire to shelter some people from the natural results of their own follies and crimes.

Men desire to amend the condition of the poor, by governing them. The tear that flows at the sorrow of another, is the brightest jewel of nature; and the heart has no more ennobling feeling than a wish to relieve distress. The noble mind desires wealth and power only to mitigate the sufferings of its kind. The most ardent of our race have the warmest and most affectionate hearts; so it ought to be, or the energies of the mighty would scorch, not delight us. This union is a beautiful illustration of the natural goodness of man. But unfortunately, the struggle in which we are obliged to engage to acquire wealth and power too often sours the temper; we forget what was the end of our pursuit, and we come to love power more because it has been associated with our struggles, than for the benefits it may enable us to bestow. The justice of men is easily bribed by the benevolence of their intentions; and the heart that is warm in its wishes for the welfare of others, does not observe that the head is totally ignorant of the means to promote it. Hence wealth and power are often sought by unjust and unholy means. We are told by a German historian:

> "That Alexander went forth, as he solemnly declared, to conquer the world only that he might make it happy. And, blinded by the apparent benevolence of his declaration, authors have honoured him for it. He followed his brilliant aim through his whole life; ruin and death waited on his footsteps; and the end of his victories was a cruel military despotism. Under its government the people were never heard of; there was nothing but generals and soldiers, who quarrelled about the division of plundered nations."[31]

The same disposition, with similar melancholy results, may be traced in many of those laws which have been made in our country, to provide work and food for the poor, and in many of those charitable donations which are recorded in our newspapers. Men seek wealth by legitimately oppressing the labourer, that they may figure as makers of benevolent laws, or as the chiefs of charitable societies. Miserable is the nation where either is much needed. Nature has created each individual with powers to provide for its own wants. She has placed the welfare of millions in their own hands and has not subjected them to one or a few men like themselves.

Our senses and our knowledge extend only to the little circle about us;[32] and it is not only vain, but ridiculous, to wish that our power and our influence may be more widely extended. We can only obtain means to pour the oil of gladness into the bosoms of the sorrowful, by first of all condemning them to sorrow. It cannot be too often repeated, that it is the exactions of one class and the interference of legislators, which have made that poverty and misery these persons are sometimes so anxious to mitigate. Benevolence and vanity conspire to make men oppress and rule their brethren. The doctrines of selfishness are in truth full of love as well as of wisdom; and no sentiment deserves so much to be scouted, as that benevolence which curses with its care. There can be no hope for the permanent relief of our poor, till the rich and the mighty leave them to themselves; nor can there be any permanent enjoyment for the rich, till they lay aside the attributes of governing Deity, and be content with the dignity of men.

Those who govern are not content unless they can prevent the interference of others. It is a part of their plans, to substitute regular systematic relief for spontaneous charity. They forbid alms-giving, as encouraging begging; and they suppress sympathy with misfortune, because they would not have kindness imposed on. That to me is strange reasoning, which can lead to forbid alms-giving. Charity is valuable to the giver so well as to the receiver. It amends the outward condition of the latter, but it softens and improves the heart of the former. It appears not right that government should take on itself the administration of the poor, or that it should forbid relieving even that distress which is simulated. It may prevent a little imposture, but it destroys one of the best means of uniting man to man. It is a power usurped not only over

---

[31] **Editor's F/N:-** There is no citation provided for this quotation.

[32] **Editor's F/N:-** It might be conceived that here Hodgskin was pre-empting the idea of Dumbar's Number.

our purses, but over our sentiments and our hearts. It pretends to curb our vices, but it renders us in reality deaf to the voice of misery; it hardens us against the complaints of our fellow men; and it makes us selfish and unbrotherly. How much more is the receiver also improved by the smile of charity, than by the book-recorded gift of the overseer! "The sight of a benefactor brings joy like his gifts."

"Denn der Anblick des Gebers ist wie die Gaben erfreulich"[33]

---

[33] **Hodgskin's F/N:-** *Hermann und Dorothea* [1797]. By Goethe, p. 167.

# Chapter V.

## Hannover - Agriculture.[34]

Hannover an agricultural country. – Agriculture of economists. – Farm at Coldingen. – Sheep.– Shepherds. – The family. – Agriculture of the marsh lands. – A mode of mending the land. – Farmers respected. – Bauers contemned. – All follow the same agricultural methods.-Right of pasturage. – Course of crops. – Mode of paying wages. – Prices. – Implements.-Impediments to agriculture. – Origin of tithes. – Manners of female peasantry. – A custom of the bauers. – Plantage at Hannover.

Hannover is said to be an agricultural country; which merely means, that the people still remain in that first state of improvement in which men, after having wandered with their flocks, erect fixed habitations, and cultivate the ground, but have neither capital nor ingenuity to establish extensive manufactories, and to carry on commerce. It does not mean that the Hannoverians are more skilful agriculturists than other people, and that their ground is better cultivated; it means, that they are merely agriculturists. They praise this state of their country, as subjecting them to fewer fluctuations of fortune than that in which people unite agriculture with manufactories, and commerce.

> "They may be, and have been, overrun by a destroying enemy, and the country was restored in a year or two to its former state of prosperity."[35]

By this nothing more is meant, than that the mass of the people live in such a constant state of deprivation, that they can never descend much lower, and never fluctuate to higher enjoyments. The enemy found nothing to take from them but provisions; the land still remained for them to cultivate, and the ensuing harvests supplied them again with food. In this estimate it is totally

---

[34] **Editor's F/N:-** This Chapter was reprinted under the title *Agriculture of Hanover* in the Farmer's Magazine, Volume 21 (May 1820), pages 173-189. This covered all but the last 10 pages of Hodgskin's original chapter.

[35] **Editor's F/N:-** There is no citation provided for this quotation.

overlooked, that to increase industry is to augment food and people, – the means of enjoyment and defence, – and is to give them something more valuable to contend for.

The Hannoverians have been alarmed by the distress which has existed in Britain, and which is frequently attributed to our manufactories and commerce. But employing different kinds of labour to supply different wants, never can produce poverty and distress. And for the benefit of mankind, in order that no species of industry may be unjustly brought into discredit, those social regulations ought to be exposed to censure, which have inflicted on us so much poverty and distress.

All the different kinds of productive labour must be beneficial, but the manner in which its produce is distributed in the society is distinct from the labour itself and is the result of social regulations. From confounding these two things, and from being serious in wishing well to their country, I have heard several clever men in Hannover express a wish that they might not become a commercial people. They thought it an evil; and as some of them had some influence on the government, this mistaken view may ultimately be really injurious to the whole.

My object in this chapter is, to give a general, and I would fain hope, an accurate idea of the state of agriculture, and not to describe the management and the improvements of any individual and take them as the criterion of the whole. At the same time, I shall notice any improvements that I know, in order to make the general idea correct.

The three classes of cultivators, mentioned in the last chapter, pursue different plans of cultivation. The large farmers have in general extensive rights of pasturage. They keep large flocks of sheep, grow artificial grasses,[36] turnips, and other succulent roots, and lay down a part of their land as meadows, that they may have an abundance of hay. The bauers may sometimes sow a little clover, or lucerne, or spergel, but they seldom have meadows, and keep no more cattle than is necessary for their work, and then the common lands can feed. They keep sheep only in those countries where extensive heaths are favourable to feed them. There are some other exceptions, such as a whole meyer uniting a distillery

---

[36] **Editor's F/N:-** Artificial grasses seems to refer to artificially sown rather than naturally occurring vegetation. This can, for example, be seen discussed in the agricultural literature of the early 19th century, such as *Sketch of Lectures on Artificial Or Sown Grasses, as Lucern, Saint-foin, Clovers, Trefoils, Vetches, Etc. Etc:* (1808) by Walter Wade.

and a public house with his farm, and thus being enabled to keep more cattle; but, in general, the bauers keep only the horses necessary for their work, and the number of cattle which can be fed on the common lands. There is therefore a radical difference between the husbandry of the different classes of cultivators.

At one of the large farms the land was divided into two portions. The first had no fallows, but the following rotation of crops: – 1st year, hoed or drilled summer fruit. 2nd, Wheat or rye, over which clover was sown in the spring. 3rd, Clover. 4th, Wheat or rye. 5th , Barley or peas. 6th, Oats, or sometimes rye; – then as before. The whole land under this course is dunged twice. The other course was, 1st, Fallow, as a preparation for 2nd, Rape seed. 3rd, Wheat or rye. 4th, Rye, dunged. 5th, Flax. 6th, Rye, dunged. 7th, Beans, dunged. 8th, Rye. 9th, Oats; and then comes fallow again. These courses were followed on the farm of Mr. Amtman Meyer, at Coldingen. The soil was a brown-coloured loam, free from stones, fruitful, easy to work, and easily kept clean; but in wet weather it quickly became foul, if neglected. A large portion of meadow land bordered on the Leine and was subjected to be over flowed by that river. The land under tillage was more elevated.

This farm was hired of the crown and situated about eight miles from the town of Hannover. It contained altogether about 2,600 acres, with a right of pasturage over extensive meadows, from the time they were mowed till the 15th of May, when they were laid down for hay. Seven pair of horses and eight of oxen were  kept as working cattle. No cattle were fattened. A portion of the land was let for feeding cows, the superior tenant not liking the trouble of this part of husbandry. His favourite pursuit, and that which rewarded him best, was sheep, of which he had about 2,200 head.

The original breed were the small German sheep, which, from being numerous in the neighbourhood of the Rhine and Saxony, are called Rhenish or Saxon sheep. They were crossed by Merinos, and now bear fleeces as fine as those of the Merinos themselves, weighing on the ewe, 2 or 2½, and on the ram, 4 or 4½ pounds. No attention was paid to fatting the carcase, wool being the principal and only source of gain. The peace, and communication with England, had enhanced its price, and the last shearing had been sold so high as 4s.7d. per pound, which was nearly double its former price. The carcase weighs on an average 40 pounds, the larger ones 60, and sells for about 9s. to 15s.

The shepherds were all dressed in long white linen coats, and white linen small clothes, and wore large hats cocked up behind, and ornamented by a large steel buckle. They all looked respectable and clean. They were paid in proportion to the success of the flock and had thus a considerable interest in watching over its improvement. They received a ninth of the profits, but they also contributed on extraordinary occasions, such as buying oil-cake for winter food, when it was necessary, and such as buying new stock, a ninth of the expences. The head shepherd had two ninths of the profits.

Some other workmen on this farm were paid in proportion to their labour. The thrashers, for example, were paid with the sixteenth part of what they thrashed. Other labourers were hired by the day, and they received about 7d. In harvest time they may make 8d. Some are paid by the piece, and then receive at the rate of 2s. for cutting and binding an acre of corn.

A water communication might have been had from this farm to the town of Hannover, and from there all over the world, but the magistracy had stopped the river by a stone wall at some distance above the town, in order to supply the town mills with a sufficiency of water. It should have been done by a lock. All the country above the wall is now excluded from the advantages of a water communication, and all its produce must be brought to Hannover by land-carriage.

In a country of commercial enterprise this would have been an evil, in Hannover it was neither noticed nor complained of. With this diminution of the natural advantages of the farm at Coldingen, it would perhaps be impossible to find land more favourably situated than it. A skilful and enterprising hand could command at pleasure the waters of the Leine, but they fertilized or wasted at their will. The bailiff was a good farmer; the farm was kept in very good order, according to the common practices, but I did not observe much of that animated seeking after improvement which distinguishes enterprising men. Yet it would be unjust not to mention the care with which the breed of sheep and their wool have been improved. Great expence had been incurred to bring rams from Saxony and from Spain, and the whole of the sheep were of the improved breed.

Consistently with the plan of mentioning such improvements as I have heard of, I may here add to those already mentioned, that Mr. Amtman Wedemeyer at Katlenburg, and Mr. Backhouse at Göttingen, are both good agriculturists, who are acquainted with the writings and the practices of the greater part of Europe and pursue the best practical methods of cultivation which are known.

I should do injustice to the hospitality with which I was entertained, if I neglected to record it. Mr. Amtman Meyer, the tenant of the farm at Coldingen, is one of the best agriculturists of Hannover; and though other occupations prevented him from accompanying me, he sent his steward over his farm, and was politely ready to give me every information my previous knowledge enabled me to ask. We are possibly in England rather given to believe, that the people of other nations are less affectionately attached to the comforts of home than ourselves, and that the decencies and charities of a domestic circle are nowhere observed but in England.

From the many well-ordered amiable families which I have seen in Germany, I am disposed to think we underrate our northern neighbours in this particular. An attention to order in their domestic arrangements is common to the Germans; and of this the family of Mr. Meyer was a good specimen. I partook with them of a well-ordered family dinner, and passed the afternoon agreeably entertained by the urbanity and politeness of their conversation. His son had been in the English service, his daughter was intimately acquainted with our language, and the whole family resembled the family of a well-educated country gentleman. Before sitting down to table, all the persons, standing behind their chairs, threw their eyes on the ground, and asked in silence a blessing on the meal. This is a common custom all over Germany.

In the Catholic countries the very poorest people, carriers, servants, and others, when they come from the stable, or when they run in from the harvest field to dine, plump down on their knees, take off their white caps, turn their faces to a corner, and repeat a long prayer. No one begins to eat till all have said grace. When the meal is finished all again go on their knees and return thanks. In the northern and Protestant parts of Germany kneeling has not been seen. Few people, however, sit down to meals without a short prayer, nor rise from them without a compliment. That you may have a good appetite is the morning's wish, and that the meal may be blessed, *Gesegnete Mahlzeit,*[37] is universally the wish at rising from table.

As the farmers of free property are very generally confined to the marsh lands, and to Friezland, and as the soil, situation, and agriculture of these districts are the same, in describing the agriculture of the second class of farmers, I shall necessarily describe the agriculture of the marsh lands.

The land under the plough in the districts on the Elbe is generally divided into long slips fifty feet wide, between each of these slips is

---

[37] **Editor's F/N:-** *Gesegnete Mahlzeit,* translates as *Blessed Meal.*

a ditch which extends the whole length, and the land between the ditches is laid up round, so that every precaution is taken to keep it dry. The ditches supply rushes and coarse grass, which are used to litter the cattle.

Fatting cattle for Hamburg is one of the pursuits of the farmers of the marsh land. Sheep are little attended to, each farmer keeping only so many as supplies his own family with wool and milk. Every day-labourer has one or two, which he uses for the same purpose. They are constantly chained in pairs and pick up their living on the dikes and other unenclosed spots. When the labourer cannot command such a spot, he is obliged to hire from the farmers so much land as will feed his sheep, but this is a favour not always obtained.

The sheep of the marsh lands are much larger than the sheep before mentioned. They weigh, when fat, from 80 to 100 lbs. and bear a coarse fleece of from 5 to 6 lbs. weight. From being more kept for their milk than to fat and kill, they are very generally poor, and when sheared, look most wretchedly. They resemble the marsh sheep of Britain. The only cheese made in any part of Hannover, except Friezland, is made from sheep's' milk, and the shepherds say that the wool of the animals milked is never so fine nor so abundant as when they are not milked.

Throughout Germany, everybody possessing a little spot of ground makes it his first object to cultivate himself everything his family needs. The people do not seem yet to have attained a thorough conviction that, if it be cheaper, it is better to buy than to grow. This state of mind may be promoted by the communication not being rapid, and the markets not certain, but each man prides himself as on a point of honour, in supplying his own wants, without having recourse to his neighbour. Individuals are like the rulers of nations, who imagine the happiness of their subjects will be endangered by a mutual and cheap supply of wants, and they, therefore, preserve a surly independence, not only at the expence of much labour, but of all the kindnesses and affections which grow out of men assisting each other. According to this principle, each farmer grows, amongst other things, so much flax as supplies the consumption of his own family.

With these little exceptions, the great objects of the marsh land farmers is to fatten cattle and grow corn and seeds. Meadow land, consequently, lets for more money than any other, and much is kept in grass seven or eight years. It is then broken up, and, 1. oats is sown on it; 2. wheat or rye; 3. wheat or beans, and the land is dunged; this change of crops continues without intermission till the land has got foul, generally with couch-grass.  On an average, this is every ten years.

It is then fallowed till June, when it is sown with rape seed.  To prepare for this crop, it is ploughed at least six times, and very often nine, and it receives a large quantity of dung.  At this time, also, the land is mended by another means.  The soil is composed of three distinct strata, which are everywhere found like the deposits of three overwhelming floods but lying at unequal depths.  The first is clay, mixed with sand, and is very fruitful; the second is a stiff cold clay, that is said to be absolutely unproductive ; the third is very fine white sand, mixed with the blue slime of the rivers, and with the remains of vegetable substances.  The third strata is usually found at a depth of from three to ten feet, and when mixed with the clay at the surface, renders it more productive.  To procure this sand, holes of six feet diameter are sunk, till it is reached, when it is thrown out, and the second strata of cold clay thrown back to supply its place.  Many such holes are made in a field, till a sufficient quantity of the sand has been spread over the surface.  Sometimes the ditches supply enough, and the process then resembles precisely that which has been practised in Lincolnshire by Mr. Cartwright.[38]

It appears that the material employed both on the shores of the Elbe and in Lincolnshire, has a great resemblance, and is found lying in a similar situation.  Such a practice has long been in use on the marsh lands belonging to Hannover; and it appears to have been suggested to the farmers there by observations similar to those which suggested it to Mr. Cartwright.  It was found in digging the ditches, and it was thought that the sand would loosen and render the clay easier of cultivation.

Although artificial grasses grow luxuriantly, they are very little used.  Clover is sometimes sown on the fields, intended to be laid down, but it is mowed as green food, or fed off, and never made into hay.  The reason assigned for this is, that the cattle will not eat it when they can get grass-hay.  There is little occasion to cultivate it, because there is much land lying on the river, or in other places, of which every farmer has his portion, which will serve no other purpose but to grow hay.

There are some parts where the land, once under the plough, is never laid down to grass.  This is the case particularly in Hadeln, where the course of crops is constantly, I. wheat, 2. beans, 3. rye, 4. and 5. rape or cole seed, then again follows wheat, and so on,

---

[38] **Hodgskin's F/N:-** See *General View of the Agriculture of Lincolnshire, by the Secretary of the Board of Agriculture,* [1808] p. 301.

without intermission; of course, the rape implies a partial fallow, as it is not sown till between the months of July and August, and till then, the land is repeatedly ploughed, cleaned, and manured.

In Friezland a rotation of crops similar to this last is followed, but here the inhabitants approximate more to the customs of Holland, keep quantities of cows, and make butter and cheese. Much land has there been recently won from the Ems, which possesses a vast degree of fertility. It is said to give back rape seed three hundred times multiplied, and barley sixty, when the fourth part of this is reckoned in ordinary land the usual increase. The Friezland or Dutch breed of horned cattle is celebrated for its size, beauty, and for the quantity of milk the cows give. This breed, with the cattle from the Tyrol and Switzerland, are favourites in other parts of Germany, and they are brought from these countries to improve the breed of the native cattle. The inhabitants of Friezland have been at great expence in gaining their most fertile marsh, and no portion of it is left uncultivated.

Both here and in Hadeln, so well as an uninitiated man can judge, I should describe the agriculture as excellent, and it is excellent without any theory. The people are not writers, and they are said to have no books on agriculture. They speak the language of Germany, and may, of course, have German books, but their cultivation has preceded the knowledge of the rest of the country, and it is said to have been entirely effected without agricultural writers.

In Friezland, and the marsh lands, the farmers are men of respectability, and so are the farmers in Switzerland, Holland, and Britain, but in every other country of Europe the cultivation of the ground is, in some measure, a degrading occupation. It is more honourable to be a mercenary soldier than an industrious man. Such prejudices cause that idleness, that haste to escape from labour, and that profligacy which the rulers of the world are so ready to attribute to nature rather than to their own systems and opinions. In Germany this prejudice is particularly strong; a large farmer may be respected, but a *bauer* is a term synonymous with stupid, and is used as a reproach to children; soldiers are knights, but bauers are *Knechts* or slaves. They have apparently been regarded by the other classes of the community as beneath them, and boys in their sport, and magistrates with their laws, think they may mock and oppress the bauers.

Thus, it was very generally the custom for the magistrates of the towns to fix the price of all the produce of the land when it was brought into the town for sale, and thus boys and girls say, "The bauers ought to be made to sell cheaper, The bauers are for us to laugh at." Labouring under the disadvantages of being contemned by the society, it is not extraordinary that they should yet be reproached as superstitious, and as dull, and ignorant, nor that it should be found necessary to tell them, "that butter is neither made nor spoil ed by witchcraft," and "that to keep their cattle in good order, good feeding, and not sorcery, is necessary." Many superstitious notions are attributed to them, such, for example, as this. They believe that trees which have a whisk of straw bound round them by a naked man at the first moment of the new year, are sure to be fruitful. I saw each fruit tree in a small orchard, near Hannover, ornamented with such a whisk, and I was assured it had been done by the owner naked at midnight on the first of January. It is the agriculture of the bauers of which I am now to speak.

There is one mode of cultivation, the three years' rotation of crops, which is common nearly to all bauers. In fact, they are very often obliged, and were formerly much more obliged than at present, to follow precisely the same mode. In general, some persons possess the right to herd cattle on the lands of the bauer, and they are consequently obliged to leave them fallow every third year. I have met several instances of this, and to show that it is general, I shall translate a sentence from a German author. At the same time, it must be remembered, that this is one of those pernicious rights which have been in several places abolished.

"In most districts, domanial and noble properties have a right to herd their cattle, that is, they may send them on the land of the bauer, and he is obliged to leave his fallow unemployed, and must not plough it before St John's day. Lately, this right is in many places abolished, and he is now permitted to employ a part of his fallow in raising summer crops for his cattle." [39]

---

[39] **Hodgskin's F/N:-** *Lehrbuch des Ackerbaus und der Viehzucht*, von G. H. Schnee. llalle, 1815.

"Most of the peasants throughout Germany are constrained to follow one course of crops, and one system of cultivation. They can neither break up their fields, nor, whatever the circumstances of the times nay demand, can they in any way alter that mode of cultivation which had been prescribed some centuries before." See *Riesebeck's Travels*, [1787] Letter 84th.

They were performed prior to the French Revolution.

[**Editor's F/N:-** *Lehrbuch des Ackerbaus und der Viehzucht* translates as *Textbook of Agriculture and Cattle Breeding*.]

Wherever this right exists, the system of cultivation is the same. Winter corn follows the fallow, the bauer may choose whether he will sow wheat or rye, but winter corn he must sow. The land over which this right of pasturage extends is generally divided into three large portions, and each of the peasants has a part of each portion ; so that the land belonging to each is situated in different places, and the fallowing takes place on each of the large portions alternately. Not only the domanial and noble properties have this right, but also the properties of corporations. The land belonging to Göttingen, for example, is subject to it, so that the land on one side of the town is always sown with winter corn, on another it is sown with summer corn, and on the third it lies fallow. Where such rights exist, or existed, there the agriculture could not improve, and it must be precisely the same at least through the whole of the district over which the right extended.

The rotation of crops here mentioned is that which the bauers generally follow. They have fallow, then rye or wheat, and then oats, barley, peas, or beans, and then again fallow. Where the above right of pasturage does not exist, the bauers begin to employ their fallow for some summer crops, and this takes place, particularly near towns, or when, from other circumstances, they can command manure. Another course of crops I have met with was, 1st, Fallow, employed for potatoes, flax, or some such crop; 2nd, Wheat or rye; 3rd, Lent corn;[40] and 4th, Rye or beans. But in general, the three-year rotation, with unemployed fallow, is common to the peasants throughout the greater part of Germany.

The utility of leaving land fallow at any time is much questioned since the introduction of so many succulent roots in the common system of husbandry, and it is only justified for strong clay soils. Throughout the north of Germany, the soil approaches sand rather than clay. Never but in one spot, in the neighbourhood of Münder, did I see what may be called stiff clay; of course fallows are, in this country, according to the improved husbandry, quite unnecessary. They were imposed on the bauers by the laws. It must, however, be remarked, that their general poverty, and their want of cattle, does not allow them to make those improvements, and to provide such a quantity of manure as is necessary to cultivate the ground without occasional fallows. The right of herding, however, destroyed in a great measure the utility of fallowing, because the bauer was not allowed to plough and cleanse his field till it was late in the spring. Of course, the greater part of Germany may be described as being

---

[40] **Editor's F/N:-** Lent corn refers to when it was grown, presumably sown, during Lent. As such it probably equates to modern Spring Wheat.

imperfectly tilled. This right alone made, and makes, the whole tillage defective.

In some parts buck-wheat is much cultivated. The grains of this *corn*, if it deserve the name of corn, is made into grits,[41] and into *pancakes*, and forms the food, particularly the suppers, of most of the inhabitants of the sandy and moory districts. The peasants have also, in these districts, large flocks of sheep. The extensive heaths are useful for no other purpose but to feed these animals. They cultivate their ground, 1st, with rye; 2nd, rye; 3rd, oats or buck-wheat; or, 1st, rye; 2nd, oats or buck-wheat; and 3rd, rye. The ground is then left for four or five years and fed off during that time by sheep. It is then broken up, and again cultivated in the same manner.

In the greater part of northern Germany most of the bread is made of rye, consequently this grain is cultivated more than wheat. Almost all the bauers cultivate such a quantity of flax as their wives and families can spin.

In the provinces of Göttingen, Grubenhagen, Hildesheim, and Kalenberg, and in many other parts of Germany, tobacco is extensively cultivated. The ground in which it is to be planted is well dunged and prepared towards the middle of June. It is then planted in rows, two feet apart. It is raised from seeds in hot-beds. When it succeeds it is one of the most profitable crops. It requires too much care to be grown by the large farmers. It rather improves than injures the ground, but the peasants like to plant it on the same spot repeatedly.

They cultivate several seeds for the sake of oil, such as rape and cole seed, but more particularly the white poppy. The seeds of this plant supply the oil which the bauers most commonly use both for salads and for their buck-wheat pancakes. Tobacco, flax, and poppies, added to the crops we cultivate, give the German bauers an advantage. They have a greater choice of different fruits.

When these people keep sheep, the shepherd is usually employed rather by the village than by any one individual. The shepherds themselves own a certain number of sheep, in proportion to the extent of the flock. The bauers find food for these sheep during the winter, and, moreover, give the shepherd twelve *Klaffters*, a measure equal to a cord of wood, and about eight shillings and a penny per year. In another instance, the shepherd received yearly

---

[41] **Editor's F/N:-** Hodgskin's use of the term grits in this context would seem contradictory to the traditional view that grits are a southern American dish of Native American origin.

two sheaves of rye, two shirts, and coarse linen for jacket and trousers, but no money whatever. He owned, however, forty sheep, from which the greater part of his sustenance was derived. In another instance, a shepherd looked after the flocks of three farmers, and he received about nine bushels of rye per year, and they were to feed twenty sheep for him during the winter. In another instance, the shepherd kept the flocks of five farmers, and he lived with them, alternately changing his quarters every week. Each one gave him a lamb and twelve shillings per year. He also received a suit of clothes. Most generally the shepherds have an interest in the flock, or they have sheep of their own, whether the flock belongs to some opulent man or to several bauers. "Sometimes they have a sixth or an eighth part, sometimes they own from sixty to eighty sheep."[42]

Farm-servants are very generally paid in produce of some sort or another, which shows tolerably well the state of the country as to communication and money. I am far from affirming that this is altogether a bad state of things. Servants and labourers, when the peasants have any, live in, and form a part of the family. There is none, therefore, of that disparity of condition which is found in countries where the agricultural labourers are paid in money.

Several examples of wages for agricultural labour have been already given, and I shall here add some others. Thrashers are usually paid with a proportion of the thrashed corn. They receive from the thirteenth to the sixteenth part, in proportion to the quality of the grain. It is reckoned that a man must gain 1 scheffel, about 1½ bushel, of winter corn, and 1½ or 2 scheffel of summer corn per week, to enable him to support a family. Ten marien grosschen, or 10d. per day, is the highest wages for common labour which I anywhere heard of. Most generally, and the rate very seldom varies, it is 6d. 7d. and 8d. Women receive from 4d. to 6d. This is the price paid for digging ground, which is hard labour. It is also paid for by the piece, at the price of 1½d. the square rood. I have met instances of people reaping corn, who were to be paid with a certain quantity of flax seed. I have found the same price given for labour in Saxony, in Prussia, and in Hannover, and the book I have before quoted, *Der Angehende Pachter*, gives the same prices. Wheat was at the same time selling for about 4s. 10d. an English bushel; rye for 4s. 5d. barley 8s. ; and oats 1s. 9d. ; beef was from 3d. to 4d. per pound; veal from 2½d. to 3½d.; mutton from 3½d. to 4½.d.; a bushel of potatoes cost about 9½d.

---

[42] **Hodgskin F/N:-** Der Angehende Pachter, Halle, 1817.

I have met no accurate accounts of the quantities of corn produced in the whole of Hannover, but such accounts as I have seen I shall here give. In 1806 the produce was, of:

| | Wheat | Rye | Barley | Oats | Beans and Peas | Lentils | Potatoes |
|---|---|---|---|---|---|---|---|
| Hildesheim | 6,571 | 33,965 | 24,722 | 18,295 | 12,000 | 1,792 | 12,000 |
| Gottingen and Gruben-Hagen, without Hohnstein | 80,000 | 40,000 | 90,000 | 50,000 | 22,500 | 2,000 | 40,000 |
| Osnabruck | 5,000 | 45,000 | 15,000 | 20,000 | 8,500 | | 25,000 |
| East Friezland | 850 | 9,000 | 6,500 | 7,200 | 1,900 | Wispel. and of buck wheat 350 last. | |

This last country exports, on an average, 5,600 last of barley; 700 last of wheat and rye; 800 last of peas and beans, and 60 last of buck-wheat, yearly. Bremen also exports above 40,000 wispel of different sorts of grain, and Lüneburg exports the value of 15,000 Thalers in buck-wheat and oat-grits yearly.

I have seen models, at the house of an ingenious mechanic in Hannover, of most of the new invented agricultural implements of Britain. They are known to all the theoretical men, but I never met with any in use. Agricultural writings are much read, and very plentiful, in Germany, and the readers are acquainted with every European improvement. The plough in common use is a simple but convenient instrument. It has two low wheels; the beam is straight; the share cuts nearly horizontal, and the mould-board, which is fixed always, turns the furrow on the same side. When a piece of land has to be ploughed, it is divided into strips, and when each strip is not already well risen in the middle, the outer part of the strip, at each side, is first ploughed, so that every furrow may be turned towards the centre, and the middle furrow may be the last made. The consequence is, that the surface of every strip forms the segment of a circle; and when a large plain is so ploughed, as it were in common, these segments of a circle form regular undulations so far as the eye can see. Two horses and one man work these ploughs, although I have seen six horses employed in the marsh lands near Hamburg, with two drivers both riding. This plough costs from 16s. to 28s. The large farmers sometimes plough with two oxen, but the peasants, except in the sandy districts, where oxen can be turned on the commons, invariably use horses.

When they are very poor, and have no horses, they sometimes employ their cows. Two or more join their stock, and, with four cows, they manage to plough very well. When the occupier is too poor to keep a team, or occasionally to hire one, he works his land with the spade, and much land is dug. An elderly peasant, close to the town of Hannover, pointed with exultation to his field of flax, and told me:

"to observe how much better it was than that of his neighbour; but he is a young man and is lazy; he ploughed his piece of ground, and I dug mine. My wife and daughter weeded it, and you see how well it looks. I can get my living off my acre, but my neighbour, I am sure I do not know what he does."

Ploughing appears to me to be well and expeditiously done. The peasants make no other water-courses than those which are made by turning the ground to the centre, and the consequence is, that ground which lies low very often produces nothing but coarse grass where corn has been sown. Draining, as a part of husbandry, is only beginning to be practised, and has not yet descended to the peasants, who sometimes ask "what the gentleman means to grow in his underground ditch." The plough mentioned must have been a long time in use, because it is common all over Germany, and it appears to me to be superior to the common large wheel ploughs, with shifting mould-boards, of the south of England, though not equal to the Rotheram, or Mr. Small's, or the swing ploughs.

In Friezland they have a plough fully equal to these. It is, I believe, known in England as the Dutch plough, and as the origin of Mr. Rotheram's plough. It is without wheels, and though fit for that heavy marsh, is worked by two horses, and is so light that I lifted one without difficulty.

In the sandy districts the people have another instrument to answer the purpose of a plough, called a Haken, which is very simple. It has neither turning, nor mould-board, nor wheels; the share is long, pointed at the end, and then broad and flat. It is only fit to scratch the sand with. The iron share costs about 3s. 4d. The peasants make the wooden part themselves, during winter, and when they buy it complete its price is only about five shillings.

I only saw one two-wheeled cart employed in agriculture throughout the country. All the work is done with light four-wheeled waggons, drawn by two or four horses. They consist of three broad planks, the bottom one of which is permanently fixed to the two axle-trees; the side ones are moveable, and one of them is always taken off when the contents of the waggon have to be thrown out. Four wheeled waggons, besides being heavier of draught, are more difficult to turn than carts, and they cannot well be made to turn up so as to throw their contents on the ground. But their disadvantages are so well known that I need not discuss them. The mechanical ingenuity of the Germans, though it has long been great, seems to be only employed to build temples to frivolity and folly, and is seldom occupied with the houses or business of men. Accordingly, many of the common instruments, such as carriages, hand-barrows, boats, waggons, and a thousand others, are awkward and ill adapted to their purposes, while musical clocks, harmonicons, and panharmonicons, are most ingeniously made.

I never saw any very good cutting instruments, but walking-sticks, that serve as tubes for pipes, with a compressing pump at one end to make a fire, and a machine at the other for impaling without destroying the beauty of insects, are common.

Scythes and sickles are like our own; but there is a sort of sickle in Friezland different from ours, and which appeared to me to be superior. There is also in the same country a very convenient sort of shovel-cart, drawn by horses, which is used to distribute expeditiously and equally, over the surface of the whole field, the earth which is thrown out of the ditches. I despair of being able to convey by writing an accurate idea of these implements, and therefore I do not attempt to describe them. These are not the only parts of the agriculture of Friezland which makes that country apparently worthy of a visit from some of our agricultural gentlemen.

Generally, all sorts of grain are sown broadcast. Beans I have seen sown in rows by the hand, the holes being made by an instrument that had a row of ten or twelve wooden spikes, I doubt if a man could make the holes with it so fast as with a single iron crow, and if the ground were hard this instrument would not pierce it.

The only manures which I saw employed were common dung, the refuse of salt-pans, and once or twice lime. In the sandy districts, where very little straw is to be had, it is customary to pare turf with heather growing on it, and to lay it in large heaps in the yards and sheep-stalls and stables.

In some parts of Hildesheim there are hedges and hedge-rows of trees. Isolated farm-houses and villages are generally surrounded by trees. Forests cover the hills, but most of the cultivated land is destitute of both hedges and trees. As no instance has been met with of the peasants cultivating turnips, as they rarely drain their land, – as they have no hedges to make – their agricultural labours are much simplified. After the winter corn is sown, till the following 1st of March, they have nothing to do in their fields, and rarely visit them. During the winter months they thrash their corn, which requires, however, but little time, and is very often done so soon as it is harvested. Those who have teams, and live near wood or peat, and near towns, employ themselves in carrying fuel to them. Many, indeed most of them, weave linen. The want of hedges seems to save a great deal of labour, and there is a much smaller place as a nursery for weeds and destructive animals, but it somewhat diminishes the beauty of the country. The union of weaving and farming is an example of imperfect division of labour.

The 1st of March is the commencement of agricultural labour. "Then we break loose," says the farmer. A day has also been mentioned when the meadows are no longer to be fed off. And almost every distinct branch of farm business has some particular day on which it is commenced. Thus, the cows and sheep are not allowed in many places to go on the common lands before the 23rd of April, St George's day. This was to many of the poor beasts a joyous day; they had been shut up all the winter, and were glad again to breathe the free air. Some few old animals seemed attached to their dirty stalls, and often turned their heads back, and bellowed their melancholy adieus; but the young ones frisked and bounded past all the power of the cow-herds, maid-servants, boys, and girls, and spectators of the village, to keep them in order. How changed did they become in a few days! When the novelty and pleasure were over, they went and came with so much regularity as a well-disciplined regiment performs its evolutions. Fixed days for work mark a general similarity in the habits of the people. They also designate a rude and a superstitious people. For they regulate their labours by only a general sort of fitness in the seasons, and often sacrifice valuable time for the sake of following the calendar of the priests.

There are some little customs connected with the common lands, that I may here mention. – A cow-herd, and often also a swine-herd, are appointed and paid by each village, who come regularly round every day sounding their horns, and collect the cattle to lead them to the pasture, and who bring them home at night. When there is any necessity for watchmen, these herds do that duty, and in winter sound their horns every hour. At Christmas a new Vorsteher and a new bull are chosen in every parish; and it would appear from the examples I have seen, that these latter, like some other candidates for the favours of the sex, were of foreign extraction.

There is one little practice connected with agriculture which I cannot forbear mentioning, though I never saw it, because it accords with the German character. The first corn of every harvest which enters any town is usually conducted in triumph. The waggon which carries it is decorated with flowers, the people go out to meet it, and they accompany it into the town in a gay and joyous manner.

From the superiority of the agriculture of the marsh lands, where the property is free, and the farms of a moderate size, it is easy to be inferred, that neither the large nor the small farmers of the rest of Germany are best calculated for the improvement of their art. The large farmers are generally either noblemen or amtmen, who possess knowledge, but want that stimulus to exertion which is derived from a necessity to labour. They keep establishments which are too large to be perfectly superintended and guided by one person. Their situation in society does not depend on the produce of their farms, and they are not therefore extremely anxious to make so much money by them as possible. On the other hand, the small farms and the poverty of the bauers impose on them a constant necessity to labour. Their theoretical knowledge cannot extend beyond mere reading and writing, and such little facts as they may pick up in the routine of providing for the cares of the passing day. The single fact, that by far the greater number of them unite some other occupation, principally weaving, with farming, shows clearly, that neither good cultivation nor improvements in agriculture can be expected from them. Their farms are too small, and they are too poor. The manner, therefore, in which the land is divided and appropriated in Germany necessarily causes defective husbandry.

Many of the causes which impede the improvement of agriculture in Germany are similar to those which impede it in other parts of Europe. That great cause, the contempt with which the occupation of the bauer is treated by chambermen and soldiers, has been mentioned; and I shall only here add two, one of which is common to the rest of Europe, but seems to weigh peculiarly heavy in Germany; and the other is peculiar to some parts of that country. The first is tithes, which are still very generally and rigorously collected in kind. Some instances have been met of compensation. They no longer belong to the clergy, but to the sovereign or to the nobles. They principally, however, belong to the sovereign, who shews himself to be, according to his language, the father of his people, by his care to gather their harvests into his barns. Fruits grown on the fallow are not subjected to tithes. They appear, however, to fall peculiarly heavy on the German peasant, from the distribution of property.

In other countries farmers have a command over labour; and though the labourer may suffer, the farmer gains from his toil a portion of that tithe he must pay; but the bauer is both farmer and labourer, and he suffers all the loss which in other countries is divided between these two classes. Whatever takes any of his produce from him, helps to keep him so near the verge of want, that it is peculiarly pernicious to him, and to the art he practises.

Christianity was forced on the people of northern Germany at a time when writing was common; and the origin of tithes in that country is perhaps better known than in any other. They were imposed by a conqueror. The zealous Charlemagne subdued the Saxons, and he made it a condition of the peace which he gave them, that they should become Christians, and give tithes to the priest. They have had a similar origin in other countries or were won from credulity by cunning working on the fears it had artfully inspired.[43]"

The power which the magistrates possess in many districts, to employ the bauers in mending roads, or corvees, is a cause which is peculiar to some parts of Germany. The ill effects of this, as the Germans call it, gezwungene Arbeit, is too well known to make it necessary for me to do more than again mention that it exists.

The Jews are some of the largest capitalists of Germany; and the law, which in many parts of northern Germany, in Hannover, for example, though not in Prussia, forbids them to hold land, and, I believe, even to take it in mortgage, must prevent them vesting their capitals in agriculture, and thus impede its progress. They can have no good security for money lent on land. This is a palpable instance of the venom of anti-social regulations corroding the body-politic from which they issue.

I have frequently made observations on the manners of the bauers, and I shall here add something further on the subject. With the exception of some parts of Westphalia and of Oldenburg, they invariably live in villages. Their houses have very frequently the same form, and their insides are laid out somewhat in the same manner as those of Friezland, which have been already described, but they are smaller. At some particular corner you find a crib bed

---

[43] **Hodgskin's F/N:-** I transcribe the passage which relates the above fact. The historian had before described the conquest.

"Insondenheit schien es den Sachsen làstig, dass die Priester der Religion, die man ihnen aufdringen wolte, zugleich einen Zehnten ihrer Früchte haben sollten, Ungeachtet Carls Freund der Engländer Alcuin, selbst Carln rieth, darauf nicht zu bestehen, wurde es doch als eine Bedingung des Friedens mit durchgesetzt; wiewohl es doch kaum scheint, dass diese Zehnten würklich in allgemeine Uebung haben gebracht werden können."—Pütter, Vol. I. page 67.

for the man who looks after the horses, when one is kept, and his bedding consists as much of the provender of his cattle as of blankets and sheets. In the bauer houses there is little other furniture than a stove, a stool, a table, and the cooking utensils.

Chimneys are very rare. The smoke finds its way out under the roof, or at any hole it meets with, or it is deposited as tar and soot on the beams and rafters. Generally, the houses are built of an oak frame, filled in with closely rammed clay or bricks. They have high thatched roofs. Fires are very frequent in most parts of Germany, and, owing to this manner of building, when once they breakout, it is impossible to stop them. The government of Hannover has commanded that houses shall be built of bricks and covered with tiles. But a family which cannot command these materials must not, on that account, be left without a roof, and accordingly, in spite of this command, I have seen people, after a fire, again building their houses with wood, and again thatching them with straw.[44]

The Germans have now been collected into towns for at least ten centuries, and still longer into villages, and one is almost tempted to believe, that, in the latter, the same form of building is preserved which the first rude settlers adopted. The progress of man in all the arts which minister to the comfort of life is necessarily slow in those countries in which military foppery, operas, and learned trifling, is thought, by him who rules the taste of the country, to be the only things worthy of his patronage.

In such countries, the great mass of the society have absolutely not enough common sense to know how to preserve themselves and their property. Their own wants and comforts are the last things to which they can attend. All their time is occupied in ministering to the profusion and luxury of others.

How rude and insecure is the house of the bauer, and yet, after toiling for ages, he has neither means nor knowledge to build himself a more convenient habitation. The single fact, that the great mass of the productive part of the population of Europe is involved in comparative ignorance and poverty, is a reproach to the class of men who have so long undertaken to guide them in the ways of knowledge and wealth. The bauer is not insensible to his interest, but he wants the means to follow it. Within a few years he has much improved his agriculture, he has adopted the cultivation of tobacco and potatoes, and he is only stupid and ignorant because he is degraded by the opinions of society. After these remarks it

---

[44] **Editor's F/N:-** *The Farmer's Magazine's* reproduction of this chapter ends at this point.

must still be allowed that a German bauer is somewhat superior to an English agricultural labourer, and in comfort, and in the scale of civilization he is much superior to an Irish peasant.

Village roads correspond with the houses; when they do not lead to an amt-house, they are in general most wretched. In the vicinity of Hannover itself, they are sometimes so bad, as almost to have the appearance of canals. In the villages and small towns, the inhabitants of which are agriculturists, all the dunghills are placed in the streets. A similar custom exists in France, and in some of the narrow streets there, the only road was over heaps of smoking putrefaction.

The ancient Germans are said to have respected their women almost to adoration, and perhaps the poorer women, without now receiving this respect, continue to deserve it. The wives and the daughters of the bauers perform with them all the labours of the farm. They dig, and sow, and reap, and plough, and thrash, just as the men do, except that the men reserve to themselves the lazy honour of going with their horses. But they do much more than the men, they look after their houses, and no sooner have they nothing else to do, than they turn to their spinning-wheels that always stand near them ready to be used. Men may be, and very often are, seen idling away their time, but it is a rare thing to see an absolutely idle German peasant woman. They quite merit what Schiller has said of them, which is in many points an accurate picture of their employments.

> "Und drinnen wallet
> Die züchtige Hausfrau,
> Die Mutter der Kinder
> Und herrschet weise
> Im hauslichen Kreise,
> Und lehret die Mädchen,
> Und wehret den Knaben,
> Und reget ohn' Ende
> Die fleissigen liánde,
> Und mehrt den Gewinn
> Mit ordendem Sinn.
> Und füllet mit Schätzen die duftenden Laden,
> Und drehet um die Schnurrende Spindel den Faden,
> Und sammelt im reinlich geglåtteten Schrein
> Die schimmernde Wolle, den schneeigten Lein,
> Und füget zum Guten den Glanz and den Schimmer,
> Und ruhet mimmer."[45]

The women not only work more, but they look more after the business than the men. Their own linen, and very often the whole of the clothes worn by the family, even the coats of the men, are of their manufacture, and the mother of a family in the country of Germany is the person who both regulates it, and whose labour feeds and clothes it.[46]

Had the many governments of Germany, who now constantly call themselves paternal, only claimed the higher honour of being maternal governments, their subjects would long ago have discovered the illusion of such language; and would have been fully persuaded that the most expensive and least productive member of the family had no analogy whatever with its mother.

It is possibly a necessary consequence of having so much to do, that the female peasantry are by no means clean either in their persons or their houses. Their hair appears only to be arranged for baptisms, marriages, and other feasts, and at all other times to be matted, dishevelled, and dirty. Their clothes on working days are utterly neglected, they are dirty, torn, and negligently put on. They are generally short, have broad faces, with a want of expression, and seem much more calculated for constant labour than for one moment's love.[47]

---

[45] **Hodgskin's F/N:-** Schiller's Gedichte, Das Lied von der Glocke:
"The modest wife, the mother of the children, governs wisely within the house; she teaches the girls, and cherishes the boys, and always employs her industrious hands. She adds to the gains by her regularity, she fills scented chests with treasures, and spins her thread by the buzzing wheel, and collects snow-white linen and glancing wool in the clean shining press. She unites ornament with usefulness, and never rests."

[46] **Hodgskin's F/N:-** I was once conversing with a German woman whose husband had been in the army, and in describing him, she said he had been Wacht-meister. I required a further explanation of this word; she said he was like *die mutter des regiments*, the mother of the regiment, and I then understood that person who in our army I believe bears the title of quarter-master serjeant.

[47] **Hodgskin's F/N:-** The following is the opinion of a German on this subject, but as he appears to have been a southern German, his opinion may also be suspected of partiality:
"Blue eyes, and fair-hair, are throughout more frequent than black eyes and hair. There is little expression in the features, but much heaviness and sloth; nowhere are there so many faces which say nothing as among the peasantry of the flat country. Fine forms must not be expected, and where these are found, the hard work which the females are compelled to perform soon destroys them. In great towns, and among well educated people,

When the women of Germany are collected in towns, they are pretty and well made, and the female peasantry of the north are only ill favoured from the labour they perform. It is perhaps impossible to calculate how much the happiness of both sexes would be increased if the women had only so much time to spare from their toil as might be required to keep their persons and their houses clean, and so much knowledge as to enable them to know the value of doing this.

When they go to church, or to market, they put on gay clothes, and hang their ornaments in their ears, but so soon as they come home, the ornaments are carefully laid away, the rags and the dirty clothes are again resumed, as if they dressed themselves for the world, and not for their families and friends. It is a strange feature in the character of ignorant people, that they are anxious, by every little sort of attention, to obtain the good word of a stranger, of the respect to a person whom they may see once a month, and they never give themselves the least trouble to please those with whom they constantly live. They buy ornaments, and want food, clothes, and firing. They give gluttonous feasts on one day and are half starved the rest of the year: and vanity seems stronger even than hunger.

I have mentioned at page 188, Vol. I.[48] an instance of their amusements, and it is customary in winter evenings for the lasses to collect with their spinning-wheels at some one house, and the young men follow them, to talk and amuse themselves. They are a social people, and such an assembly is a pleasant sort of party, without any of the expence or brutality of drunkenness.

Quietness, patience, and submission seem eminently characteristics of the female peasantry. In their houses, or abroad, or in the markets, where they collect in great numbers, each one bringing her own few eggs, or fowls, or skeins of thread, or sausages, or whatever else she has to sell, you never see a quarrel, and seldom hear a loud or an angry word. There is the buzz of a multitude, but no voice rises above it.

---

charming countenances, and regular forms, are met with as in other countries. But even here, that fire, that life, that spirit, which give the greatest charm to female beauty, and which are found only in southern climates, are entirely wanted." Länder und Volkerkunde, Vol. XIX. p. 58.

[48] **Editor's F/N:-** This equates to page 112 of this work within our *Collected Works of Thomas Hodgskin,* Volume III.

All the peasantry can read and write; though they are said to use the latter only to record what money is due to them, and the former only to amuse themselves with those scandalous anecdotes, generally of the bar or of the church, which are thickly strewed in the calendars. I have mixed with them, as much as a stranger well could, who did not understand their language; (for Low German, or some provincial dialect, is what they speak;) I have occasionally seen them read their Bible, but never discovered any signs of much knowledge amongst them. I have heard of a journal kept by a bauer in Mecklenburg, but it may be doubted, with all the schools belonging to Hannover, to be afterwards described, if the country ever did or ever will produce, under the present form of government, such men as Burns, Bloomfield, and Hogg.

Talents and animation do not by any means belong to them. I always found them civil and friendly, but calm and dull. Whether I stopped to talk to them when they were at work, or met them in public-houses, or entered their own dwellings, or had them as companions on any road, they always answered all my questions very civilly, but without warmth, without interest, and almost without remark. My being a perfect stranger, and different from themselves, seemed to cause very little surprise, and to call forth few questions. I have often told them I came from afar, and endeavoured to excite their curiosity, but it very rarely went beyond asking me what corn we grew in England, or if ours was not a fine rich land. They are guilty of few errors or absurdities, are very humble before the amtmen and their superiors, and rarely express any other discontent than at the dearness of what they have to buy and the cheapness of what they have to sell. They are too regular and mechanical to allow anything more to be said of them, than that they eat, drink, sleep, labour, and speak, with a sort of sulky civility and composure.

They have one custom, which appears to have arisen from the services they were and are still bound to perform for their landlord, which is probably worth mentioning. The regulations concerning it are precise, and I know several instances of it. So soon as a bauer grows elderly, and no longer well able to do all the active and laborious part of the work, he resigns his farm to his son, preserving to himself a part of the house and a certain income. He can only preserve, however, a certain part of the house and income; and though he may divide what he has himself gained among his other children, he cannot give from the farm, *Meyer Hof*, any of the stock, or implements necessary for its cultivation. This seems a sort of regulation which makes the heir and his parents in a manner independent of one another, and not unfrequently sets discord between them. There can be no rules for the division of property which will ever be of equal value with leaving it entirely free. It ought to be disposed, of according to the discretion of the owner.

I must mention in this chapter one establishment which is of itself very good, and which has introduced into the kingdom, by the care of the government, a great variety of useful and good fruits; but it at the same time shews what imbecility of mind is produced among a people by that unlimited interference which has been described as characterising the government of Hannover. The people, of themselves, had not sense enough to establish a common nursery for fruit trees. What superb establishments of this kind are met with near London! What care is taken to rear and propagate the most delicious fruits! Compared to these, that of Hannover is trifling; but these are private establishments for the purposes of gain, and that is a royal establishment for the benefit of the subjects. It is known by the name of the Plantage, and is situated at Herren-hausen, two miles from Hannover. It is cultivated at the expence of the sovereign, though fruit trees may be purchased at it. Several thousand young trees are annually given to some particular parts of the country where they are most wanted, and the amtmen distribute them to certain parishes, and to those people who need them. If it were possible for one moment to forget, that the power to perform such acts of beneficence towards the people is in reality derived from extorting their substance from them; if it could be supposed that governments and sovereigns create those things they are so free to bestow, there is nobody who would not be ready to worship the givers as above humanity. Now they can only be regarded as re-bestowing, with large professions of bounty, the twentieth part of what they have before taken, that they may enjoy in peace the remaining nineteen parts.

# Chapter VI.

## Hannover - Manufactories.

*Linen the staple of Germany – Quantity manufactured in Silesia. – In Westphalia. – Cotton. – Wool – Paper. – Iron. – Imperfect division of labour. – Wages of: – Imperfection of German manufactures wrongly attributed to the national character of the people. – Caused by the monopoly and interference of governments. – The guilds.*

There is much cause for melancholy, and even for despondency, when we look on the decay of any great national establishment. It is with a feeling of this kind I read the accounts (which I have met in more than one book) of the decay of the linen manufacture, which may be considered as the great staple of Germany. This feeling is not a little heightened by observing, that the people whose ingenuity has driven the Germans from the market have profited so little by their success, that they are involved in greater calamity than their unsuccessful competitors.

The manufacture of linen is not confined to particular places; it is carried on in every bauer's house. "The same hands that cultivate the field, that cut wood, and thrash corn, turn from these occupations to the weavers' loom. They are agriculturists to-day, and to-morrow manufacturers." The peasants are in winter weavers, the women weave, and they also spin at every moment when they have nothing else to do, "without their various employments destroying their dexterity." The linen which they do not themselves need is collected by dealers and sent by them to all parts of the world. Silesia and Westphalia are the principal exporting countries.

In 1805, the value of all the linen manufactured in Silesia amounted to 10,676,000 R. Thalers, (£1,779,000,) and of this, 6,091,559 Thalers (£1,015,000) were exported. There were in the same year 34,910 looms, and 30,000 families employed. The spinning was done by 500,000 persons.[49]

---

[49] **Hodgskin's F/N:-** Demian's *Handbuch der neuesten Geographie des Preussichen Staats*, pp. 66, 67.
**[Editor's F/N:-** Fuller reference Johann Andrea Demian's *Handbuch der neuesten Geographie des Preussichen Staats*, (1818), Berlin. This title translates as *Handbook of the latest geography of the Prussian state*

But the writer adds, "This great branch of industry, the chief source of the wealth of Silesia, is at present far less than it was before the battle of Jena. The want of a market reduces it almost to nothing."[50]

The linen manufactory of Westphalia was equally prosperous at the commencement of this century. Between the years 1792 and 1798, the yearly average of bolts of linen brought to the linen halls for inspection was, fine linen, 18,570, middling fine, 22,767, and coarse, 19,680, with 5,331,548 hanks of thread[51]. There is reason to believe, that this quantity is now diminished by one-half.

I have met with no modern accounts which can be relied on of the quantity of limen made in Hannover, but the amount of the value of what was shown at the different linen-halls in 1793 was 295,116 R. Thalers, (£49,189). Without being able to tell precisely to what degree the quantity manufactured is now diminished, I yet know from various sources, that not only plain linen, but damasks and table-linen, which were formerly made in various parts of Hannover, are now much less made.

The diminution of the linen manufactory has been attributed to the late war, which prevent ed the linen from finding its way to the West Indies and America. This cause for the want of a market was aided by our machinery, which enabling us to sell our cottons cheaper than the Germans could sell their linen, has in some measure diminished its consumption. A proof of this is, that many Germans now wear cotton shirts, who a few years ago never wore anything but home-made linen. This alteration must be most mischievous to the peasants. Thinly scattered as they are over the country, and destitute of any large capital or ingenuity, there can be little hope that they can supply the place of this manufactory with any other equally advantageous. Perhaps it is desirable that they should attend exclusively to agriculture; but, till the land is appropriated in larger portions, and used on easier conditions, and till they acquire a sufficiency of capital and skill to enable them to live solely by farming, they must suffer much by losing one of the means they formerly possessed of contributing to their own maintenance.

---

Presumably the quotes in the previous paragraph were Hodgskin's translations of passages from this work.]

[50] **Hodgskin's F/N:-** There have lately appeared some accounts of the King of Prussia having given a sum of money for the relief of the linen manufacturers of Silesia.

[51] **Editor's F/N:-** A Hank of linen was usually about 300 yards or 270 metres.

The manufacture of cotton is increasing. There is one considerable manufactory at Osterode, and at various places in Hannover smaller ones are established. Several have, however, failed. In the dominions of Prussia cotton is manufactured very successfully and is on the increase. It is so well made in the provinces on the Rhine as to compete successfully with that made in our country. There were twenty-two spinning machines established, in 1818, on the left bank of the Rhine, belonging to Prussia. In Silesia the number of looms employed, in 1805, was 3,490, and the value of the cotton prepared amounted to 975,998 Thalers, (£162,666).

The manufactory of wool is next in point of importance to that of linen; but of this I have not been able to collect any details which can be relied on, except for Prussia. In the provinces on the Rhine, woollens are manufactured equal to ours.

It is surely a high honour that the manufactories of England should be the standard by which other nations judge their own. In the former *department de Rure*, the manufactory of wool employed, in 1812, 50,000 persons, and the value of the product was 30,000,000 Francs. Both in Saxony and in the dukedom of Berg, casimirs are extensively made. In Berg, in 1812, there were seventy manufactories of cloth and casimir. Brandenburg has also several woollen manufactories. The value of the woollen cloth, of every sort, manufactured in Silesia in 1805, amounted to 4,982,933 Thalers, (£830,489).[52] A coarse woollen cloth, which is the usual wear of the peasantry, is made in all parts of Germany. Sometimes it is made by the bauers, and sometimes by regular cloth makers.

That the manufacture of woollen cloth in Hannover has decayed, is evident from the fact, that formerly there were not less than 800 clothmakers in Göttingen; now there are but two manufactories, which do not altogether employ 400 persons. When I visited them it was autumn, and all work was fully suspended, that the people might gather in the harvests. Here, again, we see the advantage of machinery. We can bring the wool of Hannover to England, manufacture it into cloth, and send it back there for sale.

Paper is made in considerable quantities in all parts of Germany, but it is chiefly of the coarse kind. The finer sorts are made on the Rhine. Thirty-three paper-mills are enumerated in Hannover, seven of which belong to the crown, and paper making is on the increase.

---

[52] **Hodgskin's F/N:-** Demian, 69.

Ironstone is found in most of the mountains and hills of Germany. The principal places, however, where iron foundries are established on an extensive scale in northern Germany, are the Harz, Westphalia, particularly in the neighbourhood of Siegen and Altenkirchen, and in Silesia. From the mines of the Harz belonging to various sovereigns, no book is known in which the whole of their products are enumerated. Those which belong to Hannover are divided into three districts or berg-amts;

1)  That of Clausthal, all the mines and foundries of which deliver 21,357 marks of silver, 22,597 hundred weight of lead, 582 hundred weight of copper, 100,338 hundred weight of various sorts of iron, yearly;

2)  That of Cellesfeld, the mines and foundries deliver 10,841½, marks of silver, 16,144 hundred weight of lead, and 142 hundred weight of copper, yearly;

3)  That of Goslar, the products of the mines in this district belong to Hannover and Brunswick in the proportion of four-sevenths to the former, and three-sevenths to the latter. The quantity of their yearly produce which belongs to Hannover is estimated at 6½, marks of gold, 2,039½ marks of silver, 3,205 hundred weight of lead, 1416 hundred weight of copper, 2,987 hundred weight of zinc, and some hundred weight of sulphur, copperas, and potash.

Hannover also possesses some other iron and copper works, which may supply 700 hundred weight of copper, 500 hundred weight of brass, and 2,000 hundredweight of iron.[53]

These products are not the tithe of what the north of Germany supplies. While I regret not being able to furnish a correct account of the whole, enough has been said to prove that it is deficient in none of the materials of a manufacturing country.

Porcelain and common earthenware are made in various parts, particularly in the royal manufactories at Meissen in Saxony, and at Berlin. Some of the potteries of Hannover presented rather strange examples of the imperfect manner in which labour is yet divided. At one which I visited, near the small town of Münder, five men were at work, who made, in the course of a year, 26 fuder of a coarse earthenware. Each fuder contains 36 hundred weight.

The workmen had to bring the earth they used three miles. They went every summer and brought as much as served them the whole

---

[53] **Hodgskin's F/N:-** *Neueste Land und Volkerkunde*, 19th Band. Weimar,

year. The only machines they had to prepare the earth were knives, with which they cut it into thin slices, and thus were enabled to separate all the stony and rough particles. It was cleaned by the same hand that dug and moulded it, and that placed it in the oven. Other examples have already been given of an imperfect division of labour, which must undoubtedly be considered as a cause of the slow progress of many of the manufactories of Germany.

One of the manufactories whose increase deserves to be mentioned is spirits. In every part of the north of Germany distilleries have increased and brewhouses decreased.

The wages of the workmen in iron have been mentioned in the 10th Chapter of the First Volume, and I shall here add such other wages of manufactural labour as I learnt. Carpenters and such trades gained in Hannover from 18d. to 2s. a-day. The latter was, however, for extraordinary work. Shoemakers working by the piece earned from 3 to 4½ Thalers (10s. to 15s.) per week; tailors about 13d. per day and their breakfast. A law of the guild of tailors forbids paying them by the piece. Glassblowers working by the piece make, when trade is brisk, between 4 and 5 Thalers, 13s. 4d. to 16s. 8d. per week; coal-miners, who were paid at the rate of 28 gute groschen for every *himpten* of coals, made, on an average, little more than a shilling a day. It is, however, to be remarked, that many of the journeymen live in the families of their employers, and then receive so much per year. I have found the sum given varying from £5 to £8 Sterling per year for journeymen mechanics. From some accounts which I have seen of the wages of labour in the year 1796, they appear not to have increased since then in nominal value, and to have decreased in real value. In fact, the rate seems remarkably equal and steady throughout Germany.

The fact mentioned above, that many of the journeymen tradesmen still live with their employers, is a specimen of the equality and homely state of society in Germany. The progress of refinement, if such an alteration can be called refinement, seems to be to banish this homely state. It once existed in England. Both masters and journeymen, I believe, like our present mode better, and an individual cannot decide that their judgment is wrong. I can but remark, however, that when masters describe the former state as a "grovelling situation," they like the present one better, chiefly because it ministers to their pride; and, while they boast their democratic feelings, it lessens the distinction between them and their employers, and makes a more marked boundary between them and their journeymen. It renders more perfect that aristocracy of wealth, which is already stronger in our country than in any other.

It can only be known from the experience of future ages, if this aristocracy, now first coming to its full growth, be not more pernicious than that aristocracy of birth which is sinking to decay, and which has so long been the plague of the world.

After visiting the greater part of the manufacturing establishments of Hannover, it would have given me pleasure could I have recorded anything of them that indicates rapid improvement; but to me it appears as if they were yet in a most backward state. There is not a single steam-engine in the whole country, and, with the exception of the rolling machine at Oker, and the boring machine at Konigshütte, I know of nothing that deserves the name of an improvement. The greater part of the people supply their own wants and make little or nothing to exchange. It is admitted by German authors, that Hannover, and a great part of Germany may be added, is not a manufacturing country. They attribute this to a want of enterprise in the people; they admit that it is an evil, but they charge it on the natural character of their countrymen. Other persons follow on the same ground, and the indolence, which is perhaps derived from other causes, is all attributed to nature.

To me it appears to be of much more importance to rescue nature from those unfounded imputations, which ascribe to her the characteristics of evil, and which, classing man as little better than a sloth, make him worthy to be a slave, than merely to enumerate the number of iron bars or bolts of linen which are made in a year: and I shall, therefore, here offer some observations on the causes which have impeded the manufactural industry of the Germans.

When we turn our view to the localities of Germany, and find the most valuable metals, such as iron, copper, lead, – the most useful minerals, such as coal, lime, salt, – and the most beneficial plants scattered profusely throughout the country, – and, at the same time, merely glance at what is performed in it, we must conclude that its natural advantages have never been adequately employed. This is indeed an admitted fact, and the Germans themselves attribute it to a natural heaviness of character. It has already been mentioned that this characteristic does not apply to the people of Hamburg, who are as keen specialists as any of the world ; and if we turn our view to the twelfth, thirteenth, and fourteenth centuries, we shall also be convinced that it did not then form any part of the character of the inhabitants of the free towns of Germany.

Then the inhabitants of the smallest towns, such as Stade, Lüneburg, Uelzen, to say nothing of the more distinguished Nuremberg, Magdeburg, and many others, and the progress they made in industry and the arts; were distinguished by a commercial and enterprising spirit, which equalled that of any other people of Europe. In proportion, however, as these towns came to be governed by a self-elected magistracy of lawyers, or fell under the power of some sovereigns, their trade decayed. Many of the motives for which men desire wealth were destroyed by the change in their political relations, and their enterprising spirit ceased with their freedom. Prior to the seventeenth century the Germans were next to the Italians in mechanical ingenuity and the useful arts.

Southern Germany then surpassed northern Germany, but since the Reformation, which brought freedom with it, or rather protected, in some measure, what before existed, the latter has surpassed the former. At present, the inhabitants on the Rhine do not want enterprise.

The Germans who emigrate and cultivate Russia and America, and the individuals who acquire fortunes in other European lands, are as enterprising as any people of the world, and an opposite characteristic only distinguishes those who live in Germany from the numerous governments of that country regulating and hampering every branch of industry.

Some examples of the minuteness of their interference have been given in the chapter on Government, and to these may be added the fact, that no man can establish any new species of industry in almost any part of Germany without the royal sanction. The monarchs are manufacturers and monopolists, and they allow nothing to be undertaken that might render the value of their monopolies less. The monopoly of salt is a striking example, and I have been informed, that the principal motive why the coals, which are found in abundance in Saxony, are not permitted to be imported into the territories of Prussia, bordering on the Elbe, is, that the importation would reduce the price of the domanial woods. When it is considered that every sovereign of Germany is a monopolist, and that the principle of regulating every branch of industry is in full operation in every one of its numerous governments, we may rather be surprised that, under such a disadvantage, any portion of the Germans should have retained either enterprise or industry, than that they should be slow and indolent.

Several individual instances have fallen under my observation of enterprise whenever there was room to exert it. No persons are more accused of wanting this quality than the bauers; yet, whenever they have had an opportunity, they have adopted the cultivation of tobacco and summer fruits. They have improved much within this last fifty years. I may also quote the enterprise of an individual who was rather favoured by government.

Mr. Chief Factor Schachtrupp has lately established at Osterode a white lead and a shot manufactory, which is not only complete as a manufactural establishment, but is built with great neatness and taste.  The vinegar for acidifying the lead was made in the house, the grinding mills, though all the machinery was of wood, were very good, and the article was entirely prepared for sale in the same building.  Shot were made after the English method, by being dropped from a great height, and might possibly compete, as it was evidently the proprietor's intention they should, with English shot.  The bags in which they were to be packed were marked with the king's arms, and "Patent Shot, London."

Numerous attempts, also, which have been made without success, to establish manufactories, are proofs that the people do not naturally want enterprise.  This acknowledged feature of their character is rather to be attributed to their governments, than to nature, or original sin; though these are the imagined causes to which all men refer those evils which they are either too indolent to inquire into, or too vain to imagine can be brought on by themselves.

It has not been from a want of wish to promote the manufactural industry of their subjects that the sovereigns of Germany have erred, but from ignorance.  They have established boards of trade and departments of ministry for its encouragement, they have given premiums on particular productions, they have directed how linen is to be made, and that people must not burn their cloth in pressing it.  In short, every manual art seems to have been more subjected in Germany to prescribed forms than in any other country.  The monarchs have carried the tactics of the camp into the concerns of commerce, – they have tried to drill it into neatness and order; – they have constrained and partially destroyed it, till little more remains of it than the drill-serjeants.

There was a time when our own government was equally ignorant, when it prescribed all the arts of life, but the intelligence of our people has surmounted the difficulty it threw in their way, and we have grown rich and ingenious in spite of regulations.  To this day in Hannover both woollen cloth and linen must be made according to prescribed forms, and they are both examined to see that they are so made.  This regulation, which was made by consumers, was intended, according to the declaration of the law[54] itself, "to ensure the consumer good cloth at a reasonable rate."

---

[54] **Hodgskin's F/N:-** This law was made in 1768, and so late as 1816 regulations were made for the manufacture of linen.

With such restrictions, we surely need not seek in nature for any occult cause why the Hannoverians are neither enterprising nor ingenious.

It was a part of this same system of policy to fix the price of every article consumed. Formerly the magistrates of the towns did this on every article of food which was sold. At present, it is done by the police, and prices are regularly fixed by it on meat and bread. The facts on which its judgment is founded are unknown, but "the wish to procure good articles at a cheap rate," is undoubtedly the motive for the interference. We can hardly say the police is to blame in doing this, for it only fulfils the wishes of the inhabitants.

They all think the markets ought to be under the control of the magistrates. On the same principle strangers are forbidden to purchase anything in the market at Hannover before twelve o'clock, on pain of being fined. Everybody who purchases to sell again is also forbidden to lay in his store before the same hour, and this is also done that the inhabitants of the town may buy cheap.

There may be traced, not only in the present regulations, but in the regulations of times past, a constant opposition of interest between the towns and the bauers, and it is still an opinion of their inhabitants, that, but for these regulations, the bauers would impose on them. They trust nothing either to the interest or the virtue of men but expect everything good from the interference of the magistrate. These minor but impolitic regulations seem not to be sufficiently remarked.

Most of the enlightened writers of Germany are inhabitants of towns, and it is probable this circumstance has had an influence on their judgments. They do not seem to be yet interested in procuring a free market for all sorts of produce. The bauer is himself ignorant of his rights and his interests. He belongs to that class which has nobody to speak for it, because it can reward nobody. He neither reads, nor buys books, and literary men as necessarily suit their commodities to the market as any other sort of labourers.

It is the inhabitants of towns and rich people who reward the labours of the literary man; and while a few writers are found who flatter the passions of the mob, by much the greater part of them flatter the prejudices and passions of the wealthy and the powerful. It is one of the most absurd of modern opinions, that they who have nothing to give will be the general objects of adulation; and that they who have both the power to punish and reward will always be told disagree able truths. The passions and prejudices of the pen-holding and wealthy part of every society seem to be sacred idols, to which the passions and prejudices of the rest must submit without inquiry. They have long been exclusively worshipped and are now become the legitimate guides of all men.

It must be from the natural resources of a country that its manufactories can be established, and if the whole of these are seized on at the outset by people who produce nothing, it is obvious that the country never can be manufactural. Sovereigns can never manufacture to advantage. Every person they employ is necessarily destitute of that impulse to exertion which is derived from individual interest, and subjects can have neither enterprise nor ingenuity when all the materials on which they can be exerted are monopolized by the crown. One great material of manufactories is metal, and this is monopolized by the sovereigns throughout Germany. When the mines themselves are not the property of the monarch, yet all their produce must be delivered to him; and sometimes, as is the case on the Harz, at a fixed price. Most of the sovereigns of Germany are manufacturers of cast and wrought iron, makers of porcelain, and salt, the owners of large portions of territory, and sole proprietors of most of the forests.

The sovereign of Hannover is both papermaker and miller. He fattens his own fowls and makes his own butter. He has lime-kilns at Lüneburg, and brick-kilns at Herrenhausen; he employs factors in various places to dispose of his products; in short, he is the only extensive manufacturer and merchant in his own dominions. All the original sources of wealth are, therefore, monopolized by the sovereign, and as these are employed in supporting an idle state, it is impossible that the people can be manufactural.

If the produce of the country were the property of individuals, it would only be consumed by those who were employed in creating more. The interest of the sovereign not only operates on him to make laws which check and restrain the industry of individuals, but he monopolizes the whole resources of the country, and he can at least have only himself to blame that they are ill employed.

According to the genius of his government, most of the produce of the country is divided in small, very small portions, amongst his numerous servants, who are obliged to support a certain dignity of appearance and can never accumulate capital. In truth, he is the only capitalist of his dominions. His monopoly and his laws are two of the great causes why the "exertions of his subjects do not keep pace with his wishes for their improvement."

It is a strange prejudice which makes nobles think themselves disgraced by being farmers or merchants, and honoured if they receive from the monarch an appointment to inspect his salt-works or his mines, or to manage one of his estates. It seems to be still stranger, that they should imitate the sovereign in all things but one, and disdain to be merchants or manufacturers when he is the greatest merchant and manufacturer in his dominions. But this may have its source in a dread of competition; he honours soldiers with medals, but a noble who should engage in trade would be excluded from royal favour.

Men have unfortunately brought themselves to reverence the decrees of sovereigns somewhat more than the laws of nature, and hence the honours sovereigns bestow on some occupations have brought dishonour on others. Tradesmen, mechanics, and merchants are in general both poor and despised in Germany; they are promoted to no dignified places; – they receive no honours, and they acquire very little wealth. No merchant whatever has any political power, and hence his occupation is contemned.

A gentleman of Hannover, who held a situation under government without being a nobleman, told me he had taken what was considered as a most extraordinary step, in sending one of his sons into a counting-house at Hamburg. Not merely nobles, but all those persons who may be called professionalists, look on manufactures and on commerce as degrading. And hence all the ingenuity of the people is directed to the army, to the law, to literature, or to medicine, and everyone seeks to escape from dishonoured employments. There can be no question that this opinion has originated in the rewards bestowed by the sovereigns on particular professions, and it must be considered as one cause of a want of mechanical skill, ingenuity, and enterprise.

I have dwelt perhaps rather longer on these causes than I ought, but nothing seems to me so likely to be pernicious to the welfare of our race as an unfounded opinion, that nature gives us those bad qualities which are caused by systems of government; and that, at the same time, teaches us to look to government to remedy an evil which, if it be really natural, must be beyond its power to cure.

The manner in which the capital of Hannover is disposed of prevents accumulation. Persons who can live on profits are rare, and what would be called a rich merchant or manufacturer in Britain, is unknown in Hannover. I am far from thinking that large capitalists and numerous destitute workmen are desirable. A large quantity of useful machines, and of necessaries, and luxuries, divided into tolerably equal proportions, are much to be desired, but when they are collected in the hands of a few, they neither minister to greater production, nor to happiness and morality. Hannover wants the benefit of a large capital, but she is equally free from the curse of large capitalists.

It cannot be supposed that the people who are both farmers and weavers are less happy than those who only plough or weave; – that it diminishes the enjoyment of the individual both to prepare the clay and mould the jug, but the imperfect division of labour which has been mentioned, must be considered as a cause of less production. The minute division of labour which exists in our country, and the direction of the labours of many to complete one article, is what is wanted in Hannover. This is generally obtained through the means of large capitalists, but they are by no means necessary to its existence. We must distinguish, therefore, between the two things, and while we wish the mild and gentle people of Germany may acquire a large capital, and adopt a more minute division of labour, we must hope they will so acquire the one, and adopt the other, that their produce may not centre in the hands of one or a few individuals.

The chapter on Manufactories seems to be the proper place to say all that may be necessary on the trade corporations, *Zünfte*, of Germany. It is not necessary minutely and particularly to describe them, because similar corporations exist, or have existed, all over Europe; and I shall only remark those particulars in which they appear to differ from the corporations of the rest of Europe; and which must have had, and must still have, a powerful influence on the skill, ingenuity, character, and manners of all the mechanics of Germany.

You meet travelling on foot on every road a great number of young workmen; some are dirty and ragged, others are decently clad, some have money enough to pay their expences, others are privileged to beg. All these are set in motion and kept in motion by a law common to the corporation of every trade. According to this law, every apprentice is obliged to travel, or, as it is called, *wandern*, for three years from the expiration of his apprenticeship, in search of knowledge, before he is allowed to settle in any city as a master in which guilds are yet in existence. This is one of the most important regulations of these guilds in which they differ from the corporations of our own country.

From the minute division of landed property which has been described, it might be expected that Germany would be, like Ireland, overrun with a famished and a degraded population. It is certainly far less so than our sister island; and possibly much of this evil may have been prevented by the wisdom of a regulation also common to all the trades. This is, that no journeyman shall marry. If he do, if he even impregnate a woman, – he is banished from their society, he can obtain no employment in the trade, and he has no resource but common daily labour to save him from starving.

These two regulations, which seem very important, are not, however, invariably praise-worthy. It is not a rational objection to a man marrying, that he is a journeyman, though it be a very rational one, that he is not able to maintain a wife and family; and many men set up for masters before they otherwise would, in order to obtain the privilege of marrying. Most of the mechanics and tradesmen throughout the countries where the guild laws are in existence, have seldom more than enough, with their labours, to support themselves and family. I have met with shopkeepers who were comparatively rich, but opulent mechanics, though the nation be frugal, are extremely rare. Part of the eagerness which has been remarked to become masters, may be attributed to the restraint on journeymen marrying.

There is possibly no method by which men who have a sufficient stock of previous knowledge, and who desire to increase it, may improve themselves more than by travelling. It appears to have been from this idea that the law was made which obliges every young man, after his term of apprenticeship is expired, to seek work abroad as a journeyman, for three years, before he can settle as a master. Many people of this description, however, must be perfectly unfit to travel, and it leads them into much dissipation.

It is degrading, and often destructive to the upright independence of young men, to wander about the country with a privilege to beg. I have had various opportunities, in fact, of witnessing the dissipation which the practice of wandering produces, to say nothing of the idleness necessarily occasioned by so frequently being out of employment. All the trades have different rules as to the manner of treating their wandering brethren when they arrive at any town in which guilds are established. Some make it a rule to give them only a lodging, others a lodging and a certain sum of money, and others, as the Smiths, assemble at their house of call whenever any brethren arrive, and pass the night in jollity and mirth.

All travelling journeymen have regular passports called wandering-books, and the regulations by which they are to be governed, such as not to stay longer than twenty-four hours in any one town, if they do not find employment, such as to beg in a regular manner, and apply to the magistrates for what is called the *Zehrpfennige*, subsistence-money, are printed in the first page. Such passports were formerly given by the magistrates of the towns and were then called certificates. I have reason to believe, from some police reports that I have seen, that a great part of all the persons sent out of different towns as vagabonds are wandering journeymen.

The German mechanics, from seeing various cities, from mixing with a variety of men, possess in general a great deal of knowledge, and of freedom in opinion and action; but they are poor in spirit, averse to labour, and more given than the other classes of the society to joviality and dissipation. The advantages of travelling, when men themselves like it and choose it, and are fit to travel, are very great, but to compel the whole of so large a class of men as the journeymen mechanics to travel, by a law, is so absurd as to prescribe precisely the same regimen to the sick and to the healthy.

When it was first made, also, there was little other communication between towns than what arose from people visiting them; there was no post, no press, and no periodical publications to give an account of improvements; and then, compelling the younger members of the guilds to travel in search of knowledge was much more rational than at present. One great advantage, apparently, of this law is, that it keeps the journeymen on a level with the demand for their labour. The assistance afforded them by the corporations when they are compelled to wander, protects them from absolute distress, and, constantly circulated about the country, they are always conveyed to the spot where they are most wanted. Yet we know from experience, that this beneficial effect can be produced by the mere demand for labour, without a law to enforce and compel men to go where they are wanted.

The makers of guild laws have erred, as almost all law-makers err, from not distinguishing two things which are in themselves essentially distinct and different. These are, a desired line of conduct, and a law to compel that line of conduct.

It is one thing, that a man ought to do a certain action, it is another and a perfectly distinct thing to make a law to compel him to do it, or to punish him if he neglect it. It is, for example, much to be desired that bank-notes should not be forged. The effects of not doing this are confidence in the bank, security to property, and preserving a very convenient money in circulation; but it is perfectly a distinct thing to make a law that men shall not forge bank-notes, or to sentence them to be hung if they are detected in doing it. The effect of this is, to encourage a line of conduct directly contrary to that desired.

Experience has shown it; and when men are told they must not do any certain action under the penalty of being hung, they are immediately persuaded that it will be a great advantage to them to do it, provided they can escape detection. Neither the makers of guild laws, nor the makers of laws for nations, will ever make good laws till they seize and preserve this distinction, nor till they invariably ascertain what will be the effect of making a law forcibly to produce a desired line of conduct.

The guilds are not at present universally established in Germany, though formerly there was not a single trade through the whole country, not even that of floating rafts down rivers, but what had its own guild laws. Whether this corporation compelled their apprentices and journeymen to wander in search of knowledge, I am not informed; but it monopolized the management of all the floating wood, and nobody dared conduct a raft on the Danube or Elbe without being one of the brethren.

Guilds are abolished through the whole of the Prussian territories, and in Bavaria. The monarchs have laid a tax on every trade, by requiring every person to pay for permission to exercise it. They pay soldiers, but tradesmen must pay them.

Guilds were abolished wherever the French power reached, but they are now again restored in various places, in Hannover for example, to all their former privileges. There are some towns free from them, but they are the offspring of towns, and are still generally found in all the large ones. They were originally combinations of men, so well for political as for other purposes, but they have long ceased to take any part either in the government of the towns, with the exception of the Hanse towns, or in the government of the country.

Two of the guild laws, whose influence is most important, have been mentioned. A third regulation is, that every person wishing to practise any art, whose members form a guild, must serve three or four years as an apprentice to learn that art; and there is no one, not even that practised by merchants, which has not a guild; so that every species, almost, of industry, is subject to this restriction. No journeyman can be employed who has not served a regular apprenticeship. Some trades, such as butchers, bakers, chimney-sweepers, are called close trades.

Others are open. In the former only a limited number of masters is allowed in any one town, from a supposition that more could not obtain a living; in the latter the number is not limited. Some curious examples are known of the former mode. For example, in Lüneburg the privilege of brewing was attached to particular houses, while the right to distil brandy was hereditary in twelve families, and no other person than the twelve representatives of these families could keep a distillery. Such limitations as these, which were very general, appear to have been made by masters in order to secure themselves a subsistence.

After serving an apprenticeship, and travelling as a journeyman, every person who wishes to establish himself as a master must first make some finished piece of work, called a Meisterstück, to prove his capability to work. If he is not the son of a citizen, he must buy the right of citizenship in the town where he wishes to settle.

The price, of course, is various in different towns. It has long been a law that certain trades shall be only carried on within the walls of towns, and no journeyman dare do a piece of work on his own account. He must be employed by a master regularly established in a town. Formerly this privilege was confined to fewer towns than at present, and formerly those masters who settled in the country were obliged to enrol themselves in the guild of some town and contribute to its expence. There were formerly still more hindrances to becoming a master. A man was obliged, for example, in some towns, to have a house of his own before he could be a tailor, and to prove himself not to belong to any family which had been ennobled.

These regulations were originally made by members of the trades themselves, and not by the governments. They have failed in their laudable efforts to ensure good workmen by sending them to travel, and by making them give proofs of their ability. I can safely assert, that all the common trades, such as tailors, shoemakers, bakers, smiths, have not attained so great a degree of perfection in Germany as in England. What may also possibly be deemed a proof of their uselessness is, that milliners, who have no guilds, are as clever in Germany as in other countries.

It has been justly observed, that most of the great improvements which have of late years been made in the machinery and manufactories of England, have been made by persons not apprenticed to the arts they have improved, consequently, even the fewer restrictions as to apprenticeships which are found in England than in Germany, by hindering ingenious men from following the bent of their inclination, have been pernicious to improvements. The most manufacturing part of Germany is the country about the Rhine, and there, I believe, guild laws have been long abolished. The guild laws, therefore, of Germany, extending to every trade, may be considered as having in part caused the Germans not to make the same progress in manufactures as we have made. And as they regulate so many of the actions of men, they may also be regarded as aiding to produce that unenterprising character which is ascribed generally to the Germans.

The partial abolition of these regulations, and the works which have been written in Germany on the subject of guilds, prove that our neighbours are sensible of their injurious nature, and that, in this respect, so well as in respect to many other minor regulations, they are making a rapid improvement. In looking, however, at what has been written, it is impossible to avoid remarking, that the observations have been chiefly or wholly made by men whose profession was learning, and that it would be difficult to find an instance where the mere citizens in Germany have thrown light on this subject, as they have in England.

In fact, I have talked to several tradesmen on the subject, and never met with but one individual, and he was a journeyman, whose years of wandering were expired, and who could not get settled, in which the tradesmen did not approve of the guild laws. The momentary abolition of them by the French gave a sort of licence to journeymen. Everyone who could pay the tax on trades set up for a master, and a vast deal of poverty and misery were the consequence. This fact by no means proves the wisdom of the guild laws, though it throws some light on the effects of abolishing them by an arbitrary decree. It is, indeed, at present, an admitted fact in Germany so well as in Britain, that all such regulations as the guild laws prevent much good.

The organization of men according to their trades, gave the citizens of the middle ages a spirit and a power which enabled them to protect themselves and promote civilization. At present every man finds protection in general opinion supporting the laws of the society, and these combinations now do nothing but promote monopoly. It ought not, however, to be the government which should abolish them. Its interference is above all things to be deprecated, and its only duty on this subject is to refuse its support to them and leave them to be abolished by the rest of the society refusing to submit to them.

# Chapter VII.

## Hannover - Commence.

Number of ships formerly. — Facilities for trade. — Commerce of rivers. — Regulations and tolls on the Elbe. — Regulations on the Weser. — Toll. — Vessels employed on the Aller — on the Leine. — Limitations to the trade on the Ilmenau. — Tolls on roads. — Impediments to commerce in Germany. — Advantages of Britain. — Effect of Hanse towns on the commerce of Hannover. — Canals. — Roads — Posts.

The causes which impede the productive power of any country, necessarily limit its commerce, and that of Hannover is, therefore, not of much importance. The great mass of the inhabitants supply their own wants; they desire nothing and have nothing to give ; and though this may promote individual independence, it makes commerce unnecessary and impossible. It is a matter of surprise, and even of wonder, when the manufactories of Hannover are so trifling, that a department or the Hannoverian ministry should be set apart for them, and that a college of commerce should have been in existence when there was little or no commerce to regulate.

It was imagined that the industry of a nation was to be directed by its rulers; and they, therefore, began by making regulations for what did not exist. Before the acquisition of Papenburg and Friezland, the commerce of Hannover was almost nothing. Its people made several attempts to carry on trade, but they seem all to have failed. They have at various times fitted out ships to participate in the whale-fishery; the sovereign has supported these enterprises; they have been continued for a season or two, and then laid aside as unprofitable. These efforts seem to have been regarded as something very mighty, — as synonymous with the expedition of the Argonauts, or the voyage of Columbus. The ships have been accurately described; the quantity of stores they required was carefully enumerated; and no circumstance concerning them, which could serve to give posterity a correct idea of the mighty enterprise, seems to have been forgotten.

In 1796, the electorate of Hannover possessed, exclusively of one or two whalers, two vessels that were employed in carrying goods on freight. Their united tonnage did not exceed 300.[55] Now that Papenburg and Embden are united to Hannover, she is almost elevated to the rank of a ship-owning nation. The former want of ships has not been owing to the government not having encouraged the people to build and navigate them. It has given premiums for both. Nor has it been owing to any want of good harbours and rivers.

One side of the mouths of the Elbe and the Weser, and much of both sides of these rivers, in their course, have for many years formed part of the old dominions of his Majesty. The situation of the two free Hanse towns diminishes in some measure the value of these rivers; but, while they oppose no natural obstacle to the trade of Hannover, more than the advantages they derive from the freedom of their government, they ought to promote competition, and enrich rather than impoverish Hannover. Hannover has other ample means of communication. The Oste and the Medem, which are both navigable for a considerable distance, flow into the Elbe, so near to its mouth that they may rather be said to flow into the sea. The Oste is navigable for more than thirty miles and communicates with the heart of Bremen. Ships can enter it and be perfectly safe.

Hannover also possesses more than twenty rivers, flowing into the Elbe, the Weser, and the Ems, which are navigable for some considerable distance; and the Aller, the Leine, and the Ilmenau, are navigable into the very centre of the land. Nature everywhere provides some sort of compensations for apparent evils, and she has sent so many gentle streams through the flat sands of Hannover, that it appears one of the countries best adapted for inland navigation of Europe. I shall here quote the opinion of a German to strengthen my own. He says of Hannover:

"that its situation and qualities favour manufactories and commerce. Situated in the north of Germany, a great part of the foreign trade of all the southern parts is carried on through it. With large navigable rivers on the east and on the west, – with the open ocean to the north, surrounded with fertile and rich lands, and possessing itself various

---

[55] **Hodgskin's F/N:-** Patje Kurzer Abriss, p. 424. This book was published in 1796, and no accounts of the commerce of Hannover later than it have been published.

products, it ought to be both a manufactural and a commercial country. Yet it is neither."

Nothing more will be said of the external commerce of Hannover, than that the whalers have long since been laid aside, and that Papenburg and Friezland may together possess 500 vessels of all descriptions. Friezland alone had, in 1813, 280 vessels, which together carried 22,000 lasts[56], and were manned by 1,750 men. In 1817, 54 vessels were employed in the herring-fishery, and as many more in other fisheries; but I have been assured both these branches of industry have decreased. No later accounts of its commerce have been met with than for 1781, which are given, I believe, in Oddy's European Commerce.[57] The trade on the rivers of Hannover is not only of more importance as to its quantity, but it dis plays more accurately the impediments which have been thrown in the way of the commerce, not only of this country, but of Germany, and the remain der of this chapter will be confined nearly to it.

It appears from what has been written on the subject, that one principal motive why the government of Hannover was anxious to acquire Friezland was, that it might have a sea-port. In fact, Hannover before possessed sea-ports, but the people had never adequately employed them, or profited by the advantages of their situation. This is to be attributed to the nature of the government; and it is not to be expected, that when it has prevented its ancient subjects from having commerce, that it will be able to augment that which its newly-acquired subjects before possessed, and which it has been the great object of its ambition to acquire.

This commerce is divided into two parts, that which centres in Hannover, and that which passes through it. The territories of Hannover intervene between the two Hanse towns and southern Germany, and most of the commerce which these two towns carry

---

[56] **Editor's F/N:-** A last, in this context was a large shipping weight, often over 1,800kg, that appears to have varied dependent on the cargo shipped.
[57] **Editor's F/N:-** To give it its full, rather lengthy title:
European Commerce, Shewing New and Secure Channels of Trade with the Continent of Europe: Detailing the Produce, Manufactures, and Commerce, of Russia, Prussia, Sweden, Denmark, and Germany; as Well as the Trade of the Rivers Elbe, Weser, and Ems, with a General View of the Trade, Navigation, Produce, and Manufactures, of the United Kingdom of Great Britain and Ireland, and Its Unexplored and Improvable Resources and Interior Wealth: Illustrated with a Canal and River Map of Europe.
It was published in London (1805) and Philadelphia (1807) by Joshua Jepson Oddy (c. 1735/50–1814).

on with the rest of the country necessarily passes through Hannover. A portion of it is performed by land, and a portion by water carriage. The Elbe, the Weser, the Aller, the Leine, and the Ilmenau, are the rivers which principally serve this latter purpose.

Although Hannover has little to do with the commerce of the Elbe, some little facts are known connected with that commerce, which deserve to be mentioned. It is a regulation of the Prussian sovereign, that all commodities, with the exception of millstones and pottery, coming from Bohemia or Saxony, by that river, must be unloaded at Magdeburg and loaded in Prussian vessels, navigated by Prussian seamen. It may, therefore, be inferred, that the greater part of the commerce of that river is carried on by vessels belonging to Magdeburg. In 1815 Magdeburg possessed 75 boats and barges of all descriptions. In 1818 a steam-boat was established to pass between Hamburg and Berlin.

In America such useful inventions have been established on many rivers for several years. There is no possibility of ascertaining exactly the whole commerce of the Elbe, but, after seeing its waters almost unemployed, I should suppose, that on some of the rivers of America there is as much commerce as on the Elbe. The rivers of America are free; the Elbe has always been subjected to various princes. Riesebeck says, in his 46th letter, that the King of Prussia at one time laid such heavy tolls on vessels going from Hamburg to Saxony, as entirely to stop all the commerce between these two places which was carried on by means of this river. It then went through Hannover and Brunswick.

Other sovereigns have probably laid tolls on it as heavy as those of Prussia, and probably they may be as numerous as those belonging to Hannover, which amount to six. With such impediments, notwithstanding the length of its course, the fertile and various countries through which it flows, and the number of ages its banks have been peopled, it is not at all surprising that there is probably more commerce on some of the rivers of America than on the Elbe.

Before 1806, it was calculated that 364 vessels arrived at Münden by the Weser, 104 by the Werra, and 128 by the Fulda, yearly. And the manner in which these vessels, at least those which pass between Bremen and Münden, are regulated, is one of the most curious measures of policy I have met with. Nothing is left to competition or to alacrity. The most idle and most neglectful boat men are as often employed as the most industrious and skilful. The banks of the Weser belong to different sovereigns, and it is to give a portion of the trade to the subjects of each, that the regulation has been made.  First, a boat belonging to Prussia is loaded, then one belonging to Hannover; the third belongs to Prussia, and the fourth to Hannover; the fifth must belong to Hesse Cassel.  The subjects of these three powers alternate in this manner till the thirty-fifth boat, which must belong to the town of Bremen, and so must the fortieth, when the rotation is again resumed, and is in this manner perpetually repeated.

This is not all; the right to navigate the different rivers Fulda and Werra belongs to different people.  The Hannoverians and Hessians may both navigate on the Werra, but only Hannoverians are permitted to use the Fulda.  In Münden, to which the principal part of this commerce, so far as Hannover is concerned, belongs, a certain number of barge-owners only are allowed, and it is probable a similar regulation exists in the other towns that take part in this trade.  This is not the only impediment.  There are no less than twenty-two tolls on the Weser betwixt Münden and Bremen, seven of which belong to  the sovereign of Hannover.  There are also some below the latter town, one of which, at Elsfleth,[58] has already been mentioned.

At every toll every vessel is stopped and her whole cargo examined.  On an average, more than one hour is employed at each toll to examine each vessel; so that everyone loses one whole day in passing between these two towns.  This is mere waste, a loss of time to all the parties, more injurious probably than the duties which the merchants have also to pay.  I have been informed that not one of the sovereigns who levy these tolls, except the King of Prussia, has ever employed one farthing of the money thus collected in clearing the river.  It is exacted merely to enrich them, or rather to employ and pay a certain set of dependants.  It is said the expence of collecting the tolls equals the receipts.

Münden is the most considerable trading town of Hannover, sending yearly to the other parts of Germany 450,000 *centner* of goods; 150 waggons and 600 carts go from it to South-western, and 14 waggons and 118 carts to South-eastern Germany.  The linen sent to Bremen is estimated at 1,000,000 florins yearly.  The other articles sent to Bremen are, colours, dry goods, tobacco, potash, lamp-black, paper, Nuremberg ware, iron, wood of various kinds, millstones, and Rhenish and Necker wines.  Coffee, sugar, and other colonial products are the principal articles brought from Bremen.

---

[58] **Hodgskin's F/N:-** Vol. I. p. 276. [p.158 in this *Collected Works* edition.]

There are about forty vessels employed on the Aller, the greater part of which belong to Bremen. There are three tolls on this river, between Celle and where it unites with the Weser, and all belong to Hannover. In the year 1791, Bremen sent to the town of Hannover, by the Aller and Leine, goods to the amount of 342,804 Reichs Thalers; to Celle, goods to the amount of 438,472 R. Thalers; and to Verden, goods to the amount of 32,047 R. Thalers. The three towns at the same time sent goods to the amount of 401,527 R. Thalers to Bremen. The town of Celle, which stands on the Aller, has some transit commerce. In 1807, 10,849 waggons, drawn by 57,319 horses, passed through the town. Goods to the amount of 775,000 florins were at the same time conveyed by the Aller.

On the Leine, about twenty-four vessels capable of carrying eighty tons each, though they are seldom more than half loaded, pass and repass in a year between the towns of Bremen and Hannover. They are about sixty miles apart, and there are no less than five tolls in this distance. Every vessel is stopped and examined at each one of these. They all belong to the sovereign, but are let by him, so that his own goods must pay his own tolls. On an average each vessel has to pay in descending the river about 200 Thalers, or more than £30 Sterling. In ascending the charge is double.

The number of vessels trading on the Ilmenau has been already mentioned when speaking of the town of Lüneburg.[59] They are divided into three classes, and each of these classes is limited by an express regulation to carrying certain commodities only. The number of barge-owners is strictly limited. Fifteen possess the exclusive privilege of employing their boats in carrying merchandise; and there are six others who are allowed to participate in this when there is an abundance of goods to be conveyed. Twelve are allowed to trade with corn, and eight have the exclusive privilege to convey salt and bring back wood.

Other regulations prescribe, that no boat shall take more than a certain quantity of goods on board; though, when they are plentiful, it is allowed to take a greater quantity.[60] These are to be considered as regulations of the people themselves, rather than of the sovereign; and they may be taken as specimens of the manner in

---

[59] **Hodgskin's F/N:-** Vol. I. p.182. [p.109 in this *Collected Works* edition.]
[60] **Hodgskin's F/N:-** *Kurze Beschreibung und Geschichte der Stadt. Lüneburg*, von Manecke, p.67.
[**Editor's F/N:-** Urban Friedrich Christoph Manecke (1816) *Short description and history of the city. Lueneburg.*]

which they have blindly endeavoured to monopolize all trade, and prevent all fair and honourable competition.

It has before been mentioned,[61] that the trade of Lüneburg has gone to decay; and this is partly to be attributed to the unwise monopoly. It made carriage dear and induced the merchants to seek a cheaper road. The following regulation, however, was made by the sovereign. An individual lately employed a boat to convey goods from Uelsen by the Ilmenau to the Elbe. He had no sooner adopted this method, then the government made him pay a tax for his boat, and so completely took away his profits, that his enterprise received no reward. The motive for the tax was, that the royal tolls on the road might not suffer. Lüneburg is supposed to gain 33,275 R. Thalers by the transit commerce, and to employ a capital of 217,000 Thalers in its own trade.

I cannot give the reader any very accurate general account of the quantity of goods conveyed on these rivers; but the above are some specimens of the impediments under which the river navigation of Hannover labours. Similar tolls and impediments are known to exist on every river of Germany; and most of them, like those on the Weser, are taken for the benefit of the sovereigns. They are in general domanial, or the private property of the crown. Their proceeds are never accounted for but employed as the sovereign pleases.

A remarkable example which I met of these tolls was on entering the territories of Hungary. Because it formerly had a different master, tolls had been established at its confines, and they were still exacted. In passing by water between Vienna and Presburgh, the vessel was stopped and examined at the borders of Hungary. The examination occupied two hours, though the boat had been loaded at Vienna. The cargo of the raft on which I passed from Munich to Vienna was nothing but trees, deals, and three bales of goods; yet we were frequently detained both in Bavaria and Austria for hours, to have it examined.[62]    Boats whose cargoes were more

---

[61] **Editor's F/N:-** See page 109 within our *Collected Works of Thomas Hodgskin,* Volume III.

[62] **Hodgskin's F/N:-** If the reader pleases he can compare these simple facts with the mighty projects which are described at pages 243, 244, of Dr. Bright's *Travels in Lower Hungary,* as being at that time in contemplation of the Austrian government, to improve the navigation of Austria.

On the one hand we see real impediments thrown in the way of that commerce which the people have it in their power to practise. On the other, we see magnificent schemes proposed, which the people must, however, pay to have executed, to procure them a commerce they are sure, under

complicated than ours were sometimes detained half a day. Such are some of the means by which the commerce of the rivers of Germany is yet impeded.

Tolls on roads are perhaps not less numerous, though less pernicious, than tolls on rivers. The loading of a waggon is much sooner examined than the cargo of a ship. If these tolls were analogous to turnpike gates, and the money collected at them was employed to keep the roads in repair, they ought not to be objected to ; but they are in general domanial tolls, the produce of which goes into the pocket of the sovereign, and he repairs the road or not as he pleases. I do not know what number of these may anywhere exist, but I can state, that in Hannover they are numerous, and rigidly levied.

Because the sovereign's tolls might not suffer, the government of Hannover recently gave an order that all the commerce between Bremen and Celle should be carried on by a certain road only.[63] Such domanial tolls are common on all the roads of Germany, and in some parts, they belong to nobles. One instance has been mentioned;[64] and in the whole of Prussia there are yet eighteen noblemen who possess the right to tolls which are already levied, though I believe they have no power to levy new ones, or to increase the old.

In Saxony there is also one, but in Hannover all the tolls at present belong to the sovereign. Tolls are generally heavier for foreigners, under which term is included the subjects of other German powers, than for natives; and sometimes it appears that the sovereigns cannot agree on the conditions under which their respective subjects may be allowed to traverse the dominions of each other. Thus, the post which ought to go from Bremen direct through Oldenburg to Embden, a distance of seventy miles, goes all round by Osnabrück, which is at least twice as far; and it requires three days, without employing a messenger expressly for the purpose, to convey a letter from one of these two towns to the other.

---

the present system, never to have any capital to carry on.

If these mighty unions of the Danube with the Elbe were to take place, and the toll system to be put in practice on them, they would probably be more costly than land carriage. Canals, and roads, and rivers, are things governments ought to leave to their *subjects*, and ought to leave them *free*.

[63] **Hodgskin's F/N:-** Gesetz Sammlung, 29 Abtheilung, No.14.

(**Editor's F/N:-** Law Collection 29 Division, No.14.)

[64] **Hodgskin's F/N:-** Vol. I. p.112. [p.72 in this *Collected Works* edition.]

At present there is no government of Germany that permits goods coming from other parts of Germany freely to enter its territories; and many of the governments prohibit some of the productions of their neighbours, as salt, from entering their dominions. Formerly this state of things was much worse. More tolls were levied than at present; and the greater number of petty sovereigns which then existed almost limited the market for every commodity to a few square leagues.

Let any person conceive what would be the effect on the commerce of the Thames if there were twenty tolls between London Bridge and the Nore, and that every vessel which ascended or descended the river had to stop and be examined at every one of these tolls, and he may know accurately the extent of the impediments which the water tolls of the sovereigns of Germany throw in the way of the commerce of the country. It is true that none of the rivers of Germany are frequented so much as the Thames; but it is at the same time certain much more commerce would have been carried on by means of them but for these tolls.

Let any person further conceive custom-houses placed at the borders of every county in England, custom-house-officers examining every loaded waggon; and let him further conceive tolls at other places not the borders of counties, where every waggon must be equally examined, and he may then also know accurately the impediments which the land-tolls of the sovereigns throw in the way of commerce.

Germany has been in these points peculiarly unfortunate. It has been divided into many petty governments, each of which has been anxious to raise a revenue by all manner of exactions, and to acquire superiority by impeding the rise of others. Each has endeavoured to check the prosperity of its neighbour; and thus, there is not and never has been a free intercourse between all parts of Germany. Neither roads nor rivers are free; commerce is free only in a few square miles; and the merchants of Germany have always wanted an extensive home market and have rarely been able to engage in foreign trade, because they could never acquire capital enough to live on it till the returns came from abroad.

It would be a much greater benefit to the Germans to have a free intercourse with all parts of their own country, than to restrict the importation of English goods. Their interest would be more promoted by the abolition of tolls and border custom-houses than by the utter exclusion of foreigners from their markets. Possessing a fine country adorned with the noblest rivers of Europe, speaking the same language, and forming, in fact, but one people, they ought to have a most extensive commerce.

Nature has not divided the Prussians from the Austrians, and the Austrians from the Bavarians. They are all equally her children. She has given them rivers without a fall in their whole course, as a means of communication. She has made the products of the different climates objects of desire where they cannot be produced. She has given them minerals in their mountains, vines on their hills, and corn in their plains; but the proper enjoyment of all these advantages is denied to millions of active and intelligent beings, by the petty cares and petty avarice of two or three dozen princes and their ministers. It may be right to respect these personages, but it is treason to ourselves not to respect much more the whole race of mankind of which they form so small and so insignificant a part."[65]

It is from attending to the state of other countries that we learn properly to appreciate the advantages of our country; all our rivers and roads are in our own territories, and we have long enjoyed the inestimable advantage of a free intercourse with one another. The unrestricted commerce which the inhabitants of every part of Britain carry on with every other part is an advantage which no other number of persons equally large enjoy in Europe.

Even France, now that the Revolution has knocked off so many of the shackles which ignorance, and tyranny, and avarice, had imposed, does not yet enjoy absolute freedom of communication. Articles consumed in towns are subjected to a greater duty than those consumed in the country. It is consequently necessary to examine all loaded vehicles that pass through them, in order to ascertain that they do not contain any of these articles which they may leave behind and defraud the revenue.

Our unrestricted commerce, and the power of making roads, of establishing public vehicles, and of conveying goods in them at pleasure, which is enjoyed by our people, but which is monopolized by the crown in every other European country except Holland, are the real causes of much of our superior prosperity. It is of importance to remark, that this greater prosperity has been occasioned by the mere absence of governing. The comparative

---

[65] **Hodgskin's F/N:-** I have lately read of projects to unite, by means of canals, the Rhine and the Elbe with the Danube, and to establish a complete water communication throughout Germany. The project appears admirable, only it seems to me the height of folly to expect it will be carried into execution by the diet at Frankfort, or the united sovereigns. It will never succeed unless it is done by the people.

poverty of Germany arises from its being too much governed; our government has had about as much influence on this part of our welfare as it has had on sunshine and rain; in fact, it has done all it could to augment its interference, and thus to diminish our prosperity. Whatever it regulates becomes bloated or withered, and what it leaves to the unfettered sense of the people prospers.

It is from Germany, also, that we may learn how dreadfully pernicious to the welfare of man the numerous governments of the world have been. Not one of the rivers or roads of Germany can be profitably employed, because they all pass through the territories of different sovereigns. When we trace the commercial advantages that are derived from men being united under one government; when it is clear, from national animosities having ceased whenever different nations have been united under one sovereign, that they all arose from their having different governments, how much may it be desired that all the world should have but one government.[66]

All men have a similar interest, and there is no natural or good reason why our sympathies should be bounded by the Channel any more than by the Tweed; nor why a name and an imaginary line should make men the enemies of each other. They need but to chase away their numerous masters to make them all sensible that their interest is everywhere the same. I should not wish to flatter either the cunning of states men, or the ambition of conquerors, by persuading them that they might accomplish so desirable an object as uniting all men under one head.

It is not desirable that the maxims of a Castlereagh or a Hardenberg[67] should become the laws of social intercourse, nor that we should all be beat into one square mechanical form by the leaden sceptre of some peaceable usurper of dominion; nor all drilled into the same shape, appetites, and opinions, by the medals and rations of some active and iron-hearted conqueror; nor is it even desirable that the profound wisdom of our House of Commons should dictate the conduct of the world, but it may be hoped, that, as the race advances in knowledge, it will lose the idle reverence with which it now worships some individuals, and submit itself only to reason as its natural lord and sovereign.

---

[66] **Editor's F/N:-** These passages, regarding Hodgskin's apparent approval of a single World or Europe-wide Government (an European Union as it where), seemingly appear contradictory to his earlier admonishment of regulations that are intended to be applicable to large numbers of people. These may obviously be deserving of further attention and research.

[67] **Editor's F/N:-** Castlereagh and Hardenberg were the Foreign Ministers for Britain and Prussia, who coincidentally both died in 1822.

The commerce of Hannover, however, labours under one disadvantage peculiar to itself. This is, the situation of the two free Hanse towns on two of its principal rivers. Two such cities as Hamburg and Bremen should naturally only give activity to the commerce of Hannover. They ought to promote competition, and they possess no advantages of situation greater than many places belonging to Hannover and situated on the same rivers. Harburg might be equal to Hamburg, and many places at the mouth of the Weser superior to Bremen. But the inhabitants of the two Hanse towns govern themselves. Commerce has long been their only pursuit, and they knew at a very early period how to protect and encourage it. They left it tolerably free. Their governments gave them advantages over places situated in the territories of Hannover, and while those which had formerly some commerce as Stade, and Lüneburg, and Lehe, have gone to decay, Bremen and Hamburg have continued to flourish. The situation of these two free towns thus drawing to themselves all the commerce of these two rivers, for all the inhabitants of Hannover command whatever they want from abroad through them, has had a pernicious influence on its commerce. They now possess so much capital, that, while they preserve their independent political existence, competition on the part of the inhabitants of Hannover is hopeless, and success impossible. But, under the present circumstances, they are wiser than to attempt it: they would rather share the advantages of these two towns, and they no sooner accumulate a little capital than they hurry from the restrictions of the monarchy to the security and freedom of the republics. This is not a supposition. I have met with several in stances of natives of Hannover settled at these two towns, and I have been assured of the fact by a Hannoverian gentleman of considerable knowledge.

The only canal in the old dominions of Hannover, exclusive of some trifling cuts to supply towns with water, is situated in the province of Bremen. It was planned with the very wise intention of uniting, by means of two small rivers, the Schwinge and the Hamme, the Elbe and the Weser, and also of uniting the Oste to the Hamme. It was begun in 1766, rather more than half a century ago, and not yet completed, has hitherto served no other purpose than to drain the morasses of the neighbourhood, and bring some more land into cultivation. It seems to have been a wise undertaking and has only failed from having been the work of the sovereign instead of the subjects. There seems to be a singular fatality attending the measures of sovereigns; they rarely undertake what is useful to the community, and when they do, it is seldom that they accomplish it. It has been already mentioned, that, in the newly acquired territories of Hannover, particularly in Friezland, canals are frequent and much used.

The roads of Hannover are often complained of by travellers. In fact, a great part of the road which extends from Hamburg to Hannover is made in the sand, without any stones being laid, and is, therefore, very bad for travelling. It is, however, improving. The same may be said of the roads which go from Hannover by Hildesheim, and by Peina into Brunswick. Though roads are at present making in these directions, they must as yet be considered as mere tracks, where carriages and waggons follow one another, but the drivers of each choose, in a space of almost a quarter of a mile wide, which track they will follow. From Hannover to Göttingen, and so on to Cassel, the road is good; that to Bremen and to Cuxhaven is in many places like that to Hamburg, a track in the sand, and where this is compact, it is good, where not, execrable. Under the government of the French, a regular stone laid road, to extend between Hamburg and the town of Bremen, was begun but never finished, and now being out of repair, rather annoys than benefits the traveller. A good road is begun from Hannover to Stade. Excellent roads lead from Hannover to Hameln and Münder, and Minden. The road to Osnabrück may be classed among middling good roads. The country roads of the marsh lands, particularly Hadeln and of Friezland, are good, but in general all the bye and parish roads, or, as they may be more properly called, amt roads, are everywhere very bad. Communication is slow, and in some places difficult, yet, in general, it is tolerably regular through all parts of the country.

Letters are carried by boys or men on horseback; this is called the riding post, and they leave Hannover for all the different parts of the country, twice, thrice, or four times a-week. Coaches, called the travelling post, *fahrende posten*, resembling the double bodied coaches of London, but stronger and heavier, with a *cabriolet*, as three covered seats are called, and a large *boot* behind, leave Hannover for Hamburg, and that neighbourhood, for Hesse Cassel, and southern Germany, for Bremen, and then Holland, Friezland, &c., for Brunswick and Prussia, for Lüneburg and Lubeck, for Hameln, for Hildesheim, for Minden, twice a-week. These coaches are hung on springs, and generally carry six persons very comfortably in the inside, and two besides the coachmaster, or conductor, in the cabriolet. They travel, including stoppages, at about the rate of four miles per hour. As treaties relative to communication exist between the different governments of Germany, packages may be forwarded by this conveyance to any part without any sort of mistrust.

The *Post* belongs to the crown, of which it is considered as regalia; it is under very precise regulations, and the hours appointed to set out and arrive are punctually attended to. To prevent imposition, it is positively regulated how much money is to be given to the postilions at each stage. The postmasters, who live at different places, and provide the riding and the travelling Post with horses, provide horses also for those travellers who use their own carriages. There are no other coaches resembling stage-coaches but this fah*rende Post*. In most of the towns, however, where there is much traffic, carriages with two or three horses, called *Gelegenheiten*, and possibly companions to go wherever you wish, may generally be procured. These are not, however, so certain, nor do they go so quick as the travelling post. When there are so many persons going by the travelling post that a seat must be accepted in what is called a *Bey Wagen*, a covered cart without springs: travelling by this conveyance is very unpleasant. When a seat, however, can be procured in the cabriolet, or the coach, the *fahrende post* is, after walking, or your own carriage, the best mode of travelling, not only in Hannover, but in Germany. Waggons, and sometimes carriages, may also be procured at the post stations.

# Chapter VIII.

# Hannover - Schools.

*Education promoted by the clergy. — Regulations concerning. — Children obliged to go to school. — A learned landlord. — Institutions of the town of Hannover. — Lyceum; date; description; two customs of: — Palace-school described. — Hofrath Feder. — Girls' school of the old town; of the new town; an opinion of the inspector. — Parish schools. — Or phan-house. — Sunday-school. — Military and Garrison schools. — Seminary. — Böttcher the founder who; for what intended; described; self-teaching principle at; good effected by; small funds of:-Quantity of children taught on the whole. — Manner of teaching — Precision of-Head reckoning. — A novel method of teaching reading. — Religious instruction ; effects of on children ; on young men. — Punishments. — National education. — Observations.*

Vestunni has remarked, that

> "the Reformation in the northern parts of Germany came not from the princes; but from the people, and that no persons followed and promoted the new doctrines with greater readiness than the inferior orders of the clergy. They saw themselves poor and despised by the higher orders, who revelled in superfluity, and who, possessing wealth and political power, could only be successfully attacked by the aid of the people."[68]

To bring them to support the new doctrine, it was necessary to convince them of its value. Hence numerous preachings, and hence it was in the towns, where the people had knowledge sufficient to judge of the reasonings which were presented to them, that the Reformation made the most rapid progress. It was soon discovered, that many of the people to whom it was necessary to appeal, were unable to read. The clergy laboured earnestly to

---

[68] **Hodgskin's F/N:-** *Handbuch der Vâterlandischen Geschichte*, Vol. III. p. 72.

instruct them, and so early as the year 1559, the church ordinances for the principality of Kalenberg, enacted by the influence of the clergy, contain directions for the establishment and support of schools throughout the country. It is said to have been at a later period that the princes first became thoroughly sensible how much education promoted that obedience which they are accustomed to regard as the first of virtues. Certainly, the clergy of the north of Ger many began the business of educating the people and were afterwards supported in it by the governments.

Were it not a well-known truth, that nearly all the founders and reformers of religious systems have been always, in part, incited to their exertions by the love of worldly dominion, it might be invidious to remark, that we owe one of the great improvements of modern society to this passion. The reformers struggled for influence or for empire over the minds of their countrymen, and to change the form of the church government. To effect this, they needed the support of the people, and were obliged to teach them to enable them to judge of the claims which the reformers made for their support. This was the origin of the labours of the clergy to educate the people, not only in the provinces which now compose the kingdom of Hannover, but in all the north of Germany; and since then they have prosecuted this good work with constant attention, and a considerable degree of zeal. This is a fact which seems to justify all the praise which can be bestowed on the simplicity and efficacy of the government of the church in Hannover.

According to existing regulations, every person is obliged, before the age of eighteen years, to undergo the church ceremony of confirmation, the examinations previous to which are very strict. They suppose an acquaintance with the church catechism, and to become acquainted with this it is necessary to read. Consistency demands, that when a service of any kind is required, the power to perform it should either be possessed or be given, and care has therefore been taken to supply the population of Hannover with the means of instruction.

No village of any consequence is destitute of a school, and several, such as Langenhagen, not far from the town of Hannover, have more schools than churches. Some resemblance to Scotland will be found in regulations which compel the inhabitants of two or more villages, one not being populous enough to support a schoolmaster, to unite for this purpose. When no dwelling-house is provided for him, he lives and feeds with the inhabitants in turns, according to fixed regulations; though I believe no instance of an itinerant schoolmaster is at present to be found, as formerly, who has no other school-house than the village inn.

In order to ensure support to the schoolmasters, all the inhabitants of every village who are capable are obliged to pay for the instruction of their children, from the time they are six till they are fourteen years old. And so rigid is this regulation, that people have sometimes been obliged to pay the schoolmaster of their parish for the children they have had instructed by some other person. These payments, though small, together with a house and garden, which the parish is obliged to provide, are generally the only support of the schoolmaster. It belongs to the clergyman to decide if any of the people are so poor as to be unable to pay for the instruction of their children, in which case, in conjunction with the head men of the parish, when there is no specific charity, he provides out of the common fund for their instruction.

There is also a law which subjects those parents who neglect to send their children to school to a trifling punishment, at the discretion of the magistrates. Fortunately, however, parents are becoming sensible of the value of instruction, for there is now much less necessity to enforce this law than formerly. It is so old as 1681, and, in compliance with it, lists are kept by the schoolmaster of the children who attend, and these lists are submitted to the inspection of the magistrates.

When people are compelled to pay a schoolmaster, it is right he should be qualified to instruct them, and no person is, therefore, allowed to take this office on himself who has not previously been examined and found qualified. Generally, village schoolmasters are educated at the Seminary, an institution to be afterwards described, and they are selected from there, and appointed to the different parishes by whoever is the patron of the school. Sometimes a nobleman is patron, but more generally the patron is the consistorium.

Schools for the poorest of the people, in which the teachers, though appointed by the consistoriums, are paid by the scholars, are found in all the towns as well as in the villages, and there is no town of the least importance in the whole kingdom in which better schools are not found. These are known by the name of Lyceums, or high-schools, and in general they have been established by the citizens and magistrates, in whose hands, at present, the control and the appointment of the masters remain. Here the classical languages are taught to a certain extent, and the first foundation of that education is laid which is afterwards to be completed at the university.

In the towns of Celle and Hannover there are medical schools, in which regular professors give instruction in medicine, surgery, and anatomy. Dissection is performed. With these schools are combined institutions for the instruction of midwives. None of the latter are allowed to practise without having studied at such an institution for six months. This regulation seems likely to ensure something like a decent one to every considerable part of the country.[69]*

There are schools for the instruction of veterinary surgeons; and care is even taken to give a regular and systematic education to gardeners. The celebrated university of Göttingen, which is in the kingdom of Hannover, completes the means of education. It deserves also to be mentioned, that many young women, of genteel families, and but little wealth, go into other families as boarders, for the purpose of learning house-keeping, of which they afterwards make their account by superintending the house-keeping of more wealthy people. There may be even said to be a sort of mania for schools. They have been instituted in some parts of Germany under the direction of the government, to instruct in all sorts of arts; from cooking to making shoes, and from rearing bees to jumping with skill and grace. People, who may be classed almost as poor, have private teachers for their children.

Music is almost invariably taught. As I have sometimes seen fingers that contrasted finely, from the dirt imbedded in them, with the ivory of the piano-forte, I have wondered at the strange combination of ragged clothes, naked feet, and want of cleanliness,

---

[69] **Hodgskin's F/N:-** Something of this sort appears at one time to have been much wanted.

"Julius, the sovereign," says Spittler, speaking of the period between 1570–1580, "had, as his yet unprinted police-regulations prove, provided for midwives and nurses. Till then there were no others in the principality of Kalenberg, at least in the country, but shepherds, – *Schäfer knechten*, – and oxen men, – *Ochsenjungen*, who, from the experience they had acquired with their herds, were called to the help of women when nature denied her more certain succour." — *Geschichte des Fürstenthums, Hannover*, Vol. I. p. 276.

Venturini also informs us, they were not only midwives, but surgeons and physicians.

When children are to be baptized, they are carried to the church by the midwife, and as, on this occasion, she always receives very handsome presents, in order to encourage those who have regularly studied and received permission to practise; it has, therefore, been ordered that none but the sworn midwives of the town of Hannover may carry a child to be christened.

with so elegant an accomplishment as music.   Most of the innkeepers, who, with their families, are generally dirty, may be called accomplished people.   A learned landlord whom I met at a village called Mehly, may be quoted as an example.   He addressed himself to us in French, to his children he spoke Latin, and to his dog Russian, or something we did not comprehend.   He gravely assured us, and appeared inclined to prove, that a miserable close room was a very elegant apartment, and when we could find nothing to eat but eggs and beer soup, that everything was to be had at his house.   He then retired to another apartment, and, apparently unwilling that we should go away ignorant of any of his accomplishments, he sang a song, and accompanied himself on the piano-forte.

Sufficient means are therefore employed to educate the people throughout the kingdom, but a more correct idea will be obtained of the present state of education, if that of the town of Hannover be more fully described and taken as a criterion for judging of the whole.   When the number of children instructed can be calculated, – when the population of the town is known, – when what is taught, and the manner of teaching, are described, – then a tolerable correct judgment may be formed of the general state of education in the whole country.   It is probable, from a variety of little circumstances which may be easily imagined, that the number of children educated in Hannover is somewhat greater than may be found in other towns not capital towns; but it is still certain, that in all the other towns the children educated bear a large proportion to the whole population.

The Lyceum, or high-school of the old town of Hannover, dates from the year 1500, and was one of those schools in which the instruction was regulated after three principal heads. "It was commanded, first, that piety should be taught, next knowledge and art, and, lastly, politeness and manners;" – a mode of proceeding directly the reverse of modern boarding-schools.   This school as established by the citizens and magistrates for the education of their sons; the funds which support it, the regulations of the school,-the appointment of the masters, and its entire control, – all belong to the magistrates of the old town.   It has before been shown in what manner the government influences and controls them, and, connected as they are with the government and with the consistoriums, one of these magistrates being actually a consistorial counsellor, this school, though nominally under the control of the magistrates, may be considered as under the control of government. Although it was founded so long since, as it has not the privileges of a corporate body, and is subjected entirely to the living magistrates, it has been constantly altered so as to keep pace with modern improvements, and it is not behind the knowledge of the day.

Two hundred and fifty boys are educated here, who are not exclusively sons of the citizens. Some few come from the country, and five out of the whole were children of noble parents, but generally their parents occupy the middle ranks of society, and they are chiefly intended for the learned professions. They were generally between the ages of seven and eighteen years. The course of instruction which is here followed is considered as preparatory to going to the university, and consists in the Latin, Greek, French, and English languages, mathematics, history; *literature*,[70] declamation, religion, and music.

The expences of this school are, for boys of the first class, about £3 Sterling per year, and there are gradations between this and £1.6s. which is paid by the youngest scholars. The regular salary of the director is about £200 per annum, and there are several gradations for the other instructors, till the lowest is reached, which is not above £60. There are ten different teachers at this school.

The parents of the boys are subject to another little expence, and the masters receive some more profit; but as this is made and received as a voluntary offering, it is not mentioned as salary. The scholars of each class subscribe a small sum, and thus make up a purse of money, which is then presented to the teacher of their class on his birthday, in rather a solemn manner. They collect in the evening at the school, and, having previously provided a band of music, march in procession to his house, and compliment him on the day. Their offering is accompanied by a suitable address and accepted with suitable thanks.

If the teacher is not the director, the whole procession goes first to his house, and the music is played under his window, and he also must come forth and return thanks for the honour conferred on him. Such little ceremonies and pleasures appear well calculated to smooth the rugged paths of instruction. Parties so different in age and pursuits as scholars and teachers, and who so often regard each other as instruments of annoyance, are thus united by mutual pleasure. The youngsters are pleased with the music, with the procession, and with the public thanks of the master; the master receives a handsome present, and is honoured in the minds of his fellow-citizens by the respect of his scholars; and by such means, trifling as they may appear, the necessity of coercion, and the

---

[70] **Hodgskin's F/N:-** This consisted in observations on different celebrated poets, illustrating their works by geographical and chronological remarks.

feelings of hatred for instruction, are entirely banished. This custom of making presents and going with music and torches to salute the masters, is common to most German schools, and certainly deserves the praise of being a very useful custom.

There is another little custom which appears to me to be full of all that is endearing and good. On the anniversary of the burial of one of the former teachers, the teacher who had supplied his place, accompanied by all the young men who had attended the instructions of the former, visited his grave, crowned it with garlands, and the teacher spoke a eulogium on his predecessor. This honour is only paid to those gentlemen who behave well, and he, therefore, who pronounced the eulogium, must find in his own act the strongest hope of a similar honour, and the strongest incitement to deserve it. There can be no doubt that such little ceremonies are much superior to the commemoration dinners of English schools.

There is also a better sort of school for boys, in the new town, in which about 200 are instructed. This has not been founded more than thirty years. It is supported by the funds of the new town, and is placed under the control of its magistrates, and of the consistorium. It has been already mentioned, that the magistrates of the two towns of Hannover are distinct, and that those of the new town are appointed by the crown. The members of the consistorium are also appointed by it; in fact, the chief magistrate of the new town is also a consistorial counsellor, and this school, therefore, is entirely under the control of the government. The boys are between the ages of five and fourteen years; they are divided into four classes, and are taught the Latin language, history, geography, grammar, reading, writing, arithmetic, religion, and singing. It costs for each boy from 10s. to 15s. per year for instruction, books, &c. The money is paid to the rector, on account of the magistrates, who pay all the expences. It has four instructors, none of whose salaries exceed £70 per year, with a house to live in. Three out of the four have, however, other employments, and the fourth, the rector himself, receives children to board, to whom he gives private instruction.

The palace-school was founded about twenty years ago, by Mr. Salfeld, the present Abbot of Loccum, and has gradually increased, from very small beginnings, till it is capable of educating 200 children of both sexes. Actually 180 boys and 74 girls receive instruction here. The sexes are placed in different apartments; a mistress presides over each of the rooms in which the girls are taught, though the instructors are often the same for both sexes.

They are both taught the French and the German languages grammatically, reading and writing accurately, arithmetic, geography, the outlines of natural history, drawing, religion, and singing. The boys learn English, Latin, and mathematics; the girls knitting, sewing, and other useful arts proper to females.

Some few children are educated free of expence, and it costs the others, for the first class, about £4.3s. per year; for the second class about £2.10s.; for the third class about £1.10s.; and for the fourth, or youngest class, nearly £1 Sterling per year. The money is paid on account of government, which provides a building, and otherwise pays all the expences.

The inspector of this school is an amiable and venerable old gentleman, whom I have before mentioned as royal librarian, and to whose politeness I believe every stranger who visits Hannover is indebted. Chance rather made me known to him. If the character of nations can only be known from the character of individuals, and if no man should judge but from his proper experience, I might say there are no people with which I am acquainted, who exceed the inhabitants of Hannover in politeness of heart; and I might quote the venerable Hofrath Feder as one of the best specimens of his countrymen. He is known among his compatriots by the epithet of Noble, and the tribute of respect which I am here allowed to pay him does me far more honour than him.

The instructors of the palace-school have all some other means of subsistence than their salaries, which are therefore not great. They depend on the quantity of lessons they give, and seldom amount to more than £30 per year.

The children instructed are from seven to fourteen years of age, and they are generally of the middling and better classes; they are, however, of all descriptions, and some Christians might possibly be edified by contemplating the mixture with the children of Jews. In all these schools, children of all the religious denominations which are in Hannover are indiscriminately mixed. Even the Catholics and the Jews attend what is called the religious instruction of the Protestants.

In a school for girls, in the old town, 400, divided into five classes, are educated. They are between the ages of four and fourteen years; women teachers preside in each room, and teach female work, while masters give instruction in those branches of knowledge which have been mentioned as taught in the palace-school. This school is for children of the middling classes of citizens, and its expences are not more than thirty shillings per year, for children in the upper classes, and fifteen shillings for those in the under ones. The school house was built in 1802, at which time also this school was first established. It was both an instructive and pleasing spectacle to see so many young girls collected in large airy rooms, and the whole attentively occupied with learning. This school is under the superintendence of the magistrates, who also pay, out of the funds of the town, all extra expences.

There is a school for girls also in the new town, similar to that of the old town. It educates 350 children, who are generally of the middling and poorer classes. It costs, for each child, from twelve to eighteen shillings per year, and they are taught all those things which are taught in the palace school. The inspector, who very politely gave me all the information I wished, informed me,

> "that formerly the girls learnt embroidery, but he thought it rather unfitted them for plain work;" and our aim, said he, and the same aim characterizes the whole instruction of Hannover, "is to make the children fit for good mothers and good housewives. They are taught nothing beyond their sphere; but as I know a constant use of words alone is not good for the young mind, I introduce plants and flowers into their school-room, whose names and qualities are explained to them, and which they must cultivate and attend. This familiarises them with nature and teaches them what no books can teach them."

The person who thus spoke was a consistorial counsellor, and superintendent of the new town of Hannover. Of course, he was the judge of what was the proper sphere of all the children of the school. It is pleasant to see age and dignity at the good work of instructing children in so delightful a manner. These large schools for girls seem a peculiar part of the education of this country.

Schools where the expence does not amount to more than about five shillings a-year, and in which the children are taught reading, writing, grammar, arithmetic, outlines of geography, and natural history, and religion, are found at each of the five parishes into which the town of Hannover is divided.

There is an orphan-house which educates sixty children, and even the few either idle, depraved, or neglected beings, who are found in the workhouse, are formed into classes, and receive instruction.

There is a school, also, where young men are taught, on Sundays, the elements of mathematics, and of design, with reading, writing, arithmetic, &c.

A military school is established for persons, either intended to enter the army, or already serving in it. All the officers, even the non-commissioned officers, are obliged to attend this school, and it is open to all the private soldiers who please to seek it. To frequent it recommends a soldier to his superiors. This school is perfectly unlike the pompous institutions which are called military schools in other countries. The teachers, with the exception of the language-masters, are all officers, who have few other emoluments than their pay. The whole expence does not exceed £200 per year. The French language, mathematics, fortification, military and civil architecture, with chemistry and natural philosophy, as far as they are connected with the military profession, are taught or explained.

If report may be relied on, some Hannoverian officers who were educated here, although the expence is so small, were amongst the most useful of any in the whole army of the Duke of Wellington. It certainly puts our stupendous establishments to shame; and, while the officers are obliged to learn, that they may obtain the honour of teaching, it proves that economy in forming institutions is valuable for other things besides the mere saving of money.

There is also a garrison-school, supported by the government, in which the children of soldiers are educated.

By far the most important, however, of all the institutions of Hannover for the purposes of education, is that which is called the Seminary, and which deserves a more detailed description. Ernest Christopher Böttcher, a retail tradesman of the town of Hannover, was the founder of this institution, as the funds which he bequeathed to it continue to be one of its principal supports. He was born at Great Lafferde, in the bishopric of Hildesheim, in the year 1697; he is described to have been a very pious noble-minded man; and he died at Hannover in the year 1766. He had projected something like the seminary so early as the year 1746, and from that time till his death he was constantly engaged, in conjunction with several good men, in endeavouring to realise and give value to his project.

He was assisted in his labours by a Dr. Goetten, at that time a consistorial counsellor and first court chaplain. In fact, he was the intelligent man, whose knowledge and activity carried into effect the views and wishes of the other. The original regulations for the masters of the seminary were of his writing. Teaching was first commenced in the year 1751. Many changes have been made in the modes of instruction since then, but the main principle which distinguishes the seminary, namely, that of combining a school for schoolmasters with a school for children, remains unchanged.

Various and considerable improvements have been suggested and carried into effect by some of the most distinguished members of the Hannoverian church, who have been either teachers or inspectors of this school. Among them the name of Koppe may be mention ed, who, while he was animated by a sort of ambition to make himself, as his contemporaries said, the Pope of the North of Germany, did not disdain the humble and useful labours of inspecting the instruction of the seminary, and suggesting methods to improve it.

It consists of two distinct parts, a school for children and a school for schoolmasters. In the first 500 boys and girls of different ages, divided into classes, are taught reading, writing, grammar, arithmetic, church-music, knitting, sewing, &c. &c. It is optional with the parents of the children if they pay for this instruction or not, and it does equal honour to the goodness of the instruction, and to the judgment of the people, that many who are able, do pay for their children, and send them to the seminary to be educated. The whole sum, however, which has been so contributed in any one year, has not exceeded £20, and generally has not amounted to more than the half of that sum.

The persons who are instructed so as to qualify them to teach others, are divided into two classes. The first is composed of young men who wish to become teachers; the second of the best of these young men, selected after some month's examination and study, and now destined to be the future schoolmasters of Hannover.

The first are called Preparandi, and are very generally the sons of schoolmasters, who desire to follow their father's employment, or of small trades men. In the spring of 1818 thirty-three of these received instruction. Each one pays, on entering, one pistole, about 16s.8d. and for this sum they have food, lodging, and instruction, given them for six months, which are always the six winter months. The best amongst them are selected, at the end of this period, to fill any vacancies there may be in the other class, and the remainder return to their homes, or seek employment in parish schools. As the greater part of the schools for the poorer classes are provided with masters from this establishment, such a manner of selecting only intelligent lads, appears likely to secure a constant supply of clever schoolmasters. In summer, the children of the poorer people are allowed to remain from school in order that they may assist in the labours of the field; and during this period the village schools are not unfrequently committed to the care of these young men, while the masters repair to Hannover to improve themselves in the Seminary.

The second, or superior class, amounting to thirty, selected as mentioned, are called Seminarists. They dwell constantly in the house, and have lodging, food, and bed-linen found them, and when any of them are employed, as the oldest and best amongst them are, in instructing the children of the Seminary, of whom they are in fact the only teachers, they receive a small gratuity of 1s.8d. per week. They are allowed by the inspector to teach in private houses, when this can be done without interrupting the lessons they are obliged to attend. They are much sought after for this purpose, and many of them fill the stations of subordinate teachers at all the schools I have before described.

Both these classes of young men are taught those things which they are afterwards to teach to others, and they are taught, and severely, and much practised in the best-known methods of teaching. They are taught reading and writing correctly, grammar, arithmetic as far as algebra, geography, natural history, Latin, church-music, singing, both vocal and instrumental, particularly organ-playing, calculating by the head, or without the help of slates or books; they receive some instruction, in a little compendium which has been published, of the laws most useful to the country man, and, above all things, they are perfected in what is called religious instruction. A great opportunity is also afforded them of acquiring more knowledge, but the aim of the institution is strictly confined to make them good schoolmasters for the people. A piece of ground belongs to the Seminary, and here they not only raise the greater part of the vegetables they consume, but they are taught to graft trees, to cultivate a garden, and such other similar things as may be useful to themselves and others.

One practice which is very good, is the manner adopted of making each of them in turn play the master's-part with the others. One of the lessons selected for this is religious instruction, which, as it is a sort of catechism, necessarily demands a great attention to the use of words, and great accuracy of thought. Each one in his turn has to teach, or rather question the others. He gives to the inspector, the night before, an abstract of the questions he means to ask, and informs him what part of the catechism he proposes to talk about, and explain, and the manner in which he intends to explain and enforce it. This allows the inspector to know before-hand what faults he is likely to commit. The whole of both classes assemble in presence of the inspector, and the young man whose turn it is begins catechising, and when he has finished, he sits down, and is informed by the inspector, in the presence of the whole, in what he has erred, either in his matter or in his manner, and thus the whole, by questioning, teach one another, and from the lecture of the superior, which was well given, each profit by the excellencies so well as by the faults of all.

This is a frugal establishment. The young men learn and practise economy; a complete system of superintendence is established; and every attention is paid to forming their minds for their situation, and to make them moral good men.

There is an instructor for arithmetic – another for singing and organ-playing; and these, with two inspectors, are the only instructors who are paid both for the schoolmasters and for the children, except the trifling gratuities which are given to the elder seminarists. The two inspectors must have been educated for the church; and some of the most respectable members of the church have filled these situations. The present curator of the seminary (a person who, without receiving any salary, is the chief of the establishment, who examines the accounts, and answers for the conduct of all the inferior parties to the consistorium, and who is the first dignitary of the church of Hannover) once filled the place of inspector of the seminary, and rose to eminence, like many of his brethren, by the useful labours of teaching charity children.

In fact, whatever opinion may be formed of the education of the north of Germany, the clergy of that country deserve most of the praise or of the censure which may be thought to belong to it. They have needed no rich bishopricks to stimulate them to do their duties, and they afford a shining proof that large money emoluments are not necessary to make a set of men either useful or dignified. The salary of the inspectors is about £60 per year, and apartments – a very small sum to support a gentleman, which the inspector is considered to be. Yet such a salary, and few of the teachers in the whole town have more, seems quite large enough to encourage in the gentlemen who are employed in teaching a great deal of zeal.

The seminarists remain three years to study. The inspectors have a power to recommend them into families as private teachers, and to retard or promote their advancement. Joined with occasional reproof, this power is sufficient to produce perfect obedience. The first inspector keeps a regular journal of what the young men do and notes their progress or their neglect; which enables him to know how everyone has conducted himself during his residence in the seminary. When any school vacancy occurs throughout the kingdom, an application is generally made to him for some person to fill it, and he recommends those who are most deserving to the best places. This journal also is shown the curator, and from it he forms his judgment of the character of the young men, and of the management of the institution. He may be appealed to by any scholar who thinks himself injured by the inspector, and he can lend the whole weight of his authority to support the decisions of this gentleman.

Since the establishment of the seminary, it has educated, or improved the education of, more than 2,000 persons, who have been employed in teaching others; and, during the same period, it has probably educated 10,000 children. There is no better method for improving a whole people than this of instructing schoolmasters, and the good is therefore incalculable which has been accomplished by this establishment of the illustrious Böttcher. The whole people appear to have but one opinion of its utility, and perhaps no stronger proof can be given of the improvement which it has effected in schoolmasters than this. As a stranger I could always distinguish the moment I heard any teachers whether they were educated in the seminary or not. What made them conspicuous was a clearness of method, a great gentleness of manner, precision in all their words, and a great extent of useful knowledge. They almost merit the title of perfect teachers for common schools. I may quote as an example the teacher of the common school at Göttingen. This gentleman taught or explained to a class of 200 girls, for the purpose of showing their progress to some gentlemen, in the space of two hours, reading and writing correctly and grammatically, natural history, geography, arithmetic, and calculation by the head, all in a precise neat manner. Then he pitched the time and joined the whole school in singing a psalm.

To effect all this good, the whole funds of the seminary, bequeathed to it by Böttcher, enlarged by the gifts of the government and of several well-disposed persons, amount only to a capital of 40,000 thalers, or at five per cent. an annual income of £1833.4s.[71] – a sum that would not suffice to pay one of the

---

[71] **Hodgskin's F/N:-** The sum here stated to be the funds of the seminary is what the inspector very politely informed me, and it includes their buildings, ground, and everything that belongs to it. In the history of the seminary, published by the present curator, Abbot Salfeld, in the year 1800, the whole income is stated at only 2,201 thalers, 21 grosschens, and 4 pfennige, and the expences at 2,500 thalers, or £416.13s.4d. – a sum that, allowing for the augmentation of prices since that period, cannot, even including the capital vested in buildings, &c. equal the sum stated in the text as the funds of the seminary. There is, however, some reason to think that the Abbot has made a mistake, because the various sums he mentions as forming the

teachers of some of the charities of Great Britain. So much good in the way of instruction has rarely been effected by such small means, and it is only to be regretted that the general state of the country does not allow the seminary to be used as a means of spreading accurate political knowledge; – that the good it already does should not be enlarged by the young men being taught those sciences whose truths have been methodised and made the property of the race by Smith, Say, Malthus, Paley, and Bentham.

This institution has been the parent and the model of many similar ones in many parts of Germany. There is scarcely a capital town, and certainly no kingdom or country of any part of the north of Germany, which has not at present a seminary for schoolmasters; and certainly the plan of uniting a school for masters with a school for children, carried into effect as it is here, deserves, from its utility, to be as well known throughout Europe as any institution it contains.

But admirable as it is, and much as the names of Böttcher and Goetten deserve to be celebrated, they are little, if at all, known beyond the confines of their own country; while those of Bell and Lancaster are everywhere heard of. It is the daily and free press of Britain which, recording all our actions, has made the names of our countrymen known; which has added to the value of our literature, and made its stores be examined by every other people. Without a free press, therefore, even virtue and utility remain concealed, and lose much of their efficacy, because nobody is encouraged to imitate them.

The governors of the world, and the makers of laws, illustrious as they are, will never have their names transmitted to posterity but by means of a free press. There is no foreigner of the least political reading who is ignorant of the names of the conspicuous members of our House of Commons; and Maddison, Jefferson, Monroe, are known all over Europe. But who has ever heard of Claus von der Decken, or Frederick Franz Dieterich Bremer, the ministers of the mighty kingdom of Hannover? And there is nobody perhaps who is not sensible that if the names of its sovereigns descend to posterity, it will only be as kings of a country in which the press was free.

The present curator of this establishment is the chief of the consistorium of Hannover, and one of this body is always appointed by it to this office. This institution, therefore, and, with it, from the influence which it exercises over schoolmasters, prescribing what is to be taught and what must not be taught to them, the education of

---

funds of this institution do amount to more than 40,000 thalers.

the whole of the poorer people is placed under the direction of the church, and under the control of the government.

The institutions for education in the town of Hannover, independent of boarding-schools, provide means of instruction to at least 2,100 children, the great mass of which are between the ages of six and fourteen years, and belong to the middling and poorer classes of people. The whole population of the town does not exceed 21,000, and certainly, therefore, the means of instruction are abundant and cheap. In fact, there are very few children to be found who do not go to school, and hardly any grown-up person who is unable to read and write.

I have heard it remarked by a clergyman who had been catechising all the children of his parish, that he was surprised to have found a very few who hardly knew how to read. This was for him a singular circumstance and proves the extent of instruction. Girls share in all the advantages of these schools, and they are by no means behind boys in their acquirements.

The whole of these are day-schools. The children live with their parents but go regularly to school for instruction. Boarding-schools are only used by the children of the upper classes. The children acquire book-knowledge from their teachers, but their habits of action are learned from their parents. They do not grow up unlike them from living with strangers. For the destruction of all the love of children for their parents, which is the basis of so many virtues, no system of education, except that of Sparta, was ever so well calculated as our present system. And among the causes for the immorality of our people must be enumerated our plan of educating children in boarding-schools. Parents cannot be surprised when children are undutiful, for they allow strangers to perform all their duties; and they wilfully separate themselves from their children during all that part of the life of the latter, in which their character and opinions are indestructibly formed. The whole of the school buildings are good, and all the rooms airy and healthy; and care is taken of the health of the children, by allowing them a short time to jump about between the hour of entering the school and returning home.

From the trifling expence of these schools, it may be imagined that they are something like the preparatory schools of England – a cheap method of amusing infants; but the quality of the education which they supply is of a superior kind. I visited nearly all these schools with a wish to observe them. I was everywhere politely received, and nothing left me to desire but a better memory to retain all the information that was cheerfully given me. One scheme of instruction, one sort of method, more or less perfect, according to the talents of the master, prevails in them all.

It has already been mentioned what the children are taught at the different schools, and it may here be repeated, that, in the meanest of them, reading, writing, arithmetic, grammar, and the outlines of geography, are taught. Singing is never neglected, and many of the younger boys, and all the girls, are taught knitting, and the latter are also taught sewing, shirt-making, &c.

The children are all divided into classes according to their age, and the time they have been at school; and each of these classes has a different employment for every hour; consequently, no lesson lasts more than one hour without interruption. In the better schools each class has a different master, and different instructors for the different branches of learning, or at least only two or three similar ones are taught by the same master. In the minor schools, however, there is but one instructor to the whole school.

When what is to be taught is anything which can be learned alone, such as the rules of grammar, a portion of the catechism, or the facts of geography, the teacher selects a portion of it, which he reads to the class; and they often write it down after his dictation, and this they are obliged to learn when they are out of school. On the following day the instructor examines the whole class to know if they have learned the lesson. The examination is promiscuous or made in such a manner that no one is sure he will not be questioned, although but few are. The probability of being questioned, and the reproof which the children receive if they are not capable of answering, obliges them all to learn; and the frequent repetition which even those who are not asked hear made by others; even the mistakes of the inattentive, when rectified by the master, serve to inform the whole class, and fix all that has been taught in the memory of all.

In fact, a great part of the teaching is examination; the pupils learn alone. Very often the master proposes the question and allows volunteers to answer. Now begins a struggle for distinction: The volunteer rises from the seat, or stretches forth the little hand as a signal of readiness; often the whole class are on their legs, or their little hands are extended with an earnest prayer, *Ich bitte bille*, – to be selected to answer; and nothing gratifies them more than this favour, except the praise bestowed on their success.

Here the first seeds of emulation are sown, and all struggle to reach the goal of honour without unfairly jostling their neighbours. Hundreds of little children, with blue eyes and fair hair, who appeared almost too timid to speak, struggled through the whole hour for a good word, or to be thought well of by the stranger. If the men who doubt the efficacy of instruction and honour on man, – who drawing from their own polluted bosoms continue to affirm he is made to sin, – who desperately persevere in the use of whips, prisons, and the gallows, as the only means of making him righteous, were frequently to see such scenes as these of the schools of Hannover, they might probably mistrust their barbarous institutions; and acknowledge that they themselves were the exceptions to the human race, not the criterion by which it was to be judged.

What is very good in this method is the precision which belongs to the plan of question and answer. Grammar is one of the things thus taught, and those who know how complicated the German grammar is, must be aware that he who has learned it perfectly has made no inconsiderable progress in the knowledge of words. By this method all the children acquire such a knowledge, which is undoubtedly one cause why the Germans in after life learn foreign languages so readily.

A great degree of precision pervades all the descriptions which this people give. I have noticed this quality repeatedly in the conversation of all classes, particularly when I have been visiting their institutions; and have, in general, found the description so accurate as almost to render seeing them of little or no service. This quality is derived from their education. Precision, in a very high degree, is the characteristic of the instruction given at the seminary and may therefore be described as common to the instruction of the whole kingdom.

The question and answer method also gives the scholar the use of his knowledge; it gives constant practice. Boys and girls repeat them to each other. It gives fluency and ease in the use of words and seems altogether much better than the mere learning long pieces and passages by heart, which are repeated to the master.

Most of the schools for the poorer people are called *Arbeit* or *Industrie-schule*, – work schools. They are so named, because the females are taught hand-work, as well as instructed in books. The mistresses show them what they are to do, and they do this while they are listening to the instructor or answering his questions. This has the great merit of calling many useful talents into employment in very early life, of keeping the children quiet, of fitting them to earn a livelihood, and of reconciling the poorest parents to sending their children to school. They are not only able to make something useful to themselves, but often times of earning so much by their little labours in school as they could do by going on errands, herding cattle, &c. What the children gained by their outdoor labours was always the excuse made by the parents, if not the real motive, for not sending them to school.

Two brothers of the name of Wagemann, in Göttingen, and the consistorial Rath Sextro of Hannover, have been the means of introducing this plan into practice. I was assured by many people, as well as by Mr. Superintendent Wagemann himself, that this method has done a great deal to improve the industrious habits and morals of the people.

What I have called calculating with the head (*Kopf-rechnung*) deserves to be further noticed for its utility. The master proposes questions, complicated in proportion to the previous knowledge of the pupils. In the earlier stages of instruction, the children are obliged to repeat aloud all the steps of the calculation till they find the answer; afterwards they merely think over them themselves. The questions are generally something suited to life; and the children, particularly the females, acquire a great dexterity in answering them. They find this of very great utility in shopping, as they are able to calculate of ten times quicker than the tradesman with his slate.

Singing, and the elemental parts of music, are also taught to classes; and this deserves notice from its obvious utility. It seems possible that much, even of the practical part of music, such as placing the fingers on instruments, so as to produce certain sounds, may be taught to several persons at one time. And it is certain, that when any part of it is taught to one person in the presence of others, and when several are taught the elemental parts together, the power of audible perception is improved in all, and the acquisition of any part is facilitated to all. There can be little doubt that the quantity of music, and of musical instruction which exists in Germany, refines the ear and the taste of the whole people, and facilitates to them the acquisition of the power to play on any instrument. This may deserve the consideration of those persons who are engaged in teaching music. There is possibly no one but wishes the knowledge of it was more general in our country than it is, and that the present very expensive method of teaching it by one master to only one pupil at a time could be improved and made cheaper.

There is also a method of teaching to read, which deserves, from its philosophical accuracy and efficacy in practice, to be mentioned and explained. Men spoke before they wrote, and though the first inventors of an alphabet might have made a separate written sign to correspond with each simple sound of their own language, yet these signs at present, or modern alphabets, do not stand for the most simple sounds into which any European language can be reduced. Many signs for simple sounds also stand for other sounds. Some vowels have several sounds; and no consonant, though each is a distinct sign, stands for a simple distinct sound. The name we give to single letters is not that sound which they have when they are combined into words. Any person who pronounces the letters of any word separately, and afterwards pronounces the word, must immediately perceive that no one word is composed of, or has even much resemblance to the sounds or names of the separate letters with which it is written. Written words are composed of letters, but spoken words are never composed of the names of the letters. Hence, when we have, with labour to ourselves, and sometimes torture to our children, taught them to read and pronounce our alphabets, they have to unlearn this pronunciation before they can read and pronounce words.

The method here mentioned, divested of all its tabular forms, and all the nonsense which has been employed to give extra importance to what is of itself a very simple and valuable scheme, proceeds on this principle. The children are taught to pronounce consonants only when they stand in conjunction with vowels. When standing by themselves, they are considered as inarticulations, which cannot be expressed by any other written signs. When children have learned to know the letters by sight, and, from hearing words, have learned to pronounce them as they are combined, they know ever afterwards, when they meet these letters so combined, how to pronounce them. In neglecting, therefore, to teach a distinct articulation for consonants, it was necessary to supply some abstract of the general manner of pronouncing them, both before and after vowels.

A Mr. Oliver, of Dessau, has been at the pains to make such an abstract for the German language, or, in fact, to teach a new series of simple sounds as the component parts of spoken words. Clearly the abstract of the simple sounds of any one language can never be adopted in any other. It is the principle only which may be transplanted; and each nation must endeavour to find out and classify the most simple sounds of its own language for itself. These alone ought to have a separate sign; or an alphabet of any spoken language should consist of a distinct and separate sign for each and for all the most simple sounds which can be found in it. As the whole spoken language is made up of these simple sounds, every word could also be written with the corresponding signs.

It is certain that the present alphabets of Europe, borrowed from the languages of other people, though they serve the purpose of writing, are by no means correct; and this principle, followed out, would dictate to each nation an endeavour accurately to classify all the sounds of its language, and employ a more correct set of written signs to signify them.

The rector of the boys' school in the new town of Hannover, Mr. Fromm, has improved Oliver's method, and continues to teach it with great success. Children of four years of age learn by it to read in four or six weeks. The method meets with opposition; though it is widely spread. I met it both in Dresden and Hannover; and the inventor continues to employ it at Dessau. It is said to impede the children in learning to spell and write correctly. But this is owing much less to the method itself than to the circumstance of its not being universally adopted. The writing-masters continue to follow the old plan of spelling, and as the children do not learn this, they of course find some difficulty in writing correctly.[72]

In all the schools something is taught under the name of religion, and this term signifies so many different things, that what is taught under this name requires further explanation. It is that part of the instruction of this country on which the teachers lay the greatest stress. It is united with the severest censure and the warmest praise. They describe it "as forming the heart." It must have a great influence on the moral character of the Germans, and it therefore deserves to be explained.

The Lutheran religion consists less of an exposition of incomprehensible dogmas than almost any other, and, therefore, what is taught the children under the term religion is very generally morality. It is found principally in the catechism, and a variety of books called the Children's Friend. Of course, the commonly received principles of Christianity are taught ; but as these are not susceptible of continued exposition to children, much of the catechism illustrates the duties of life. I transcribe a portion from where chance has led me to open it.

> "*Instructor.* — The world must have an author, by whom it has been created; why do you judge so ?
>
> "*Pupil.* — The smallest house must have a builder; how then can the world, this great and beautiful dwelling-

---

[72] **Editor's F/N:-** The teaching method Hodgskin here describes is nowadays known by the term *Phonetics*.

house for innumerable creatures, exist without a wise and powerful author?"

Another place, p. 94, treats of attention to the body, of a good name, &c.

"*I.* — Can we promote the perfection and felicity of the soul when we take no care of our body ?

"*P.* — No ; God has so united soul and body, that, through a careful attention to the body, the perfection and felicity of the soul is promoted.

"*I.* — What sort of care are we indebted to the body?

"*P.* — The care for life and health, and a proper use of its members.

"*I.* — Why for our life?

"*P.* — Because God has given it to promote our own and our neighbour's welfare. 1 Pet. iv. 10.

"*I.* — May we not freely destroy life?

"*P.* — To destroy life, when the understanding is sound, is a great sin, because God is the lord of our life.

"*I.* — Does the Christian judge those who, in folly, or in deep melancholy, destroy themselves?

"*P.* — No ; but he guards himself more carefully, that he may not fall into such an unsettled state of mind.

"*I.* — Why must we be careful of our health?

"*P.* — To keep us free from pain, and preserve us fit for our occupations, and to continue our life.

"*I.* — How must we take care of our health?

"*P.* — By using good food and drink; by moderation in eating, drinking, and sleeping; by tempering the violent and effervescing emotions of the mind; by labour, foresight, and cleanliness, which are also necessary to our being received in the society of other men.

"*I.* — Why must we keep the members of our body in a certain state and fitness for useful labours?

"*P.* — We make, by these means, our business light. They enable us to move better and make us more agreeable to others.

"*I.* — What do we want to support life, and to keep us healthy?

"*P.* — A sufficient quantity of nourishment, dwelling, and clothes.

"*I.* — By what means must we seek to obtain and preserve these?

"*P.* — By labour and economy without avarice.

"*I.* — Can we, through our own works and cares, obtain and keep a sufficient degree of nourishment?

"*P.* — No ; we must also have the blessing of God and must unite industry with piety and prayer.

"I. — What is opposed to industry and economy?

"P. — Idleness, extravagance, and avarice.

"*I.* — Are idleness and extravagance pernicious?

"*P.* — They bring want and contempt, and, at the end, induce to steal and to cheat.

"*I.* — What is avarice?

"*P.* — An immoderate desire for riches without properly using them.

"*I.* — Does avarice make people unhappy?

"P. — Yes, very unhappy; for the miser vexes and pains himself, troubles his neighbour where he can, and makes riches his god."

From the Children's Friend, I extract the following:

"A mother was once going on a small country excursion. The journey was not long, but she had to pass through a few villages. Her little daughter Regine was with her. In the first village the road was narrow and dirty. Mother and daughter wore shoes and stockings, which they did not wish to soil. The mother could pass without much dirtying herself; but she was unable to do this and carry over the child. Near at hand was a maiden keeping cows. As soon as she saw the travellers, she ran to them, took little Regine in her arms, and carried her safe into the dry. — *Question.* Do you not think that this action was worth friendly thanks?"

Such is the spirit of the two principal elementary books used in Hannover and in Germany, to teach that most important of all things for the happiness of man — the proper manner to conduct himself.

They would be scarcely worth mentioning, if, like our own catechism, they were only occasionally employed; but they are used at least for the younger branches of both sexes twice every day and must have a great influence on their character.

The reader cannot have failed to remark how many of the motives which these books inculcate for virtuous conduct depend on that tangible and powerful reason — the worldly advantages to the virtuous person. Nor is the instruction, as carried into effect, at all different from this. I select two specimens from many lessons I have heard.

A miser was described by the instructor, and then he asked, "What did he feel when he was obliged to give money for the necessaries of life?

"*P.* — He was troubled.

"*I.* — When people made just demands on him, he quarrelled with them, what ensued?

"*P.* — He made himself enemies.

"*I.* — What did he lose by not being charitable?

"*P.* — The greatest joy; hence people ought not to be miserly."

Second example:

"*I.* — Why should people not sin?

"*P.* — It was forbidden.

"I. — What was the consequence of sin?

"*P.* — Pain here, and punishment hereafter.

"*I.* — A father promised his daughter a nice garden, with all that was good. She, however, told a lie, and when she had received the garden, she was troubled, and could not enjoy it; why?

"*P.* — She could think of nothing but the sin she had committed.

"*I.* — A man with a small garden, in which he had to work, enjoyed it; why?

- 146 -

*"P.* — He was good.

*"I.* — When virtue produced such good effects, what was it?

*"P.* — A great good equal to health, and next to life."

In this manner most of the duties of life are illustrated and enforced. The catechism supplies but few examples, but the instructors, who are generally men from the same class of persons as the children, know what will be useful to them, and very often furnish excellent illustrations. The children learn answers from the catechism, but also find, according to the principles of that book, answers for themselves, and thus they are not only taught principles of conduct but learn very early in life to practise their understanding. They are compelled to find out accurate reasons for every line of conduct, and the best is every hour enforced on them.

I have thought it particularly necessary to mention the important place which this sort of teaching holds in the schools of Germany; because we appear in Britain to be rather in the habit of imagining that morality is neglected in every other country but our own. In fact, we have been in general taught to believe, that in Germany both religion and morality were totally neglected. At the same time, I am doubtful as to the effects of teaching morality as a science; it seems better to let children learn it in the common course of events, from the example and instructions of parents.

What is taught in the higher schools, under the name of religion, is different from what has been already described. This consists in reading and expounding, with such critical remarks as the teacher pleases, portions of the Bible, and of biblical history; – in detailing such events as were connected with the establishment and progress of Christianity, and in teaching rather a history of religion than religion itself. As the first mentioned course of instruction makes moral good men, so this may probably make what are called irreligious men. "Religion," said a German, "is taught in our schools, but neglected in the world." It is taught there unconnected with all those persuasions to belief with which it is usually combined; it is made a matter of reason, and of cool instruction : it is treated like one of the sciences, and becomes, like them, destitute of all influence, but what it may derive from its truth. This sort of instruction, which is very general in Germany, probably causes some of that unbelief which is so generally attributed to the well-educated Germans.[73]

---

[73] **Hodgskin's F/N:-** Goethe says in his Memoirs, "Aus meinem Leben," –

The punishments employed in all these schools are trifling, are never corporeal, and all, of every description, are very rare. It is enough not to be selected to answer for having made mistakes; – to be selected to answer for having before answered well; it is enough to be pointed out as intelligent and good, to make all the children attentive and industrious. Public examinations[74] take place every year, which also promote good conduct. Entering the school at improper hours is repressed by the disapprobation of the scholars themselves, and regular attendance appeared to be secured by the value of the instruction, or, at most, by the punishment of being placed in a corner, and by not being allowed to participate with the others in the lesson. The severest of all punishment is a total expulsion from the school.

Excellent as the school education of Hannover is, it is lamentable to connect it with the progress which the people have made in the arts and comforts of life. These have been, or will be, in other places more minutely described, and here it can only be remembered, that a large portion of their country is waste, – that its trade is as nothing, – that all machines, beyond the most common ones, for abridging labour, are unknown, its literature is at best trifling, – the people read little more than novels, or employ themselves in the classification and arrangement of insects, – and its government and laws are by no means good. Scarcely a great man is found in the country; and when this education sows the seeds of greatness, they must be nursed into life by a warmer sun and a freer air. Its army is brave, but mercenary, and the people, though kind-hearted and amiable, are in general destitute of all that noble spirit of enterprise which is one of the best qualities of man.

It has been mentioned, when the various schools were described, in what degree the government controls the education. In fact, the consistoriums are part of the government, and, in one manner or other, their members have an unlimited control over the whole education of the country.

---

Vol. I. p. 60, – that, as a boy, the New Testament was become, through preaching and religious instruction, trifling and without interest to him.

[74] **Hodgskin's F/N:-** I saw the venerable Hofrath Feder, after an examination was concluded, at which he had presided, seat himself at the piano-forte and play a tune. This gentleman was formerly professor of moral philosophy at Göttingen, and I do not know anything which appears more characteristic of a general amiableness of manners, than such a man possessing and using for his own enjoyment, and the enjoyment of others, so elegant an accomplishment.

A national education, under the sort of control which has been here specified, is good inasmuch as it models the whole community according to the wish of the controllers. Where the nation is entirely excluded from communication with other nations, it produces a certain uniformity of manners, a quiet submission, and a most perfect contentment. But it almost excludes improvement in all the great arts of life and limits the attainments of the society by the attainments of its rulers. It may prevent all the party-spirit tumults, factions, and disorders, which arise in countries partially free, from different political opinions; but it at the same time prevents the people knowing when they are badly governed, how much knowledge they want, and how much they might obtain; it prevents originality of genius, and the growth of individual talent.

A national education under the control of governments may fit men for their priests, their soldiers, their lords of the bed-chamber,[75] for their judges, and for their slaves. But until the benevolent Creator of the world shall depute a ministering angel to rule over every nation, it may well be doubted if an education so controlled is useful to mankind.

The subject of a national education, provided by a government, and controlled by it, is one of very great importance, but which appears not to be thoroughly understood. I do not mean to discuss it, but only to remind the reader, that when a government is allowed to interfere, it never knows when to stop, and the people have never power enough to resist it without causing confusion. The following fact is a proof of the extent to which governments are disposed to go, and it shews how jealous we ought to be of giving them any power over education.

The Elector of Hesse, in the latter end of 1818, ordered that no person in his dominions, beneath the rank of a counsellor, should give their children a learned education, or send them to his university; and that no clergyman should give his sons, except his eldest son, a learned education. Such a fact speaks volumes against allowing princes to control education. They will only control it to educate men for slaves.[76] It is unfortunate, that in Germany

---

[75] **Hodgskin's F/N:-** These are a much more insignificant race of beings in Germany than in England, and many of them are known by the almost contemptible appellations of Hofjunker, Cammerjunker, &c.

[76] **Editor's F/N:-** Werner Stark emphasised Hodgskin's position on this point, when he set about establishing the London Mechanics Institute:

"Men had better be without education than educated by their rulers," he [Hodgskin] says (to quote but one example), "for then education is ... the mere breaking of the steer to the yoke; the

clever men profusely praise the sovereigns for their cares on this point. If they be encouraged to patronise education, they will assuredly control it, and if this be wrong, they ought not to be supplicated for their bounties.

The seminaries for the instruction of schoolmasters which have been established in Germany, and most of the methods I have mentioned as followed in the schools of Hannover, have all been either established, invented, or improved, at comparatively recent periods. The practice of instructing young men, while they instruct children under the inspection of a master, – of making them teach and examine each other, – and the general plan of questioning some scholars of a whole class, so that all may in turn, and in the course of some few lessons, be examined, and all profit by every examination, make this method of education, though not the same as the Lancastrian method, resemble it very much, and equal it in wisdom.

Neither of these methods was copied from the other, but in both countries a want of something better was felt, and in both countries, improvements were the consequence. Their simultaneous origin proves that they were the natural consequences of the state of society, and that something of the same kind would have taken place even if the illustrious individuals whose names they bear had never existed. It is consolatory thus to see the improvements of the species depending on general laws, and that they are not subject to the accidents of time, nor submitted to the control of any individual.

The education of the other parts of Germany resembles the education of Hannover. Schools similar to those described, similar school-books, similar methods, with some little alterations, and even the schoolmasters, for they often change from one country to another, are common to the whole of Northern Germany. Each town has its Latin school, and each town has other schools, in which all the poorer children are taught at little or no expence. If the education of Bavaria resembles that of Hannover, and I believe it does, there may be some reason for the states of that country having decided, as they are said recently to have done, that there

---

mere discipline of a hunting dog, which, by dint of severity, is made to forgo the strongest impulse of his nature, and instead of devouring his prey, to hasten with it to the feet of his master (Mechanics Magazine, Oct. 11, 1823. "the education of a free people, like their property, will always be directed most beneficially for them when it is in their own hands. When government interferes, it directs its efforts more to make people obedient and docile, than wise and happy." (Stark, 1943, p.78)

was no occasion to disturb the existing establishments to introduce the improvements of Lancaster and Bell.

# Chapter IX.

# University of Göttingen.

*German universities founded by sovereigns; professors not attached to any particular sovereign. – Difference between German and English universities. – Funds of Göttingen. – Manner of living there. – Privileges of German universities. – Tribunals of Göttingen. – Number of professors; celebrated ones; what they teach; manner of teaching; specimen of minuteness; effects on character; salaries; honours. – Degradation of professors. – Consequences of patronage. – Number of students; what they learn; their importance; separation from the other classes of Society; manners; their comment; eccentricities; their unions. – Disturbance at Göttingen, by what occasioned. – Remarks.*

Fashion seems to be followed in seeking places of study, so well as in dress, and novelty in both has more influence than convenience. At least it appears so in Germany, where the comparatively modern universities of Jena, Göttingen, and Berlin, are crowded with students, while many of greater antiquity, as Helmstädt, Wittenberg, Rinteln, and Erfurth, are forsaken and suppressed. This is chiefly owing to the patronage of monarchs, each of whom, in his day, sighs for the "song of praise," and strives to secure the admiration of posterity by bounteously rewarding those learned men who are the keepers of the records of the world.

German professors and students, and I may add soldiers and statesmen, have never had, time out of mind, any other country but Germany. While they have professed the most profound obedience to their sovereigns, they have always served that one who paid them best. These tradesmen offered their wares to the highest bidder, and seldom asked any other question of the purchaser than if he were a Catholic or a Protestant. This well-known fact is mentioned merely to explain the sudden rise or fall of German universities. Every tradesman should carry his industry to the best market; – teaching, – guiding armies, – conducting affairs, are all species of industry, and no love of country, and no sacred duty towards it, can imperiously command the services of subjects when its name and character are habitually usurped and prostituted by princes to the purposes of their own ambition. No love of *country*, therefore, ever keeps a German professor within the dominions of the sovereign under whose sway he was born.

By offering sufficient rewards, each sovereign is thus enabled, when he has determined to patronise any university, to bring to it the cleverest men of the whole of Germany. In some countries, those persons who are candidates for any public situation must study in the university of those countries. For example, in Darmstadt all the people who choose to study, must go for two years to the university of Giessen. With this exception, the students have no attachment to native universities, and they who can bear the expence choose that place to study at of which the reputation of the professors is greatest. Celebrated professors are invariably sought and followed by a multitude of students, and the reputation of a university is thus established when they can be procured.

The King of Prussia has recently founded a university at Bonn, and already the professors' chairs are said to be all filled, and the halls to be attended by students. In 1810 he also founded a university at Berlin, which has since then been much frequented. The university at Göttingen was founded by George II.[77] in 1733, and learned professors were brought to it from all parts of Germany. It has since then become known to all Europe, and, owing to the continued favour of the sovereign, has enjoyed a reputation far beyond the oldest universities of Germany.

Accustomed as we are to regard our ancient universities as an integral part of our constitution, which it would be almost sacrilege to amend or destroy, this rising and sinking of universities, so that they sometimes scarcely last longer than the life of their founder, appears very strange. The facility to change is derived from the institutions being the mere bubbles of the monarchs' will. Griefswalde, in what was formerly Swedish, but what is now Prussian Pomerania, is an exception to this. It has funds of its own and is said to be richly endowed. The consequence is, that it resembles an English university. It has twenty-two professors and

---

[77] **Hodgskin's F/N:-** The reputation of this monarch is different in England and in Germany. Mr. Boswell, in his *Life of Johnson*, says, "that it is too well known that the second George never was an Augustus to learning or genius." In Hannover he is certainly honoured as an Augustus to learning.
**[Editor's F/N:-** Hodgskin was here referring to James Boswell's *The Life of Samuel Johnson* (1791).

teachers, and sixty students. Now that it is Prussian, these gentlemen will assuredly not be suffered to fatten in idleness.[78]

Leipsic also has funds of its own, and many of the others have stated incomes, though dependant on the sovereign. The sovereigns retain the power to appoint and reward professors, though the faculty may recommend them, – to alter the laws and regulations, – and they generally keep the funds for the maintenance of the establishment in their own hands.

In every state of Germany there is a department of the ministry under which the universities are particularly placed. And the sovereigns alter and regulate them at their pleasure. German universities are, therefore, essentially different from the universities of England, which are corporate bodies, regulated by laws of their own, possessing large revenues, and independent of everything but the laws of the land. Some part, however, of this facility to change, seems common to all corporate bodies of Germany. Religious corporations, corporations of towns and guilds, all of which are regarded with a sort of veneration in England, have been swept away in Germany at the will of the monarchs.

That philosophy which considers the control of sovereigns over the education of society as an evil, regards this state of the German universities as a matter of deep regret. But while it allows them to be altered and improved as men improve, it may possibly be regarded as a less evil than if they were regulated by laws which cannot be amended. Universities which living men can alter are better than those which slumber on, century after century, and take no note of all the improvements that rise on every side. German universities can always be so organized as to answer the ideas which the sovereign of the day has of what is excellent in universities; but unalterable corporate bodies, with Gothic regulations, answer no man's ideas of excellence but those of their own well-paid members.

Without placing much confidence in sovereigns, it may at least be supposed, that, checked and informed as they now are by public opinion, they are as capable of organising a university as the same class of men were three or four centuries ago. It is at all times to be regretted that an undue veneration for the regulations of men who are almost forgotten should allow the immense sums, or rather quantities of the labour of the present generation, which they appropriated for education, to be wasted in producing very little

---

[78] **Editor's F/N:-** The University of Greifswald was in Prussia from 1815-1945. It had been in Sweden from 1648-1815.

good.  There is probably no country of Europe in which larger funds are appropriated to this purpose than in England, and, owing to our rigid adherence to Gothic regulations, there is no one in which so little good is effected by them.  The revenues of the two universities of England are probably greater than all the sums expended in the whole north of Germany for the education of the people.  In one country they serve to maintain a few individuals in idleness and luxury; in the other they have diffused knowledge and morality among the poorest of the people.

The whole expence of Göttingen, and, compared with other German universities, it is magnificently endowed, is for books, for the salaries of professors, for buildings, and all other expences, about 70,000 R. Thalers, or somewhat more than £11,000 Sterling per year; a sum that possibly equals the incomes of four of the heads of houses in one of our celebrated seminaries.  At Göttingen there is no other expences than paying the teachers, and providing books, instruments, &c.  A few students are educated at the expence of some towns, and of the sovereign, and they have a free table and lodging given them; but Göttingen has no good things to bribe its younger members to a continued adherence to taught opinions.  There is no warm and well-lined stall of orthodoxy, and no means are taken to influence the students' conscience through their stomachs.  They believe according as they discover truth, and not according to the prebends, and bishopricks, and fellowships, which reward a particular faith.

The German universities are said to teach theology very well, but they cannot gild it and render it delightful, as other universities do, to many learned and estimable men.  The Germans do not squabble, therefore, who shall have it.  Notwithstanding the want of large incomes, the Germans are, however, some of the most learned theologians of the day, and the most heartily charitable and tolerant of all the people of Europe.

The only buildings belonging to the university at Göttingen are, the library, a museum, an observatory, and a council-house.  Several others belong to the medical part of the university.  There is a lying-in-hospital, a botanical and agricultural garden, and one large hall, where some of the professors give lectures; but the professors and students live scattered about the town, and, in general, the instruction is given in the houses and private rooms of the former.  In Göttingen almost every house is a lodging-house.  The students board where they lodge, or their meals are procured from some cook's shop, or they feed in taverns; but they are never collected at a common table and fed from the public funds. It is a general characteristic of most German universities, that the professors and students live where and how they please.

When teachers and students are collected in *colleges*, as in England, they may need a particular code of laws, and ought, perhaps, in all things which regards college discipline, to be subjected to the tribunals of the university alone; but the mode of living in German universities neither calls for such a separate code, nor justifies giving the students regulations and tribunals different from the common laws and tribunals of the country. Yet the separation, in Germany, of the members of a university from the other citizens, is more complete than in England.

When professors are appointed, and when the students have paid their matriculation-money; – when they have received a copy of the university laws, and have given their hand – *Handshlag* – to obey them, they are both, from that moment, with all their families, domestics, and dependants, university citizens – *Academische Bürger*, – and they are both, from that moment, set free from the control of the civil magistrate, and rendered entirely independent of any other laws or tribunals than those of the university. This is an important fact, because it partly explains in what the freedom of the universities of Germany consists, when they are, at the same time, dependant on the sovereigns. The great substantial privilege of both professors and students is, that they are subjected, in no case whatever, to any other tribunals than those composed of the professors themselves. This is an admirable security for the professors.

In every university there is more than one teacher for any particular branch of knowledge which is much studied. Although the professors are appointed, and, in general, paid by the sovereign, much of their income, at the same time, is derived from the fees which the students pay to hear their lectures. Of course, each professor is anxious to have as many hearers as possible, and all are careful, in their capacity of magistrates so well as in their capacity of teachers, never to irritate or offend the students. There is both a competition amongst the different professors at the same university, and a competition amongst those of different universities; and the students are sometimes tempted to choose the place of their study rather by the indulgences allowed than by the reputation of the professors.

Thus, Jena is praised by them, because they can enter the class-rooms in a morning-gown and slippers, and Göttingen because they are there treated with more gentle manly respect. This situation of the student relative to the professor, thus ensures him the protection of this latter, who is his only judge and master; and herein consists the freedom or the licence of all the students of Germany.

Because a professor is not limited to one state, and because the sovereigns have been greatly desirous to be praised for their patronage, the latter necessarily protect the former. There is a competition amongst the sovereigns who shall have the most learned professors, and which of their universities shall be best attended. The consequence is, that the professors, and with them the students, are protected against that power of the monarch, which is the only one superior to both. Another thing which has given importance and freedom to the members of German universities, is the immunity which they have long enjoyed to print whatever they please without their works being subjected to any other censure before publication than that of the faculty of which the person printing was a member. It is a great advantage that the censors should be brother professors, and without any power, either over hope or fear, to produce the suppression of a truth. In these points consists that independence of which the members of German universities are so deservedly proud.

In most cases, the laws of the society are the laws which are administered by the tribunals of a university; but there are also separate regulations for the conduct of the students. They prescribe almost every trifling particular of their conduct, not only in their class-rooms, but in their private life. They forbid them to collect in multitudes, prescribe how much money they may be trusted for confectionary, and how much for clothes. A man who shaves them may give them twelve months' credit; while he who only dresses their hair, as this is a luxury, must not trust them for more than six. They forbid them to wear tassels of a particular colour to their pipes, and they fix the time for which they can hire a room. They must not give or hold large entertainments without permission. In short, if the conduct of the students is not inimitably correct, it is not for want of most minute and precise regulations.[79]

There are three university courts in Göttingen to administer the laws and regulations. A certain portion of the professors form the four faculties of learning; to each faculty there is a dean, who is changed every year; and the resident chief of the university is a pro-rector, who is changed every year, and who is taken alternately from each of the faculties. The first court is called the university-council.

---

[79] **Hodgskin F/N:-** For the last regulations for Göttingen, (there have been a great many,) see Gesetz Sammlung 3 Abtheilung, No. 30, p.44.

It is composed of the pro-rector, president, all the members of the four faculties, and the actuary and the syndicus of the university, who are both jurisconsults. It meets once a-month, and transacts business relative to the whole university, so well as tries important causes, which may involve a serious punishment.

The second court is called the university deputation. The pro-rector is president. The deans of the four faculties, and when the pro-rector is not a jurisconsult, the person who is next in turn to be dean of the faculty of jurisprudence, with the syndicus and actuary, compose this court. It meets whenever it may be necessary, and it decides in cases of importance relative to justice or to discipline.

The pro-rector, the syndicus, and the actuary, form a little court, and meet twice a week to hear and decide complaints of lesser moment. All complaints against any member of the university, or against their wives, families, and servants, must be made to one or other of these tribunals. The university itself can be complained of only to the government, under whose special superintendence it is.

An extraordinary feature in German universities is the number of professors. At Berlin, in 1818, there were 55;[80] and at Göttingen there were 35 ordinary professors, 5 extraordinary ones, and 30 persons who were authorized by the government, and gave lectures or instruction on some topic or other. A dancing, a music, a fighting, and a drawing master, with a person to teach architecture, and another to teach the French language, are all nominated by government, and considered necessary to complete the education. Seven of the professors, and other licensed persons, teach theology; 14 teach jurisprudence; 18 the healing art; and 38 what is called philosophy, which includes history, languages, mathematics, political science, metaphysics, &c.

A more minute account will show precisely what is taught at a German university. I shall therefore give in the Appendix a scheme of the studies for one half-year; which will also shew accurately the manner in which teaching, as a branch of industry, is divided in Germany. The courses of lectures and examinations amount in one-half year, and they are not less numerous in the other half, to 148 different ones. A few professors give only one course of lectures, but most of them give more; and the most popular read three, and sometimes four, lectures daily. There is no branch of school-knowledge, therefore, however numerous its twigs, which has not at this celebrated university its appropriate teacher.

---

[80] **Hodgskin's F/N:-** In 1819, there were 67 teachers at Berlin – at Heidelberg, 51 – at Breslau, 52 – who advertised 140 courses of lectures.

The most celebrated of the professors at present at Göttingen are Messrs Hugo, for civil law; Meister, for criminal law; the venerable Blumenbach, for natural history; Osiander-Himly-Langenbeck, in the healing art; Stromeyer, jun. for chemistry; Eichhorn, the elder, for philology and theology; Sartorius, for political philosophy, statistics, &c.; Gauss and Harding, for astronomy; Hausmann, for mineralogy and geology; Heeren, for history and ethnography; Bouterwek, for metaphysics and moral philosophy; and Thibaut, for mathematics and natural philosophy. Each of these gentlemen may have improved the science which he teaches, or the method of teaching it. They have compiled a vast body of information, which, from being collected, is afterwards more easily diffused through the world; – but, except some philological observations made by Professor Eichhorn, some trifling discoveries in chemistry made by Professor Stromeyer, and the elucidations of some passages of the Roman law, by Professor Hugo, I am not aware that any one of them has materially enlarged the boundaries of human knowledge, or added to human power. Professor Heeren has followed the steps of his illustrious predecessor Spittler and has added considerably to historical literature; and Professor Sartorius is doing much towards spreading proper notions of political economy, the science of which he has deeply studied. The great merit, however, of all these gentlemen rather consists in having better arranged the knowledge which was already in existence, and in having corrected many learned errors of their predecessors, than in having discovered any valuable truths.

Even this is a great merit; for between the discovery of a valuable truth, and the rectification of a learned error, there seems to be no other difference than that the former may become the property of the whole race; while it is scarcely possible that any of the latter, except those which a class of men may be set apart to teach, should ever be extensively diffused. The errors which learned men rectify, and the ignorance which they enlighten, are merely the errors and the ignorance of other learned men, and rarely those of mankind.

The list of what these gentlemen teach, the manner in which the sciences are divided and subdivided, will suggest to the reader the spirit of what is taught. There seem to be no outlines which the student can fill up at his leisure – no large and comprehensive views, whose subordinate parts, acquired by secret industry, make knowledge valuable, by making it truly the property of the individual. Everything seems explained to the very utmost limit of minuteness; and the plan of teaching rather resembles the manner in which schoolmasters repeat trifles to their scholars, than that of great philosophers giving hints for study, which industry must adopt and improve.

Many of the lectures on theology and jurisprudence consist in mere verbal criticism, explanations of different readings, restorations of corrupted passages, and all that can make the old books, whether of law or of religion, intelligible to the young hearers. I am aware of the presumption of censuring, even in the most remote way, the pursuits of men who are distinguished in the world, and who only do what has been done and applauded for ages. Yet I cannot avoid thinking that very much of what is here taught is the veriest trifling which idle monks ever adopted as an amusement, and which the learned world has believed to be a heritage of wisdom from them long after their other doctrines and themselves are forgotten. It is trifling with which any man may innocently and rationally amuse himself, but which no man can be paid by a government for teaching without a waste of the national substance; and which no man can be induced, by extra rewards, to learn without a most deplorable waste and perversion of his talents.

Sciences and arts must be valued by their utility; and they possess two sorts of utility. They are useful to the people who profess them, and they are useful to the society. But in what way are geology, mineralogy, ontology, zoology, philology, mathematics, and, in short, all those branches of human knowledge which are dignified by the name of the sciences, (the fine arts may also be added,) so much more useful to the society than the common mechanic arts, than agriculture, and weaving, and shoe making, that the funds of a nation should be appropriated to pay their professors? The very circumstance, that the professors of many of the sciences and arts cannot find any reward for their labours in the common markets of the world, is a complete proof of their disutility to the society. That which is useful to men they will most assuredly reward.

In general, the utility of these sciences and arts to those persons who are conversant with, and who practise them, – the pleasure which they give the individuals who have long studied them, – and the importance which they thus acquire in their minds, – have been substituted for their utility to the society, and governments have thus been persuaded to reward what is of no general use. The character of these sciences and arts has been always given by the persons who professed them. They have held the pen for the rest of mankind and have written their own opinions as the opinions of the world. Far be it from me to doubt the positive and ultimate utility of the sciences and arts. I know what a beautiful and innocent amusement they are – how they enlarge, and soften, and improve the mind; but poetry, and novels, and music do all this, and no professors are required to teach how they should be written. It is, in fact, because some of the sciences and arts are useful that they do not need any extraordinary rewards. When these are bestowed they only stimulate a part of the system into diseased action, and its greatest beauty changes into monstrous excrescences that render the whole ugly in the sight of every sensible man. Thus, collecting worms, impaling insects, and all the veriest trifling that ever-amused children, become classed as art and science.

If it may be doubted whether the sciences and arts are so pre-eminently useful, that they ought to be encouraged by greater rewards than they receive in the common market, how much more may it be doubted of that particular science which is known as jurisprudence; whose professors, after having imposed shackles on mankind, must be paid for teaching how to rivet them? There is no greater evil than that the word of a man in all bargains and contracts should be of no value unless it is attested by lawyers. What should we think of rewarding a set of men to teach priestcraft to others – to teach them how to enchain us in ignorance? And assuredly lawcraft, or the dominion of lawyers over the understandings of men, is not a less evil than priestcraft was when it was in the pride of its power. There are no less than fourteen persons at Göttingen, the greater part of whom are appointed and paid by the sovereign to teach how to lengthen processes, how to confound right, and how to make a mystery and a property of justice.

It can be of no consequence to the present race of men how the Romans decided in any particular case; by referring to their decisions we are only prevented from examining the merit of the particular case and deciding according to it. After the experience of so many ages, after so much knowledge has recently been accumulated on the rights and duties of men, if those of the present day are not better able to decide on any question of right than the wisest lawyers of the days of Justinian, it can only be because our guides have always confined us to the decisions of these ancient lawyers. People who please may study the Roman law as an amusement; but it is certainly absurd to bestow any of the national funds on those who do study it, and still more absurd to direct, by artificial rewards, the talents of a nation to so barren and pernicious a study.

It can also be of too little consequence to the present generation how the Greek language was constructed, and how the Jews spelled and wrote, and what the half-formed and barbarous jargons of these barbarous people signify, that professors should be employed to teach and to explain them. These are rational praiseworthy studies for individuals, but most certainly they are not what a nation should honour and reward. But a large part of the professors at Göttingen are paid for explaining the writings of Jewish priests and of the Greek poets.

It is a part of the system of instruction to explain all these things in a most minute way. An explanation for every verse may occupy an hour, and the tablets and the memory of the students are amply filled, however their understandings may be neglected.

Among the lectures which it is necessary for the students of jurisprudence to hear is one on the public law of the confederate states of Germany. It was numerously attended. I should have thought I was unlucky in the time of hearing it, and I should not have judged of the whole from a part, had I not known several students of jurisprudence who assured me that what I had heard resembled the whole; and they defended the professor against my remarks on what I thought his trifling nonsense. He was speaking of the post regulations of Germany; and he described them to such a degree of minuteness, that he omitted neither the horses, the conductors, the postilions, nor their uniforms and badges. He dwelt particularly on the certificate (*Post Schein*) which is always given to every person who either takes a place or sends a parcel . Professors ought to teach something difficult to learn which they had themselves acquired by years of labour; but, in this instance, something was taught of which no stranger who had ever travelled by the post coach could be ignorant. There was no international law to be elucidated by this. The whole regulations of each individual Post being made by the different sovereigns, and, like the notices of our own coach-offices, are printed on every certificate.

When the utility of the studies at this university is estimated, they give but small hopes of any accelerated improvement in mankind from the labours of the learned. The "lights of the world, and demi-gods of fame," are employed teaching what is of doubtful utility; and most of the elite of Germany, the future "lights of the world," are wasting the precious hours of youth in acquiring a veneration for trifles that abides by them through life.

When the course of instruction for youth places equal value on the subtilities and chicaneries of jurisconsults, – on composing Greek verses, – on discriminating between stones formed by fire and by water, – on the hues of an insect, – and on the proudest lessons of moral and political wisdom, – need we wonder that men so instructed substitute the lessons of lawyers for plain honest wisdom, or that these subtilities become the rules of national councils; need we wonder that, classing the phenomena of magnetism, collecting and preserving intestinal worms, and impaling and arranging butterflies, should be deemed objects of great importance? A great many of the occupations of the learned in Germany are the merest trifling; and their love for this is chiefly to be attributed to a course of instruction at their universities, in which everything that bears the name of a science, without any regard to its utility, is indiscriminately taught. There can be little doubt that, whatever is wrong in this system, is to be attributed to the patronage of sovereigns, who have equally rewarded every learned pursuit; or rather they have done all they could to encourage trifling, that the attention of men might be diverted from more important objects. The pleasure of the prince has been substituted for the good of the society, and his views have been made the criterion of general utility.

Although most of the professors are paid by the government, very few of them lecture gratis. The students are, in general, obliged to pay for every course of lectures they wish to hear. The price is one pistole, or 16s.8d. for each course, though there are some of the medical courses which cost double, and even treble, that sum. The salaries of the professors are unequal, depending, in a great measure, on their reputation, and on the necessity the university or the sovereign has for them. Some of them are said to receive 2,000 Thalers per year; others have not above so many hundreds; and some are contented with the mere honour of the appointment.

Some of the best paid professors may, at the same time, make 2,000 Thalers per year by the students, which makes the highest money reward which is probably acquired in Germany by teaching, amount to about £670 per year. For this, however, many of them labour very hard; they read three or four lectures a day on five days of the week. In point of industry they are surpassed by no literary labourers of the world. Professor Eichhorn the elder, who is probably the cleverest man of the whole university, has been for many years in the habit of reading four lectures a-day on five days of the week; and he is also the author of more than eighty volumes of printed works on various subjects. Such a labourer can have had no rainy days.

Numerous as the retainers of every German government are, it is impossible that they can be well paid, compared with the servants of the British government. I am rather disposed to think that the emoluments of German professors, compared with the emoluments of other people in Germany, are large. £600 or £700 a-year, as the highest reward for teaching, is, at the same time, very little compared with what many schoolmasters and professors make in Britain. This poverty, if it really be poverty, is, however, compensated to the German professor by the honour to which teaching sometimes leads. A professor of theology in one of our universities may become a bishop; but, in Germany, the professors are frequently called to situations of dignity in the ministry. Spittler, who was professor at Göttingen, was afterwards one of the principal ministers of Wirtemberg; and Mr. Martens, the present ambassador from the court of Hannover to Rome, was professor at Göttingen.

The greater part also of the professors enjoy the honorary distinction of Hofräthe, and no less than nine of those of Göttingen are knights of the order of the Guelphs. No mere teacher at any of our universities has, I believe, been honoured with knighthood. This fact shows in what manner the want of large emoluments may be compensated, and also the manner in which teaching is honoured in Germany. This is not an example that we ought to wish imitated. Whenever monarchs take learning to their embraces, her illegitimate progeny are all rickety, ill-formed, and diseased; her offspring are only healthy when she lies in the arms of freedom. A gay ribbon may go farther than a pecuniary reward, and warp that knowledge to trifling, which is now dispensed in our country with a great regard to truth and utility.

This honour has not, however, saved these gentlemen from a species of degradation. A work that may be regarded as proceeding from the ministry of Hannover, said of the tumults of the Göttingen students,

> "that no official information had been given of them at Hannover, because the superiors of the university, it was well known from experience, loved rather to preserve silence than to make any reports that might be displeasing to the students."[81]

These same superiors also

> "begged of the commissioner, with great earnestness, when the students withdrew, that he would order away the hussars, and invite the students back."[82]

---

[81] **Hodgskin's F/N:-** Actenmässige, Darstellung, &c. &c. p. 26.
[82] **Hodgskin's F/N:-** Ibid. p. 79.

In short, a great many proofs may be found, from the manner in which the learned men have treated the students, that they are rather in a state of degrading dependence on them. In spite of the patronage of the sovereign, therefore, or rather in consequence of it, these learned men suffer a degradation to which no common schoolmaster of Britain would submit. Loaded, as I am afraid the reader will already find this book, with discussions, I would not say a word in explanation of this fact, were it not that a great body of men are constantly demanding of sovereigns more patronage for learning, and that this degradation appears to me to be occasioned by such a patronage.

Through every department of industry, wherever an artificial stimulus, that is, a stimulus greater that the natural demand, has been applied to encourage the production of any commodity whatever, the effect has always been, that a greater quantity of talents and of skill have been directed to its production than could at length find a proper profit or reward. The artificial stimulus is either withdrawn, or it is insufficient, and the people who have been induced by it to employ themselves in a particular way, are sure to fall into poverty and distress. The same fact is true of many of the manufactories of Britain, to which a larger portion of the skill of the nation has been directed than would have been but for the frequent unwise encouragements of the Legislature, and the manufacturers are now involved in distress.[83]

The same fact is true of the artists of Italy and France, who have been seduced, many of them, from mechanical pursuits, by the patronage which has been bestowed on the arts. All the minor artists of these countries, and under this term musicians, comedians, buffoons, and such people, must be classed, are some of the most degraded of the population of those countries. They have no other means of procuring a miserable subsistence than by flattering the lowest passions and the vilest lusts of degraded People. And the same fact is true of the learned of Germany, and perhaps of Europe.

Learning has long been patronized by princes, and they have patronized a learning not always saleable in the common markets. This is thought to be an honour for learning and has induced a far greater number of men to follow it as a profession than princes could reward, or than the funds which the opinions and the wants of

---

[83] **Editor's F/N:-** This paragraph presents what was to become central to Hodgskin's concept of Business Cycles, that finds later expression within the Austrian Business Cycle Theory. See the appendix A.1. for a discussion of this point.

the world have destined to learning, could maintain.  It is this sort of patronage, much more than any natural desire to study, or than any dazzlings of genius, which has directed so many people to follow learning as a pursuit; and more have engaged in it than could possibly be rewarded.  Hence the little value paid for teaching and for authorship, and hence the complaints of the learned of their poverty.

This cause has operated in Germany more, perhaps, than in any other country, from the number of sovereigns, all of whom are ready to patronize learning.  The consequences are the immense number of professors at each university, – their competition one with another, and, at length, their dependence on the students.  Did no extra stimulus, such as the bounties of the sovereign, induce a great number of men to follow learning as a profession, and to collect at one place, open and public competition would be admirable.  Did no law of the society make these gentlemen who are thus dependent on the students, at the same time their judges, they could have no opportunity and no power to tempt the students to attend their lectures by any other means than superior teaching.  And, without being patronized, and without having this power, they never could have been degraded as they now are ; nor could the tumultuous conduct of the students, which has been in a great measure occasioned by the dependence of the professors, have ever brought the whole universities of Germany into one moment's disrepute.

The manner in which the professors lecture is the same as that adopted at the university of Edinburgh.[84]  Each lecture lasts an hour, and, generally, the professors deserve credit for slowness and distinctness of delivery.  The diligence of a student is measured by the quantity of notes which he makes, and, to permit them to do this, the professors are very particular in dividing their discourses into separate heads, and in waiting some time under each division, that, at least, the title may be written down, and the general topics known.  I cannot in general praise the eloquence or the elegance of the manner of delivery.  Professors Hugo, Sartorius, Bouterwek, Thibaut, had paid some attention to the graces of speaking; but most of the professors seemed to me, so utterly had their voices lost all the intonations of feeling, or of passion, much more to resemble speaking machines than men.[85]

---

[84] **Editor's F/N:-** Hodgskin had attended Edinburgh University between 1813 and 1815 (Stack, 1998, p.49-51).

[85] **Hodgskin's F/N:-** "Many teachers, not celebrated, lecture much more amusingly and instructively than more celebrated men.  The manner in which these latter speak is so confused, so likely to lull to sleep, that when

The professors are easy of access, and polite to strangers, whose notice, indeed, they are said "to court as a sort of honour."[86] Before meeting with this remark, I had thought they seemed so accustomed to be visited, that they calculated on it, and were ready, like sovereigns, to receive the homage of every stranger who requested to see them. There may be a little vanity in this, but they are always extremely polite. No stranger need be shy in approaching any one of them, for he is sure to be received with urbanity and kindness, and to have every information given him he may wish to obtain.

The number of students at Göttingen, in 1818, was 1,158. Of these there were:

| | |
|---|---|
| natives of Hannover | — 472 |
| From other parts of Germany, | — 580 |
| Foreigners, | — 106 |

Of these were to study:

| | |
|---|---|
| Theology | — 220 |
| Jurisprudence, | — 554 |
| Healing art, | — 210 |
| Philosophy, &c. | — 174 |

It deserves remark, that, compared with a former year, the number of students in theology has increased as 1; in jurisprudence as 14; in the healing art as 12; and in philosophy as 10. It is not affirmed that this is a constant proportion, but there is reason to believe, from a comparison of several years, that the alteration in the number of students who study different sciences is not inadequately expressed by these numbers. [87]

---

a student has not a very great love for what they teach, he would do much wiser to hear the lectures of less celebrated gentlemen." — Der Göttinger Student, p. 38.

[86] **Hodgskin's F/N:-** Der Göttinger Student, p. 24.

[87] **Hodgskin's F/N:-** The reader may perhaps be pleased to see the number of students in some other universities. I add, therefore, an account of such as chance has made me acquainted with. In Wurzburg, in 1819, there were 576, — 128 were foreigners, 117 study philosophy, 126 theology, 149 jurisprudence, 184 medicine; in Tubingen, 700; in Jena, in 1815, 321, —in 1816, 374, —1817, 493, —1818, 634, —1819, 669. Jena,

The list of what is taught, which is given in the Appendix, is also, in a great measure, the list of what is learnt; but, as some of the branches of knowledge there mentioned are more studied than others, it is necessary to make some observations on what is most generally learnt. Although the students of theology and of medicine may have a great influence on the whole society, they are not likely to have so much as those who study jurisprudence; for almost the whole of the efficient legislators and governors of Germany, the advocates, the judges, the professors of this science, and all the young men who are candidates for any office under the government higher than that of a copying-clerk, write their names down for three years to study jurisprudence.

From the list which has been given of the studies under this head, it will not be expected that, however much learning may be got from them, they will give much wisdom. In fact, much of what is taught under the head of jurisprudence may be described to be a knowledge of ancient systems of law, or of *existing* systems of law, both of which inquiring and wise men very generally allow to be far from perfect, if not absurd.

Many things which are of themselves useless, are learnt from a necessity which exists, derived from these systems being established to learn them. Although it might be easy enough, from a knowledge of nature, and from mixing with the world, to learn what is deemed right in any society, yet it requires a particular study to know, in every case, what was deemed right by the Romans, and what is ordered by the laws, and hence a necessity arises from establishing foreign, or complicated codes of laws, for a large body of men, to devote their whole time to studying them.

Of themselves they are a barren study, and when they require such a quantity of talent as we see devoted to them in Germany, it is surely a proof that they are a great evil. What might all the powerful minds which have been wasted on them not have effected for the human race had their talents been directed to some useful and productive study? The Roman laws have done much to ungermanise Germany. They have deprived the people of their particular usages, and much of their national character. Their own

---

therefore, is rapidly increasing in reputation and numbers of students. Two hundred and twenty were to study jurisprudence, 103 medicine, 287 theology, and 59 philosophy. In the same year there were, at Vienna, 995, —at Berlin, 942, —at Leipsic, 911, —at Prague, 850, —at Landshut, 640,— at Halle, 503, —at Breslaw, 366, —at Heidelberg, 363, —at Giessen, 241, —at Marburg, 197, —at Rostock, 180,—at Kiel, 167, —and at Griefswald, 55.

legislators have taken them as models, and there is not a single modern regulation or law, I believe, of the whole country, without expressions of the Roman law. With a constitution totally different from that of Rome, Germany has been deeply inoculated with the poison of Rome's worse institutions. This is one of the many instances to be found in our times of a blind imitation of the ancients. To follow the Roman law at present is as rational as it would be to follow the Roman methods, if they be known, of weaving and of making war.

The students have no settled general plan of studying which can be accurately delineated, further than that each one attends those lectures he thinks will conduce most to his improvement. It is necessary for every young man to undergo a certain examination before the professors, and to receive a certificate of his qualifications, before he can procure any situation either under the government, or as an advocate, or as a surgeon. To obtain any respectable situation, it is necessary to study three years at some university; but, during this time, the student chooses for himself those lectures which he will attend. The young advocate must attend lectures on the Institutes, on the Pandects, on criminal jurisprudence, and on the elements of practice. In like manner, there are certain lectures which the medical and theological student must hear; there are others, such as those on general history, on statistics, and on geography, which they attend if they please; but, in general, all the students attend those professors principally whose reputation is great. Out of 1,150, the number at the chemistry class was 39, at the political class 100, and at the class for the public law on Germany, it was still greater.

There is no good student who does not attend three — most of them attend five, and some of them six — lectures in one day. They write down everything which is said; they are never idle or inattentive; rigid laws amongst themselves prevent one from disturbing the others; and, on the whole, their industry is equal to the industry of the professors.

Some few students are older than the others, but in general young men go to the university between the ages of fourteen and seventeen. They may go after being confirmed, which always takes place at fourteen, and they generally do go immediately their studies at the upper schools are completed, which rarely extend beyond their seventeenth year. Latterly, owing to the disturbed state in which Germany and all Europe has been for so many years, and owing to a large part of the young population having being obliged to serve in the armies, a greater number of young men of a more advanced age have become students.

The students of Germany have lately occupied so much of the public attention, that I am tempted to give a more detailed account of their manners and conduct than I should have otherwise thought it right to give of a few young men, or rather boys, who, through injudicious treatment, have acquired a momentary influence in society. The community is in a diseased state when the voice of the young alone is heard on political questions; when their organized bands are so powerful that they are regarded as superior to the laws of their country; and when they fill the public ear and occupy the public mind, we may be sure that the rest of the society are submissive, degraded, and oppressed.

"Wir alle sind Brüder und einander gleich," — We are all brothers and equal to one another, is the motto of the students, and the sign of their university equality. And there is a freedom of intercourse amongst them that teaches, at least for the moment, both the future prince[88] and the future citizen to respect man more than his artificial dignities. The rich and the poor students have necessarily different sorts of lodging, different companions, and seek different amusements; but, whenever they meet there is amongst them a perfect equality, and all are, as they themselves say, brothers. It is one of the best features of their character, that they are always ready to help one another, with their hands, their heads, or their purses.

Mad. de Stael has truly remarked, that men of letters in Germany are more separated from the rest of society than in any other European country. The separation is fast diminishing; learned men mix more with the best society; they are called to offices in the state: but the distinction is yet so strong between the learned and the mere citizens, that it will be many years before it can be obliterated. It is perhaps one of the most singular circumstances in the life of Kant, that one of his most particular and oldest friends was a merchant.

For, in general, there is little or no communication between such different classes of men. Most of the universities of Germany are in retired corners and small towns, where the learned are completely the superiors of the whole society, and never see any persons but their subjects, unless it is the passing stranger, who rather ministers to their vanity, by laying at their feet his homage of their talents. The

---

[88] **Hodgskin's F/N:-** Many of the minor sovereigns of Germany, when young, study at the universities.

tradesmen are, in general, in Germany, poor and despised; the farmers are bauers and stigmatized; — but few merchants are opulent; but few soldiers are learned; and, therefore, when a university is not in a large city, the learned necessarily live in their own circle, and quite separate from the rest of the society. In Germany also every class forms a *Stand* by itself. Guilds were common to all trades, and, though they have been in most instances abolished, the guild of the learned yet maintains itself with all its ancient privileges and powers.

This unhappy separation of the learned from the rest of the society, if it be not chiefly owing to the constitution of the universities, is yet much widened by it. The professors, with their separate privileges and tribunals, can have no common interest with the rest of the citizens; and the student, by this constitution, is made at once something which is not a citizen. At the beginning of his literary career his interest, his privileges, the laws under which he lives, are all different from those of the rest of the society; and if he do not afterwards fill some situation in the public service, — if he continue a literary man, he remains separate from the rest of the people through life. I met a literary man in Dresden who knew nothing whatever of the tribunals or administration of justice in his own country. And a learned professor at Göttingen was ignorant of all such matters in Hannover. From this separation, the learned have troubled themselves very little with the common concerns of life. Hence much of their learning is nothing but dreaming and mere words; it has no relation to the affairs of the world and is of no other use but to amuse the learned. This separation is therefore mutually mischievous. The learned want common sense, and common men want learning. The recent political circumstances have done much to unite the classes. The writings of the day begin to have more wisdom, and the people more useful knowledge.

With this separation the learned, particularly the students, combine very naturally, from their superior privileges, an idea of being greatly superior to other classes. Fichte,[89] a celebrated philosopher of the Kantian school, said, many years ago:

> "that the students speak of themselves as the elected of God, and that all other men are the rejected. Every other class must give way to them. Each person must be pleased with what they do, and nobody dare to displease

---

[89] **Editor's F/N:-** Johann Gottlieb Fichte (1762-1814). *His Foundations of Natural Rights - Grundlage des Naturrechts* (1796) would appear to be his most Hodgskin-like work.

them. Every person not a student, with the exception of their teachers, and the magistrates under whom they are placed, must speak them fair and honourably, and must recommend himself to their favour by carefully avoiding whatever might offend their delicate ears. This is the duty of every person towards them; but, from their exalted freedom and feelings, they may treat all persons unworthily. This is their right against every man."[90]

They are not only, therefore, separated from the rest of the society, but they have learned to despise it. The contemptuous manner in which they speak of everybody not a student, whom they call *Philisters*, (Philistines,) while they are the chosen of God, shows this unamiable part of their character in its full light.

They have no academical dress, and they therefore seek to distinguish themselves from the Philistines by any and every absurdity of clothing they can invent. Some cut their hair and dress themselves like Cossacks; many let both hair and beard grow in unpruned wildness, and have a costume peculiar to themselves, consisting of immense green trousers, a red waistcoat, and a sort of white or grey coat, with some curious coloured cap. Most of them, however, are clad like the old Germans. Their hair is suffered to hang in ringlets on their shoulders. Neck handkerchiefs are rarely worn ; but their white shirt collars, of which they are very proud, are doubled back also on their shoulders. Their little caps, (*Mütze*,) fastened under their chins by a leather strap, often assume somewhat the appearance of an open vizor, and give their scared faces, and flaxen ringlets, a curious appearance of ferocity and effeminacy.

This capricious violation of common fashions may appear to be of no consequence to those Germans who believe in the separate existence of a "noble, moral, and transcendental man." But morality is, in general, little more than an obedience to the opinions of the world; and he who disregards that in trifles, may more easily be led to despise it in matters of importance.

Men deviate from its fashions; they laugh at it when it reminds them of their follies; and at length they spurn it when it reproves their vices. German students differ from the rest of their countrymen in their manners so widely as in their dress; they are rude and boisterous; and seem to have put on with the dress of the

---

[90] **Editor's F/N:-** Hodgskin provides no reference or citation for this quotation. It is likely that it was Hodgskin's own translation of Fichte's original German text.

Cossacks, and of their ancestors, all their harsh ness and unamiability. On ordinary occasions they abuse and ill-treat the servants of public places; they are ready to take insults and to insult; they walk about the streets in parties, singing and making hideous noises; they clatter with their heels and sticks on the pavements; they strike against the window-shutters of the Philistines; they not unfrequently cheat,[91] or, as they call it, *prellen*, the citizens; and, without being wicked, they seem to forget all the common civilities and little rules of life. The frequency of duels amongst themselves, from which results their scared faces, is well known, and is of itself a proof of their general character. Some gentlemanly steady young men are, of course, to be found amongst them — some who are afterwards to fill professors' chairs and be the ornaments and instructors of their age. Some I have known whom I yet love and respect; but these are the exceptions, and the general character of the students is what has been described.

Perhaps this character strikes a person more forcibly who has lived some time in Germany. He becomes accustomed to a high degree of gentleness and amiability in the elder people, and to such softness in children, that the contrast with the students is very great. The master of a respectable academy, who had frequently had English boys to teach and to educate, told me he always found them so ungovernable that he would rather have ten German boys than one English one. German boys are, in truth, compared to ours, extremely mild and soft, and these amiable qualities are put off whenever they become students. Three years of the life of a German are passed in total freedom from all other laws but the "Comment." Before that he is a gentle child under the roof of his parents; and after that he is lost in the greater circle of the world and follows implicitly its strict and regular rules. "A few years are allowed him between the discipline of the schools, and the restraints of office, in which, while he is taught, he may also indulge himself, and preserve a joyous remembrance of accomplished follies."[92]

That they may be countenanced in their absurdities, they have a set of rules made by themselves for their conduct, (the *Comment*,) which prescribe to them to demand satisfaction of any person who insults them, by applying to their conduct such epithets as foolish,

---

[91] **Hodgskin's F/N:-** I shall justify this part of the assertion by a quotation from a work written by a student:-"Misstrauisch gegen die Studenten sind sie (Die Einwohner) allerdings in der Regel, allein mit vollem Rechte denn man prellt sie auf zu vielfache Art und zu oft." *Der Göttinger Student*, p. 21. — The English is — That the citizens are *mistrustful* of the students; but with perfect right, for they are cheated too often, and in too many ways.
[92] **Hodgskin's F/N:-** Goethe, Aus meinem Leben.

strange, extraordinary, wonderful, monstrous, laughable, and all such other terms. In short, they seem to have proscribed every term of reproof that they might indulge unrestrained in every whim, and in every folly. According to this comment, all duels must be decided by the sword; and the weapon in common use is short and made only to cut. No more than a certain number of rounds is permitted, so that the affair seldom terminates in any other way than in disfiguring their faces. This comment is the only law which is rigidly obeyed. Its violation is visited by the severest punishment the students can inflict. The culprit is put in Coventry, (in *Verruf*,[93]) and during this time no person will associate with him, nor can he demand satisfaction for any insults he may receive. They have sometimes extended this Verruf to tradesmen; and, by depriving them of all student custom, have brought them to ruin, and rendered the whole of them extremely obedient and fearful.

Their conduct is marked by many eccentricities, of which the following is an instance:

In 1812, one of the students, either involved in debt in town, or in love in the country, retired from the town, and built himself a hermitage, in the neighbourhood of a house of amusement called *Maria Spring*. He made a very neat little place of it, planted a little garden, and lived here for nearly two years. It is said the great attraction was the daughter of the house from which he used to procure his provisions and other necessaries. Certainly, he lived in this retirement for a considerable time, and then, I believe, went clandestinely away, leaving the daughter and parents to mourn over lost virtue, money, and happiness.

The separation of the students from the citizens, and their mutual differences and quarrels, gave originally occasion to the former to unite in a body for defence and aggression. The students are collected from different parts of Germany, many of which have different dialects. It was natural for the natives of any particular place to associate with their townsmen or countrymen more than with strangers. The inhabitants of the different parts are distinguished by something peculiar in their dress. From these causes there came to be formed amongst the students' different little societies called *"Landsmanschafts."* They were originally societies for pleasure, for amusement, for defence against the

---

[93] **Editor's F/N:-** *Verruf* translates as *Disrepute*. However, in the context of how Hodgskin goes on to discuss Verruf it would seem evident that the word *Boycott* would be the modern equivalent. Given that this term refers to Charles Boycott and dates from 1880, it is a term that was unavailable to Hodgskin 60 years earlier.

citizens, and sometimes for defence against other students; but they were originally and long remained destitute of any political aim whatever. Some of the young men in such societies acquired more influence than others, and thus each society soon came to have something like a leader; and through these leaders and these separate societies, the students were frequently brought to act together. Their power was soon felt, and many attempts have been made, by ordinances, and by severe punishments, to suppress the societies. The sovereigns, however, only gave importance to them by recognizing and forbidding them. They were founded in a natural feeling of attachment; they were strengthened by the power which uniting conferred; and they appeared only to have been rendered formidable by the multitude of decrees which have been issued against them.

Recent political events have, in some measure, tended to destroy the petty dissensions and divisions of the Germans. In the recent contest against the French for freedom, it was proposed in some political journals that the students should change their *Landsmanschafts* into a general union or *allgemeine Burschenschaft*.[94] Some universities, as Halle and Jena, adopted this; others, as Göttingen, retained the old plan of Landsmanschafts.

The French conscription had extended to many parts of Germany. Many of the young men belonged to the *Landwehr*.[95] In 1813, the sovereigns called the students to the field, and led them to the combat. All these causes, together with the present tendency of the writings of several German authors, have combined to give the meetings of the students a political aim. University communicates with university; and all the students, whether united in *Landsmanschafts* or *Burschenshafts*, have recently been taught to act in bodies, and without any settled and fixed aim, they have spoken and acted decidedly in favour of freedom.

It is this union of purpose which has given to the German students, when there is no other body of men united for a common end, a power of making themselves heard and distinguished in the community. They have become more than any other body formidable to those sovereigns whose anxious cares extend to everything. The ceremony of burning some emblems of tyranny at

---

[94] **Editor's F/N:-** allgemeine Burschenschaft translates as *general fraternity,* whereas *Landsmanschafts* translates as *Country team.*

[95] **Editor's F/N:-** *Landwehr* can be translated as translates as *defence of the country* or as *Home Guard.*

the Wartburg, in 1817, interested all Germany.  Men were rejoiced or alarmed at it, as they were the advocates of freedom or of tyranny.  Every newspaper was full of it, and every mouth spoke of it.  When the students quitted Göttingen, in 1818, the same attention was excited throughout the country; and the ministry of Hannover concealed very ill the alarm which the conduct of the students excited in their bosoms. They mingled in the dispute and seemed to have acquired no honour.

The students have been regarded by many people, particularly the political writers of Germany, as destined to make a great alteration in the welfare of their country, and to be its deliverers from oppression and slavery.   When I had only heard of their processions, and their feasts, and their songs, this view appeared to me in part correct.  It argued well when the whole of the future legislators, judges, and ministers of Germany, were the warm advocates of the interests of humanity.

Since I have seen more of them, I have doubted if a set of young men, intoxicated by the power and importance which they derive from their momentary freedom, and from their numbers, can ever learn the value of freedom themselves, and I am sure they never can be fit to bestow it on others.  In their own societies, they submit to the most severe slavery.  A few bold spirits keep the whole in awe.  Many of them would have gladly returned to their studies at Göttingen.  Many of them wished never to leave it, but they were constrained, on these points, to obey the directions of a few.  In the midst of their licentiousness, they are slaves, and they never can give to others that freedom which they themselves can never properly value nor possess.

But the students are also all of the privileged classes.  The future clergymen, the future jurisconsults, judges, and ministers, are all students; and never did I hear any of them, except one, express any decided opinion against the quantity of lawyers, or the complicated systems of government, which are, in truth, the plagues of Germany.   On the contrary, I heard these young men express a greater disdain of bauers and mechanics than I ever heard expressed by any other persons.   These are, however, the oppressed classes of Germany, and they, I am quite sure, have nothing to hope from students.  Their riots are symptoms of youth full turbulence — not of a love for freedom.  They are certainly an evidence of enthusiasm — of a warmth of temper amongst the Germans greater than we are accustomed to ascribe to them ; but it is the warmth of youth, the enthusiasm of hot blood and licentious living, and not of a rational and determined spirit.

The disturbance at Göttingen, in 1818, shows this, and it exemplifies their character and conduct better than any descriptions can do. It was of sufficient importance to be noticed at the time in all the public journals of Germany. Several pamphlets were published on the occasion, and it excited a sort of literary warfare. Its effects on the university are likely to be permanent; and although it has frequently been mentioned in our own periodical works, it seems to me to be of sufficient importance to demand further remark. I shall, therefore, give a short account of it. I reached Göttingen a short time after its commencement and remained there till after its termination.

On the morning of July 2, 1818, one of the students, in passing through the meat market, where there was no regular road, and only a narrow-covered path, thrust a child on one side, who was talking and laughing with a butcher. The butcher said to him, in no very polite tone, there was no road there. He replied, the "devil take you," — Kerl, dich soll der Teufel holen. Some scuffling ensued betwixt them. Some witnesses say the butcher gave blows to the student; but this is denied both by the student and by the butcher.

The student complained of the insult to the police, and was told, after the matter had been inquired into, that the police could do nothing more than give a reproof to the butcher; and if this did not satisfy the student, he must have recourse to a common prosecution. The student declared to the police magistrate that he was satisfied, but his comrades deemed the dignity of the whole body insulted.

After thinking over the matter for nine days, or till the 11th of July, they met in consequence of a public notice, in great numbers, on the evening of that day, in a public garden close to the town, and resolved on doing themselves justice. Some of their number addressed them, and encouraged them to be valiant; and they marched in an orderly procession into the town, and demolished with stones and sticks the windows, doors, and some of the furniture of a house belonging to a man bearing the same name as he bore who had affronted the student, but not belonging to him; in fact, the house of another man.

They demolished the furniture of the house, after breaking into it, in the presence of the man himself, his wife, and daughter. This gross injury to an unoffending individual, this insult and outrage to females, they called taking that satisfaction which had been denied them for an injury. After threatening the house of the magistrate to whom the butcher had been complained of, they marched, singing their songs of triumph, through the streets, and at length dispersed.

The citizens, alarmed at this outrage, so well as by some previous excesses, and each one fearing that his turn would come next, and the magistrates having no power whatever to protect them, they requested the magistrates to represent the matter to the ministry at Hannover, which was done in the warmest colours. It appears that, although the ministry had not been officially informed of many previous excesses, that it knew of them, and had resolved to seize the first opportunity to curb the students and give to Göttingen a constitution better calculated for the exigencies of the times.[96] *

This appears to have been the principal motive why it was now resolved thoroughly to sift the conduct of the students, and to make a severe example of the guilty. Mistrusting the impartiality and knowing the bias of the usual tribunals of the university in favour of the students, the ministry sent a gentleman from Hannover, with the title of Royal Commissioner, to inquire into the whole matter. He arrived on the 21st of July, nine days after the fray, during which time no further riot had taken place. He was followed the next day, very much to the displeasure of the students, by a detachment of Hussars.

The conduct of the Hannoverian ministry was much discussed on the occasion, and it was on account of employing the soldiers that they received most blame. The citizens, of course, who felt the want of protection, and the partizans of military power, justified it throughout. The advocates of the students, and generally the friends to liberal opinions, condemned it. Without being a friend to the employment of soldiers, to sabre any class of people into obedience, it appears to me that, on present occasion, there were some good reasons for sending soldiers into Göttingen.

The students had got to so great a pitch of intemperance and disorder, that it would have most certainly been impossible to subject any individuals of them to merited punishment, without the whole breaking out into riot and rebellion. They were resolved to stand by one another; and when the ringleaders of the riot were demanded, a list of nearly all the students was given in. If it were necessary to inquire into the disturbance, to punish the perpetrators of a gross outrage, and protect the citizens, an armed force was necessary. If it were necessary that the students should not be absolute masters of the town, soldiers alone could hinder them ; for the civil magistrate had no power whatever.

---

[96] **Hodgskin's F/N:-** Actenmässige Darstellung der Worfälle, &c. Zu Göttingen, p. 27.

That they remained quiet from the 11th till the 21st of July, when there was neither inquiry going on, nor punishments inflicted, is no sort of proof that they would continue so when their conduct was investigated, and the ringleaders punished. But this part of their conduct gave them great advantages in arguing that the soldiers were not necessary. Whether this step was justifiable or not, it was a measure full of unpleasant consequences to most of the parties concerned.

On the evening of the day when the Hussars arrived, the students walked in great numbers through the streets, and sang songs. This is a common custom — only that on this evening the numbers were greater than usual. They were obliged by the soldiers to separate and go to their homes. On the following day, the students petitioned the Commissioner, under promises of good behaviour, that the Hussars might be withdrawn — of course, their petition was refused. They were, on the same day, forbidden, by a public notice, to collect in numbers, either in houses or in the streets, and they were also forbidden to sing in walking through the streets. Such parties are forbidden by the usual regulations of the university, and this order only enforced them.

In the evening, however, a great many of them collected near the place where the guard of Hussars was posted, and began singing Schiller's famous robber song, "*Ein freyes Leben führen wir*," — "we lead a free life." They then ridiculed and reproached the military, and at length pressed around them in such numbers as to impede the patrols from coming in. Something like the report of a pistol was heard, and the Hussars then received orders to drive the students away, and to strike them with the flat part of their swords. The students opposed them for a moment, but soon separated; and eight of them were cut or wounded in the fray. Considering all things, the soldiers appear to have behaved with moderation.

I must here remark, that there is a great deal of difference between sending soldiers into the town, and the manner of employing them when there. Although I think their presence on the spot was necessary for the protection of the citizens, it is difficult to believe that there was any necessity for guards or patrols in the street; and that it was not wrong thus to excite opposition by an unnecessary display of power.

In such cases it is always necessary to consider what the people have been before accustomed to. The students were unaccustomed to be awed by soldiers. Though contrary to the regulations of the university, they were accustomed to amuse themselves by singing through the streets without opposition or remark; and it appears, therefore, to have been most unwise to have forbidden that at this particular time, and to have enforced the decree by the terror of the soldiers. The only justification of sending them into the town was, that they were to protect the citizens; but they were employed unnecessarily to annoy the students.

Of course, the students felt themselves grievously affronted by the assault of the Hussars, and talked of arming themselves, and taking revenge. More military were brought into the town on the 23rd, the day following, which possibly prevented this determination, and induced the students to resolve on leaving Göttingen. They put this latter resolution in practice on the same day, and retreated to some of the villages, and to a little town belonging to Hesse Cassel, called Witzenhausen, which are in the neighbourhood.

They remained here till the 2nd of August, negotiating with the *ministry* of Hannover for the removal of the soldiers. As they were disappointed in this aim, they then came to a formal resolution, that all the students who were foreigners should leave Göttingen, and that no foreigner, which includes all other Germans but the Hannoverians, should, under penalty of being put out of the comment of all other universities, and out of the comment of the native students remaining at Göttingen, dare to go to Göttingen to study for two years. To be put out of the comment exposes the young men to all sorts of insult without any redress. This was putting Göttingen in *Verruf*, and the consequence was, that the whole of the foreigners immediately left the university. The students had no doubt, from this Verruf having been accepted by the students of most of the other German universities, that, till the two years are expired, few or no foreigners would go to Göttingen to study.[97]

Such is the power, and such the actions of the Göttingen students. Individuals, both students and citizens, who had displeased them, had frequently before been put in *Verruf*, to the great mortification of the former, and sometimes to the ruin of the latter. But this, I believe, is the first instance of their having extended their power to a whole university, and of their having decreed it not to be lawful for certain classes of persons to go there to study. This conduct betrays, on their part, no want either of freedom or of presumption. I will not exculpate the ministry; but certainly, the conduct of the students must be condemned.

---

[97] **Hodgskin's F/N:-** The Verruf does not appear to have had all the success intended from it. In 1819 Göttingen had 770 students, and above 130 of these were foreigners.

They took satisfaction for an imaginary insult, which, in fact, the individual offended allowed to have been satisfied, and, in doing this, they outraged some unoffending individuals, among whom were females; they displayed no contrition at this offence but insulted the authorities they were bound to obey. Much might, and much ought to be pardoned, in young men; but this single action was but the type of their general spirit, and this was opposed to all the restraints, not only of laws, but of order and decency. This is not a hazardous assertion. I have already given some specimens of their conduct. The quotation before made from Fichte may show that a bad spirit has long existed. The turbulent character has recently been somewhat augmented by a large number of the students having been in the armies, and then returned to study, bringing with them the habits of the camp.

A respectable citizen of Göttingen told me, however, that he remembered four instances of the students withdrawing themselves from the town, and they had not returned without stipulating conditions. They had each time re-entered the town in triumph, and they expected, on this occasion, to have done the same. The author of the little pamphlet which I have quoted, whose work was evidently written with a view of justifying the conduct of the government, has enumerated five recent disturbances at Göttingen, in one of which the students routed all the armed guard of the town. This he attributes to the young men having been soldiers; but these were only specimens of their general conduct. They cannot be considered as anomalies in their character, but merely its common features thrust more conspicuously into notice.

Göttingen has, however, been long considered as much superior to the other universities of Germany in point of manners. The following is Goethe's remarks when he was a student towards the year 1765. —: '

'In Jena and Halle rudeness was arrived at its highest pitch. Strength of body, skill in fighting, and the wildest self-will, were there the order of the day; and such dispositions could only be supported and encouraged by the most vulgar riots and turbulence. The relation of the students to the inhabitants of those cities, how different so ever it might be, helped these dispositions. The rude stranger had no respect for the citizens and looked on himself as a being privileged to use every freedom, and every impertinence."[98]

---

[98] **Hodgskin's F/N:-** Aus meinem Leben, Vol. II. p. 89.

Such, therefore, as it now is, has their character long been, and from them there can arise no other hope but that they should pursue their studies, and learn what order and freedom are.

Every Englishman must be astonished at the patience with which the citizens bore, and bear, the insults, contumely, and outrages of these youths. It marks the difference between a German and an English tradesman. Had students conducted themselves in a similar manner to Englishmen, hussars might have been necessary to prevent bloodshed, or to protect the students. The citizens would assuredly have had spirit to protect themselves, and to punish the boys. But the Germans, pounded into submission with the iron pestle of authority, can neither judge nor act for themselves when undirected by a police officer, or an order from the government. From having been over governed they have become imbecile, and they have changed the activity of intelligent beings for the mechanism of slaves. The citizens of Göttingen, as a free town, in the sixteenth century, were not behind those of Brunswick and Hannover in independence. The citizens of Göttingen, as a royal town, the seat of a university, are destitute of common vigour of mind.

There are seven or eight different *tribunals* in Göttingen, exclusive of those of the university. Yet among all these there was not one which could repress a common tumult, though there is a small armed force under the orders of the magistrates of the university. There was not one of these that was fit, in the judgment of the Hannoverian ministry, to inquire into and decide on the merits of the persons concerned in the riot. The legislators of Hannover must misdoubt their own institutions, and be sensible, after all the trouble they have given themselves, of the unfitness of their own creations to answer the end intended.

When we reflect for a moment on the consequences of such a riot, had it taken place in England, we may be sure that no armed force beyond the common civil power, aided by the citizens, could have been requisite to keep a few students in order. But, where men rely only on the military, they may, and must, use them equally to oppose rebellion or repress a tumult; to stifle the clamours of a nation, or stop the throats of noisy boys. They are instruments of despotism always at hand; and that violence which ought to be the last refuge of the government, is used the moment there is the least question of opposition to its will.

No extraordinary tribunal would be required in Britain to decide on the conduct of a few students; nor can a cabinet ministry in our country ever find it necessary to listen to their complaints. The

Hannoverian ministry had to interfere between the students and the laws; they set themselves formally to negotiate with them and degraded themselves from statesmen to police officers. They brought this degradation on themselves by that meddling spirit which compels them always to direct the most minute actions of the subjects, instead of trusting them to the common laws of nature. How much more powerful does the law appear in our country, where it is exposed to examination and to censure, than in this, where it is above inquiry, but rests on the will of some individuals; and where it is an engine of government, and nothing which the people are interested in supporting.

In the dependence of the university magistrates which has been described, there was a very good reason for not allowing this matter to be investigated by them. And their dependence on the students is to be considered as the great cause, not only of this riot, but of all the past, the present, and the growing turbulence of the students. What can be expected from them but excesses and violence, when the persons appointed to govern them not only do not reprove, but are ready to palliate their excesses? And they may well reproach the university magistracy for its compliance, and the government for placing it in a situation to fear them.

It was from similar offences having been long tolerated that at length brought on them the shame of being put down by soldiers. It must not, however, be argued from the present dependence of the professors, that they should have greater salaries given them to make them above the students. This is not the reformation which is required. This would make them neglect teaching. The students ought not to be removed, as they now are, from the control of the civil magistrate. Both professors and students should be subjected to the common laws of the land, and to the same tribunals as other people. This restriction is perfectly distinct from interfering with teaching. It is much to be wished that this should be rendered wholly independent of governments, rescued both from their patronage and from their control. But it is at the same time to be wished, that the professors and students should not be separated, by different laws and privileges, from the rest of the society.

It has been mentioned, that the reason why Göttingen was chosen for the seat of a university, was the ruined and impoverished state of the town.[99] "The inhabitants were to be maintained and nourished by the professors and students."

---

[99] **Hodgskin's F/N:-** [ibid] Vol. I. p. 341.

The consequence of this has been, that the former have become utterly dependent on the latter. The students know this; they know that the prosperity or the ruin of the inhabitants of Göttingen depends on them ; they know that the citizens, so well as the professors, fear above all things that  they should withdraw themselves, and thus ruin both. This power over the welfare of the citizens of Göttingen, and its consequent arrogance, has therefore been given to the students by that act of the government which was dictated by a wish to render Göttingen flourishing by founding a university at it. It has before been shewn, that a great cause for the turbulent disposition of the students was the dependence of the professors; and this also was originally caused by a desire in the rulers to have the honour of being the patrons of learning.

Another assigned cause for the present turbulence of disposition was the great number of students who were in Göttingen. Lodgings could scarcely be found for them all. In moral reasoning, it is the height of folly to fix all our attention on the last of any series of human actions, and to leave all its causes unexplored and uncondemned; or, in this case, although the students were presumptuous, riotous, and turbulent, although they had collected in Göttingen in greater numbers than could be accommodated, it is absurd to throw all the blame of such dispositions on them, or to attribute their coming in such multitudes to chance. German boys are mild and amiable beings, and students are rendered otherwise by nothing but the constitution of the university, and their relative situation to the citizens. For this constitution, – for this situation, – the government, its vain desires and regulations, are entirely and alone to blame. Presumption and turbulence in young men are necessary consequences of possessing *power*, and the overt acts of insulting people, and of rioting, are the consequences of such dispositions. The number of students collected in the little town of Göttingen was owing to the patronage of the government, and unless men should be determined not to extend their view beyond immediate causes, they must blame the silly vanity which aspires to the honour of being the Mecænas of the age, and the regulations of the government, so well as those dispositions of the students, which these regulations cause.

These latter observations account only for the arrogance of the students of Göttingen, while a similar disposition evidently now forms, and has long formed, part of the character of all German students. But it must be remembered, the principal causes for their presumption, namely, their independence of the laws of society, the patronage of the monarchs, and their exclusive privileges as a *Stand*, are common to them all, and that many of them share in that particular cause for the presumption of the Göttingen students, which is derived from knowing that the welfare of the little town in which the patronized university is situated depends on them. A class of reasoners are constantly blaming the evil passions of our nature as the causes of our misery. They teach all mankind to curse our common mother. If it were not for fear of being paradoxical I should assert, that what are called our good passions do as much mischief as our evil ones. At least, the evil passions of the students, and, probably, many other of the evil passions of all classes of society, may be clearly traced to that disposition in the rulers of the world which most men applaud as benevolent. Admitting that the intention of patronizing universities is most laudable, it is evident that its effects are most mischievous.

# Chapter X.

## On the German Language.

*Wrong criterions employed to judge languages by. – German language not unmusical; examples. – German articles redundant. – Declension of substantives redundant. – Adjectives absurdly declined. – Changes in verbs redundant. – German language complicated. – Source of the errors. – Is a rich language. – Kant; his merits and peculiarities.*

From the influence which language has on the character and on the literature of nations, every foreign language may, with propriety, be made by every traveller a subject of remark; and, therefore, I shall here make some observations on the German language. Most persons pronounce on the merits of any language either by its affinities to that one which they have spoken all their lives, or by its affinities to someone which has been recommended as a standard of elegance and accuracy. By the learned, most of the spoken languages of Europe have been called good or bad as they resembled the Latin or the Greek language; one or other of these having in general been selected by them as the model of a perfect language. By the ignorant other languages are called good or bad as they resemble their own, or as they are supposed to have some musical properties. It is wrong to judge by either of these standards.

It would be extraordinary if language, which is the master-art of life, should have been carried to perfection when all the other arts and sciences were in their infancy. If the languages of antiquity were more perfect than our own, it might then be supposed that they were anomalies in nature and were a sort of miraculous gifts. Like other arts, however, language had probably a chance beginning, it has been improved by patient research, and refined by every generation correcting the errors of the preceding one. [100] We have

---

[100] **Hodgskin's F/N:-** In a German grammar recently published at Göttingen, by Mr. Grimm, librarian at Hesse Cassel, it is asserted, that the German language had more noble forms in the thirteenth century than it has at present, and that it was still better in the fifth than in the thirteenth century. I am disposed, however, to believe, that what the learned librarian calls nobler forms, was a greater complexity than even at present exists, which is in all languages a bad, not a good quality.

not outstripped the ancients in this point so much as in many others, from the same cause why we have not outstripped them in statuary, architecture, &c. namely, that we have in these arts confined our efforts to an imitation of what they had achieved. Our learned people have sought to model the languages, and our artists the buildings and the sculpture of modern times after those of antiquity. If the mechanic arts had been subjected to the same restraints, we should now have wanted, with many other improvements, both the printing-press and the steam-engine.

Thoughts are so intimately connected with words, so few people ever think of separating one from the other, that in general men cannot conceive any other mode of expressing their thoughts than that to which they are accustomed. Use is said to be the tyrant of language. Though it decides whether we shall adopt or reject certain phrases, it can of itself never be of sufficient authority either to justify or condemn them. If usage were to be the only authority for speech, there would probably be no error of language which might not be justified.

The German language must not, therefore, be judged of by the analogy of its own modes or usages, nor by its relation to any other language. Neither ought it to be praised or condemned from any vague idea that it possesses musicalness or harshness of sound. Neither of these is an essential property of any spoken language. The poetical, or musical, or sung language, of any people, may, and very often does, differ materially from their spoken language. The Italian language is itself an example. The spoken, or provincial Italian, can nowhere, except in Venice, be described as a musical or harmonious language. The most rugged and guttural spoken language may be musical; and if this were not possible, nobody who knows that it was for the German language many of the compositions of Mozart and Haydn were made, or who has heard the famous little song written by Goethe, called Mignon, or Schiller's more common Robber Song, sung by a company of common soldiers, but must be convinced, that the German language can with no justice be described as a harsh or unmusical language.

I should be sorry to make a paradoxical assertion, but to my ear the German language does not sound harshly; and I do not know that there are to be found in any language more musical and well sounding lines than may be extracted (among many other pieces of poetry) from both the above-mentioned songs. For example, the first verse of Mignon, particularly the second, third, and fourth lines, seem to me sounds as soft and musical as were ever uttered:-

Kennst du das Land? wo die Citronen blühn,

Im dunkeln Laub die Gold-Orangen glühn,
Ein sanfter Wind vom blauen Himmel weht,
Die Myrte still und hoch der Lorber steht,
Kennst dues wohl?
Dahin! Dahin
Möcht' ich mit dir, o mein Geliebter, ziehn."

It must be remarked, that the Germans have a softer way of pronouncing the *s* than we have. The third line is exquisitely soft and musical, and in the whole there are but three words whose sound is in the least harsh — hoch, mächt, and ich, and perhaps ziehn. The two lines in the robber song,

Ein freyes Leben führen wir,
Ein Leben voller Wonne,

are all vowels or labials. I may add three other lines that I stumble on by chance, from Schiller's little poem, Würde der Frauen:—

Zärtlich geängstigt vom Bilde der Qualen
Wallet der liebende Busen, es strahlen
Perlen die Augen von himmlischem Thau.

I give these quotations as nothing more than examples of soft and pleasing sound. I do not mean to enter further on the subject, but merely to give some examples as a justification for believing the assertion, " that the German language is harsh and unmusical," has been probably made by people who have rather judged it from its crooked and strange letters, than from having heard it spoken or sung. I am far from asserting it has no unpleasant sounds, no words that abound in consonants, but with such, it contains as large a portion of musical and pleasant sounds as most of the spoken languages of Europe.

Language is the sign for what we see, feel, or think; every distinct perception, feeling, or thought, ought to have a distinct sign ; and no two of them ought to have the same sign. Against the first of these principles all languages offend. No one of them has a distinct and different sign for every different thought, or there would be no ambiguity, though no language perhaps sins less on this score than the German. Most languages also offend very materially against the second principle, and no one more so than the German.

The definite article *the* (in German *der, die, das*) is, in fact, a pronoun relating to some object before designated, or afterwards to be designated. If any three distinct and different objects had the same name, it might be a rational way to distinguish each of them by affixing to it a different article. Thus, *der Mann* might signify the man; *die Mann,* the woman; and *das Mann*, the child. All these three beings so nearly resemble one another, and are so perfectly of the same species, that the different genders might as well be marked by those articles which are called the signs of genders as by a change in the name. The Greeks, I believe, had only one term corresponding to our child to signify both boy and girl; and to this word they affixed a masculine or a feminine article to distinguish which of these two were meant: as we say a man or a woman child. From a contrary custom of speech, it would now sound absurd to say a male boy, or a female girl: But changing an article when, at the same time, two distinct names designate the different genders or qualities which are to be designated, is as absurd as saying a male boy or a female girl.

Whenever genders are easily distinguished in nature, most modern languages have a different name for each gender. This is particularly true of the German language, which has a syllable (*inn*) that, added to words designating males, makes them signify the females of the same species. There can, therefore, be no need of any further sign, or a different *article*, to designate genders. But German grammarians have established a different rule. They have not only different names for the different genders of most animals, — not only a feminine termination, which they can apply to most nouns, — but they have also three distinct articles. They have given a gender to *words* and have called *them* by the fine deceitful names of masculine, feminine, and neuter. German substantives are divided into three sorts, and with each of these sorts of words a different article is used. And so capricious is this use, that there are many *words* which designate masculine beings, to which the feminine or the neuter article must be prefixed, and *vice versa*.

*Das Weib* and *das Mädchen*, for example, words that signify females, are themselves neuter words; while *die Bürgerschaft*, the citizens, and *die Geistlichkeit*, the clergy, both signifying a collection of males, are feminine words.

The principle on which this practice is absurd has been above stated, viz. that it is wrong to employ two signs to designate the same feeling, perception, or thought, — or the different objects here mentioned are already distinguished by different names, and the relation we mean to designate by the article being in all cases precisely the same; it is absurd to use three signs when one is enough to signify this relation. The principle is justified by the use of the English language, which has only one term for this relation. The

French language has only two genders of words, and two articles. The German language has, therefore, one sign for the same relation more than the French, and two more than the English. This extends to all substantives. It is therefore a fault, or an absurdity of principle, which goes throughout the German language.

There is reason to believe that the three different articles of the German language were originally nothing more than the different manner in which the different tribes of Germans pronounced the same word; — and that grammarians, finding three such words in promiscuous use among the people, adopted from the Greek language a scientific arrangement of these three manners of pronouncing one word, and called them masculine, feminine and neuter. In many provinces they are yet promiscuously used and confounded one with another. In the low German, which is an unpolished language, this distinction of words into genders is said to be unknown. And the absurdity seems, therefore, less chargeable on the genius of the language than on the imitation of learned grammarians.

Those relations which, in some languages, are called cases of nouns, and which, in many of the northern languages, are perhaps better expressed by prepositions,[101] may be either signified by prepositions, as in our language, by changes in the nouns, as in the Latin, — or by an alteration in the article, as is done in the German language; but it is wrong both to change the termination of the noun and to use a preposition,-and it is truly absurd to do both these, and, at the same time, also to alter the article. In the German language all the three changes are sometimes — and the absurdity is clearly shown by they being only *sometimes* made. Thus, the Germans sometimes make two changes to signify our *of*, or the genitive case — they say *des Mannes*, (*der Mann* is the nominative;) they sometimes make three changes to signify the dative, or our *to* —

---

[101] **Hodgskin's F/N:-** The question has, I believe, been often discussed. Whether changes in the terminations of words, or the use of little words like our prepositions, are best? And generally, I believe, it has been decided against the prepositions. There is, however, one strong argument in favour of the prepositions; and this is, that they serve to signify the same relations throughout the language, and always keep the ideas more distinct and better known than the method of changing the termination of the nouns. And when it is remembered that, in the inflexions of the human voice, these small words are only distinguished by a practised ear, that to an unpractised one they seem united to the words they accompany, — and that, consequently, they can have no unpleasant influence on the harmony of a language, it may appear that the use of prepositions is better than changing the termination of the nouns.

they say *zu dem Manne*; and they generally make three changes from the nominative to signify the ablative case, or our *from*, of all masculine and neuter nouns—they say *von dem Manne*. I am far from affirming that our single words *to* or *from* do not at times express different relations; but this impropriety is not remedied by the additional changes in the German words. The *zu dem* and *von dem* are as indiscriminately applied as our *to* and *from*; and the differences which they signify might be signified either by the change of the noun, or of the article, or by the use of a preposition. This unnecessary change and multiplication of signs takes place with each of the articles of the German language in most of their cases, and with many masculine and neuter nouns.

Notwithstanding this unnecessary multiplication of signs, there are some real differences which are not distinguished. Thus, feminine nouns are never changed in any of the cases of the singular number; and the different relations which we mark by *to* and *of* are not distinguished when applied to them. The article *der* for both these relations is the same. I am far from affirming that every instance in which we use one of these two prepositions, the other could not be substituted in its place. In many it could. In many, however, there is such a radical difference in the relations which *der* signifies, that they ought to have a different sign. Thus, *gehören der Frau*, is *something belonging to*, or *possessed by*, a woman. But "auf dem Meer *der* Leidenschaft" is literally on the *sea of passion*. The relations signified to the two feminine nouns *Frau* and *Leidenschaft*, by the word *der*, is different; and this is a case in which, notwithstanding a great number of changes in their words, the Germans have no change to mark an essential difference.

A single object, or more objects than one, (singular and plural,) requires but one sign to mark this difference. The English language, though there are exceptions, marks it by the addition of a single *s*. I believe the same rule is followed in some of the low German dialects; but the written and polished German language has no simple general rule like this. It not only has several different manners in which the plural is distinguished from the singular, but it uses in many cases several different signs to signify this one and simple difference. The article of all masculine and neuter nouns is changed in the plural, though not of the feminine nouns. Many of them add a syllable or a letter to their nominative, and many change one of their vowels into a diphthong. As an example, *der Mann*, the man, makes to signify the men, *die Männer*. Three changes are unnecessary, and two of them are absurd. This is not only proved from principle, from the practice of our own language, but also from those instances in the German language, (all the feminine nouns,) in which one single change in the end of the noun accurately marks the difference between singular and plural, as *die Frau* and *die Frauen*.

Adjectives are signs for qualities which are the same in each and every different substantive. Thus, the word black signifies the same quality in a man, a woman, or a child. But because the Germans have classed nouns into masculine, feminine, and neuter, and because they have adopted the absurd principle that *words* ought to accord with *words*; they change the termination of adjectives; — as they are connected with masculine, feminine, and neuter nouns, and as they are preceded by the definite or indefinite article, or not preceded by any article.

They say *ein schwarzer Mann, eine schwarze Frau*, and *ein schwarzes Kind*. Such unnecessary changes are made in all German adjectives, and in most of the cases of those adjectives. With much more propriety the adjective in the English language always remains unchanged, and in this point it is superior to most of the languages of Europe.

I have somewhere read (I believe in a German grammar written by a Mr. Steinheil) that there was a time when the terminations of the German adjectives remained unchanged. In many provinces, and amongst uneducated people, they are still used unchanged, or the changes are at least made as chance may direct. The refined form of the error, therefore, by which the termination of the adjective is made to change, according to rules, must be considered as having been introduced and perpetuated by the writings of grammarians.

Of pronouns nothing will be said, because to elucidate them would require a greater space than I can here allow myself to use. It will be enough to remark, that they are also unnecessarily multiplied and confused from the principle of making words accord with words, being followed in using them.

The different persons designated by speech may be signified by prefixing pronouns to the verbs, or by changing the ending of the verb.[102] To prefix pronouns as we do, and to change the ending of the verb as the Romans did, is one or other of them a redundancy. In *some* instances, we do both, and so do the Germans, which is

---

[102] **Hodgskin's F/N:-** For the reason relative to prepositions, mentioned in the note to p.332 [F/N No. 98, two pages previous in this edition], the use of pronouns, keeping the verbs unchanged, ought to be preferred to changing the verbs.

proved to be wrong by both not being done in many instances, and yet no ambiguity occurs. Thus, there is no difference in the verb of the German language for the first and third persons of the plural, and none in the English for either of the three persons of the plural. Either the use of pronouns, or changing the verb, is unnecessary; and both have only been introduced from following the wrong principle of making words accord with words. A great many similar remarks might be made on the modes of verbs; but, on this point, the German language is not worse than many others, and, like the pronouns, they would require too much space.

It would tire the reader to enter further into the minutia of the German language. The faults which have been exposed are faults in principles. They pervade it, they make it complicated and cumbrous, and they vitiate it throughout. Much time and much attention is required to learn all the artificial rules by which some of the words of this language are made to accord with others. These rules are contrary to the axioms of rational grammar, and they make this language one of the most troublesome instruments of thought which are in use amongst the nations of Europe. With all its faults, however, it contains many treasures; and from the progress which the Germans are making in knowledge, it is perhaps as well worth our cultivation and our inquiries as any language of Europe.

The terms employed in German grammar, the nature of the errors of the German language, and the fact that many of these were not formerly in use, explicitly prove that most of its complexities and faults have been occasioned by an endeavour to make at least its grammar resemble the grammar of those languages which are called classical. A similar endeavour has materially injured the construction of most of the languages of Europe. Our own and the languages of Scandinavia have had but few of the absurdities of the boasted grammars of antiquity implanted on their own absurdities; and they consequently remain, though very far from perfect, comparatively simple in their construction, and easily used instruments of thought.

There is no want of persons in Germany to write grammars, and to propose amendments and alterations in the German language; but so far as their writings have fallen under my observation, not one of them appears to be aware of the principles which ought to be followed in simplifying their grammar. They are rather botchers than builders, who perpetually make their language worse, from having no accurate conception of what that grammar ought to be which they try to amend. It is an opinion of their own that their language is not yet fully formed, (*ausgebildet*;) but they unfortunately think that what it needs is a greater complexity of false and unnecessary distinctions. In fact, they in general regard all these conformities of words to words (the absurdity of which I have endeavoured to expose) as the great merit of their language; and they regard the simplicity of our language as its greatest imperfection.[103]

The German language has one advantage: this is, that words to signify every idea may be formed out of pre-existing German words. The common signification of the root words being known, the combination is equally well understood. The Germans have introduced a less number of foreign words into their language than has been unwisely introduced by most other Europeans into their languages. Hence, they have preserved a greater number of their original words; and out of these they can and do make compound words to signify many of those ideas, to signify which we borrow words from the Latin or the Greek. They have preserved, in consequence of this, much more distinctly than we have done, the proper and figurative meaning which is common to almost all words. *Auslegen*, properly, to lay out, figuratively, to explain, is an example; and many more might be found. These circumstances have probably also been the cause why the Germans have many words, particularly nouns and verbs, for slight shades of difference, which are not distinguished by other people. So far as they signify a real difference, this is a most praiseworthy quality, and it constitutes what is called the richness and the precision of the German language.

It is much easier, however, to multiply words than to discover differences; hence the German language has the bad property, in common with most of the languages of Europe, of possessing many different words to signify precisely the same thing. A multitude of words which mark real differences gives precision. They prevent amongst the Germans those equivoques which distinguish the writings and speech of their word-poorer neighbours the French; but

---

[103] **Hodgskin's F/N:-** Much has been written on the subject of a universal language, and many wishes have been formed by learned and clever men, that one could be adopted. The different nations of Europe would form but one great nation had they only one language. This is a point, however, to which only many ages of constant progression can bring them. They have improved so much, that it is possible they will one day reach this point. They would arrive at it sooner if they were all and each to begin by modelling the grammars of their respective languages according to principles of reason. Usage in language should conform to right — not prescribe it. The laws of rational grammar are very nearly the same for all languages; and the grammars of all the languages of Europe ought to be constructed after the same principles.

they allow them to speak and to write much nonsense. When words are changed so often that a recurrence of them does not offend the ear, and when they are placed in that customary relation to each other which usage calls grammatical: nonsense is easily imposed on the world as wisdom. A still greater evil results from this unnecessary multiplication of words. The use of them becomes habitual : what they signify is forgotten; but it is always affirmed that they are all necessary, and accuracy of thought is constantly impeded by inaccuracy of language.

A great part of the praise which has been bestowed on Kant was occasioned by the circumstance that he was one of the earliest philosophical writers in the German language; and his style was grammatical and neat. He was enabled to choose, amongst a great mass of common words, many of which he used with uncommon significations. He created a great many more, and, putting all these in grammatical order, he produced a great many volumes, the greater part of which signify and explain very little or nothing. Such sentences as the following are calculated to impose on a great many people who judge by sounds:–

"A transcendental principle is that by which general conditions, à priori, are made, under which conditions things that are the objects of our knowledge can alone exist."

*Die Anschauung* is one of Kant's fundamental powers; he defines it thus: By whatever art, and by whatever means, any knowledge of any object whatever may exist, that to which it is immediately related, and by which all thoughts as their medium exist, is the *Anschauung*. If any person is acquainted with any such principle as is here defined, he may be able to tell by what English word *Anschauung* should be translated. I know of none; neither do I pretend to give the meaning of the first sentence. I merely translate the words. The greater part of the works of Kant are made up of such well-sounding sentences, and they appear to be an admirable illustration of those remarks of Campbell and Hume on the art of talking nonsense undetected. The philosophical writings of many other Germans contain proofs of the same fault, and they are examples of the ease with which nonsense may be written, in what is called a rich language, with a complicated grammatical structure.

The earlier and smaller works of Kant contain much more good sense than his later and larger works. He had the powers of genius within him, but they needed the nourishment of a polished, and well formed, and sensible society. Königsburgh, where he passed the greater part of his life, did not supply this. He was a king amongst professors and students and grew inordinately vain of his power of writing. We may smile at his ridiculous peculiarities, – at his holding his mouth shut, and breathing through his nose to cure himself of some asthmatic complaint, and at his eating great quantities of mustard to strengthen his memory. But we must condemn that vanity which induced him to class himself, as a moral teacher, as inferior only to Christ.

His disciples, for he yet has disciples in Germany, though, I believe, they are not numerous, praise his abilities at the expence of his virtue. Rather contrary to the opinion of Mad. de Stael, some of them regard his works as supporting, in the strongest manner, the doctrines of infidelity. And they assert that those parts of them which, in any manner, tend to support religion, were the unwilling offerings of his fears on the altars of authority. He was at one time suspended from his professorship on the score of irreligion; and it was then he professed his belief.[104] His writings contain few facts. They consist of arbitrary definitions of terms arbitrarily assumed, from which anything and everything may be proved.

There can be little doubt that the complex structure of the German language; by demanding from writers and readers a constant attention to the accordance of words; and its richness, by allowing a constant change of words, have done much towards vitiating the philosophical reasoning of the Germans. Many instances more than the above two might be given, not only from the writings of Kant, but also from those of Fichte and Schelling. The instances given, however, may suffice, particularly as metaphysics in Germany are giving place to more important political studies. The structure of the language seems to have had a great influence on German literature; and perhaps the fault of being in general prolix and wordy, is entirely owing to the cheat which is put on the understanding by giving words the properties of things. Men believe, from this delusion, that they have new ideas, when, in truth, they only change their words. And in proportion as these possible changes are numerous, so is the understanding more easily deluded.

The inhabitants of the town of Hannover have the reputation of speaking the German language better than the generality of the Germans. Like the inhabitants of Inverness, who are said to speak good English, the language which they speak is not their native language, but the language of southern Germany, or rather of

---

[104] **Hodgskin's F/N:-** I have forgotten to note from which of the two biographies of Kant, which I have read, I have extracted these little notices.

books. Low German is the language of the north, and it is still spoken by the common people in various places. Not many years ago it was the language in common and general use. Those persons who are acquainted with the Low German affirm that it is more expressive and equally harmonious with the High German. Its construction is more simple; it knows nothing of the absurd distinction of words into genders; and, as it was the language of all the little republics which have been mentioned,[105"] of a people who were more free than the inhabitants of southern Germany, it may be regretted that it is fast falling into disuse, and that its place should be supplied by the more complex language of a longer enslaved country.

The translation of the Bible, by Luther, into the dialect of Saxony, was undoubtedly one cause of making that dialect the written language of the Germans. It is perhaps worthy of remark, that, in the German, as in the English language, the Bible, as it was translated by Luther, is still relied on as good grammatical authority. It may also be worthy of remark, that the written German resembles the Italian language in being nowhere spoken with purity by the mass of the people; though it differs from it in this, that all well-educated people speak it, and, from the rapid extension of book-learning in Germany, it is becoming the spoken language of the whole population. It may be doubted if the written Italian may not be regarded, in some measure, as a dead language, whose treasures we may possess, but which, till that unhappy country shall be rescued from its political and religious degradation, will never be a generally spoken language.

---

[105] **Hodgskin's F/N:-** See Vol. I. Chap. vii.

# Chapter XI.

# Literature.

Drama-Works of Messrs Oehlenschläger and Grillparzer; of Mr. Müllner. – Guilt, a tragedy; King Yngurd, a tragedy; possess the characteristics of German literature. – Historical literature of Germany – General characteristics of its fine literature.—Its faults and beauties.

Perhaps nothing astonishes a Frenchman, who sees his beloved Racine and Corneille honoured for ages, or an Englishman, who only follows the opinions of his forefathers, in professing an unbounded reverence for the single name of Shakespeare, more than the rapidity with which dramatic authors rise to celebrity in Germany, and then sink into forgetfulness. Lessing, Schiller, and Goethe were honoured in their day, but their dramatic works seem now to be rarely performed. Since they were at the height of their fame, Werner and Körner have glanced on the horizon of literature the meteors of a moment, and are now succeeded by Grillparzer, Oehlenschläger, and Müllner, who shine at present the very suns of dramatic literature.

Of Mr. Oehlenschläger's works I know nothing; I saw none of them represented but heard them much praised. They are said to be constructed on the melodramatic principle of horror. He is himself a Dane and writes in both the German and Danish languages.[106],

Mr. Grillparzer is the author of a very tame tragedy, which bears the name of *Sappho*; but his fame principally rests on a sort of melodrama, called the *Ahn Frau*, - Grandmother.[107], The hero of this, who is the chief of a band of robbers, commits incest, murders his father, and burns the mansion of his ancestors. All these pretty amusing horrors were told in a short jumping measure, and they gave such delight to the Germans, that they were represented to more crowded houses, in 1817, 1818, than were ever collected to see the works of Schiller. The inhabitants of Vienna were quite

---

[106] **Editor's F/N:-** Adam Gottlob Oehlenschläger (1779-1850) was a Copenhagen born Danish poet and playwright.
[107] **Editor's F/N:-** Franz Seraphicus Grillparzer (1891-1872); was a Vienna born dramatist nowadays known as an Austrian playwright.

captivated with the beauty of the verse and the elegance of the sentiments. The young people learned them by heart; and as they met in society, as they sauntered in the Prater,[108] and on the public walks, they spouted to one another the well-sounding mouthfuls of sentimental horror. The decorations were good, the palace burned very splendidly and pleasingly, and the vulgar of all countries apply those commendations which belong to the pleasures of sense to the sentiments of the mind. Mr. Grillparzer was indebted for much of his good fortune to the machinist. The success, however, of such a piece, and the popularity of its rumbling poetry, was an evidence of a worse taste among the middling classes of people, in the south of Germany, than I was disposed to ascribe to them.

The two tragedies of Mr. Adolphus Müllner,[109] which were most popular, and which occupied most of the attention of the theatrical public, were called *Die Schuld* (Guilt) and *König* (King) *Yngurd*. They are very superior to the *Ahn Frau*. As it is probable they are not known to the English reader, and as they were very popular, the *Schuld* [1816] having been performed at some theatres for more than thirty following nights, and having gone through several editions, I shall give a more particular account of them. Mr. Müllner, the author, lives at Weissenfels, which formerly belonged to Saxony, but is at present under the government of Prussia.

*Guilt* derives its name from the conduct of Count Hugo, of whose whole life It must be considered as a transcript, though only the last day of it is put into action. The time occupied by the whole does not exceed thirty hours, and in this space the author has contrived, with great art, to give the whole life of his hero. His parents are Spaniards. Before he was born his mother refuses alms to a gypsey woman. The gypsey is displeased, and prophesies to the lady, that she shall bring forth her child with great pain; that, if a boy, he shall murder his elder brother, and, if a girl, the elder brother shall murder her. The first part of the prophecy is fulfilled, - Hugo is brought into the world after painful labour; and the mother endeavours to avoid the fulfilment of the latter part of it, by giving him to a noble Scandinavian lady. She carries Hugo to the north, presents him to her husband as his son, but afterwards tells him the secret; and, as he has no other male issue, he procures for Hugo the investiture of his family estates. Hugo grows up to be a handsome hero, a Mars and an Adonis. He leads armies to victory, and, "as the females weave him a myrtle crown, their young bosoms

---

[108] **Editor's F/N:-** The Prater is a large public park area in Vienna.
[109] **Editor's F/N:-** Amandus Gottfried Adolf Müllner (1774-1829) was a renown German critic and dramatic poet.

heave with the sighs of love." Even his supposed sister warms with the holy fire of sister's love, but which she feels to be impure when she discovers that he is not her brother. He is described,

> Aufgewachsen hoch im Norden,
> G'rad und stolz wie unfre Tannen,
> (Obwohl anderwärts geboren)
> Schien er früh schon auserkohren
> Zu der Zierde nord'scher Mannen.
> Offen, wie des Himmels Blau,
> Lag in seinem Aug' die Seele
> Fremdem Auge da zur Schau,
> Freundlich, fest und ohne Fehle.
> Männer priesen laut den Krieger,
> Stark, zu halten einen Thron;
> Jungfrau'n, ihm die Myrthenkron
> Flechtend im verschwiegnen Busen,
> Seufzten heimlich nach dem Sieger.[110]

His supposed father dies and deprives him of his peace by telling him the secret of his birth. The impulse of nature then drives him from Norway to Spain.

> Weg von hier, wo niemand mir verwandt,
> Zog das Band
> Der allmächtigen Natur
> Mich zum Land
> Goldner Flur,
> Das in Dunklem, früh empfangnen Bildern,
> Winkend durch den Nebeltag,
> Wor mir lag,
> Wie die Worwelt auf der Ahnen Schildern.[111] #

Instead of finding his parents, he forms a friend ship with a Spanish nobleman, (Don Carlos,) saves his life at a bull-fight, but

---

[110] **Hodgskin's F/N:-** "Though not born in the north, he grew up there, straight and proud like our pines, and seemed early to be selected as the ornament of northern warriors. His soul lay in his eyes, open to the stranger's view, like the blue of heaven, friendly, firm, and without a spot. Men praised the warrior, strong to support a throne; maidens, as they wove him a myrtle crown, concealed in their bosoms the secret sigh for the victor."

[111] **Hodgskin's F/N:-** "Away from here, where nobody was allied to me, the bonds of all-mighty nature drew me to the land of golden fields; which, in dim early-received pictures, glimmering through a cloudy day, lay before me like the past world on the shields of our ancestors."

falls in love with his wife, who, having been early betrothed, has no love for her husband, and returns the passion of Hugo. The jealousy of the husband is excited; Hugo fears his revenge, and, to save himself and gain the lady, he murders her husband. He marries her and returns with her to the north. Here the scene of the action is laid, and the drama opens on the anniversary of the murder, by displaying Elvira (the wife) alone in a large hall and having just ended playing on the harp. The last tones die away as she speaks. The opening sentence is perhaps one of the best in the whole poem:–

> Wie der letzte Laut verklinget,
> Der sich unter leiser Hand
> Aus der Harfe Saiten schwinget;
> Wie's auf klarem Teichkristalle
> Sich von eines Tropfen Falle
> Weiter stets und schwächer ringet,
> Bis es fern am Blumenstrand
> Still verschwand:
> So auch möcht' ich einst verschweben
> Und verklingen in das bessre Leben!
> Wird mich, fern vom Vaterland,
> In der Stürme rauher Wiege,
> Wo ich angefesselt liege
> Von der Liebe starkem Band
> Wird mich einst des Schicksals Hand
> Sanft empor zur Heimath heben?[112]

When this is ended, a harp-string breaks with some noise, and the instrument falls "threatening to the earth." For even instruments can be made, by skilful authors, to perform a part. This is looked on by Elvira as a sort of answer to the complaints she has just made. Guilt is full of fears. Hugo is at the moment hunting, and she is alarmed for his life, and immediately, though wrongly, concludes, as the usual time of his return is past, that some accident has happened to him.

A curious concatenation of events leads Valeros, the father of the murdered Carlos, to visit Hugo, and to arrive at this time in

---

[112] **Hodgskin's F/N:-** "As the last sound from the harp-string, when struck by a gentle hand, melts into air, - as the circles made by a single drop falling into a crystal lake, spread farther and weaker till they are lost on the flower-covered borders, so may I fade and float into a better life. Will the hand of fate never softly raise me to my natural home, from the cradle of storms, where I lie, far from my country, fastened by the strong band of love?"

search of the murderer of his son. He had been in America, and only first suspects that Carlos was murdered on seeing the corpse at his return, when the conviction "flashes on him like the rising of the meteor of the north." He seeks the murderer with a mingled desire to be revenged on him and to weep on his bosom. Without knowing that Hugo is his son, and without knowing that this son is the murderer of his brother, he feels from

"The secret impulse of nature."

he knows not what of suspicion, anger, and love. After the arrival of Valeros circumstances lead to an explanation. He discovers that Hugo is his son, and Hugo, at the same time, learns that Carlos was his brother. After talking of dying on the scaffold, after a duel has almost taken place between the son and the father, and after sundry long speeches and plans of the amiable active Jerta, (the daughter of the house which had adopted Hugo,) he and Elvira kill themselves. They exemplify, by their death, the effects of Guilt. All these murders are sometimes called by German critics the necessary rounding of the piece, — "die néthige Rundung." The only action, therefore, of this drama, except secondary and unimportant parts, is the arrival of Valeros, the explanation, and the murder at the end. All the rest is narration.

It can scarcely be denied that the whole fable is simple and plain; but these are all its merits. An absurd fatality reigns throughout, that, compelling the agents to be guilty, makes us pity, not condemn, the murderer.

> Thun? Der Mensch thut nichts. Es waltet
> Ueber inm verborgner Rath,
> Under muss, wie dieser schaltet.
> Thun? Das mennst du eine That?
> Oh, ich bitt' dich, lass das ruhn!
> Alles, alles hingt zuletzt,
> Am Real, den meine Mutter
> Einer Bettlerin verweigert![113]

The chief incident which is the foundation of all the errors and crimes which are afterwards committed, is evidently an imitation of the prophecy to Macbeth. It is, however, a bad imitation. The prophecy to Macbeth works only on his own passions. It lives in his

---

[113] **Hodgskin's F/N:-** "To do? Man does nothing. A hidden council rules above him, and he must do as this directs. To do? Call you this a deed? Oh, I beg of you leave that in peace. All, all at last depends for certain that my mother denied a beggar alms."

own knowledge, and moulds his own heart to the evil deeds which he commits. The prediction of the gipsy might naturally have so worked on the fears of the mother as to induce her to part with her child. But Hugo knew nothing of it, and when he was disposed of, all its influence ought to have ceased. It did not exist in his heart and could have no power over his passions. The author, however, has perfectly fulfilled it, and, by so doing, he has, as far as lay in his power, absurdly lent the authority of reason to the errors of superstition. He makes Hugo, by nature, a hero, and, to fulfil the saying of a gipsy, he degrades him to be the mean assassin of his friend. This hero is also made to faint like a child. He lightens his bosom by confessing his guilt, and yet he murders himself. He himself says, "The fire is burnt out, and the house stands in peace." He may hope for pardon, he might be contented to live, for the author has already degraded him to be a sentimental driveller; but that would not have answered the purposes of tragedy. He is a high-spirited nobleman, and he is made to talk of seeking peace on the scaffold, which he describes also, in his agony, very poetically. In short, we seek in vain for anything very natural either in the action or sentiment of this piece; and such a production could only have acquired popularity among a people who were as yet ill qualified to judge of its merits. The approbation bestowed on it came from that same half-informed sentimental part of the pleasure-seeking population, all whose feelings are factitious, and who gave so much applause to the author of the *Ahn Frau*.

The work is written, however, with great fluency and ease. The opening passage, which has already been given, breathes something like the tender melancholy of poetry, and the fears of Elvira, which make her see signs of death in everything, is also poetical.

> Horch, der Wind erwacht am Strand,
> Und die Nordsee donnert ferne.
> Ausgelöscht sind alle Sterne,
> Und vom finstern Himmelsbogen
> Kommt der Schnee im Sturm geflogen.
> Wirbelnd, wie der Wüste Sand,
> Stäubt er wieder auf vom Boden,
> Und, wie Erde birgt die Todten,
> Deckter das erstarrte Land,
> Aufgethürmt zu Grabeshügeln. —[114]

---

[114] **Hodgskin's F/N:-** "Hark, the wind wakes on the shore, and the north sea thunders afar. All the stars are hidden, and from the dark arch of heaven the snow comes driven in storms. Whirling like the sand of the

The boy Otto, the son of Elvira, is sketched with all the softness and gentleness which belong to German boys, and both he and the steady Jerta serve as admirable foils to the guilty Hugo and Elvira. Hugo himself appears to be an example of the fact, that the Germans are in general inadequate to conceive any character consistently great. He is a murderer, but a soft, and a subdued, and almost a whining murderer, in whom the agony of guilt amounts to lassitude of body, folding of hands, fainting, and, at length, death.

The work contains some other tolerable good passages. Valeros describes the ship leaving a port,

> Günstig linde Lüfte dehnten
> Weit des Schiffes Flügel aus,
> Und das leicht bewegte Haus
> Trug die Pilger, die sich sehnten
> Nach der Heimath, frohlich fort.[115]

Hugo describes his friendship with Carlos as like two streams that become a deep water by uniting.

> Wie zwei Ströme sich begegnen.
> Einzeln schlängeln sich die Brüder,
> Kaum den Kahn zu tragen mächtig,
> Schüchtern durch der Berge Lücken;
> Doch vereinigt rauschen sie,
> Reicher jeder durch den andern,
> Hochgeehrt durch's offme Land,
> Und mit schwerer Schiffe Last
> Spielen leicht die stolzen Wogen.[116]

There is, however, in the work much common place, and many truly low and vulgar phrases and sentiments. Jerta compares Elvira to a corpse with open eyes. (p. 46.) Elvira describes her husband as a ravenous beast, and Hugo her as a revengeful fury. (p. 68.) Many passages are written only for the sake of the miserable sound. At pages 21, 52, 75, the reader may see specimens of this failure.

---

desert, it rises again from the ground, and, as earth hides the dead, so it covers the stiffened land like the hillocks over graves."

[115] **Hodgskin's F/N:-** "Soft favourable airs filled the sails of the ship, and the lightly-moved house brought away merrily the pilgrims who were longing for home."

[116] **Hodgskin's F/N:-** "Drawn together by a secret power, our lives united themselves like two streams. Alone each winds its modest way through the openings of the mountains, scarcely able to carry a boat, but, united, each enriched by the other, they flow, highly honoured, through the open land, and the proud waves play lightly with the heavy-loaded ships."

I had the pleasure of seeing this tragedy performed, and, notwithstanding its horrors, I felt more wearied than amused. Unfortunately, it derived little embellishment from the performance. The theatre of Hannover is notoriously one of the worst provided with performers of all the theatres of Germany, and on this occasion the whole strength of the company was not put forth.

*King Yngurd*, though it deserves more praise than *Guilt*, was less popular. It has the advantage of being in five acts, and it required two nights to perform it; while Guilt is comprised in four and could be performed in one night. Theatrical amusements are cheaper in Germany than in England, and a proportionably larger part of the population participate in them. On this point the Germans are fast following the steps of the French and Italians. The theatre is a part of the fine arts and is become to the inhabitants of towns a necessary amusement. Most of the cities have theatres, and there is not a single sovereign of Germany on whose civil list the theatre does not appear as a considerable expence. It was at first a sort of plaything, a doll, for grown-up babies at courts; and, by dint of their patronage and bolstering up, it has now come to be considered as belonging to the pursuits and taste of the nation. And at present the Germans encourage the drama as much as any people of Europe.

King Yngurd is entirely the production of the author's imagination. He tells his reader "not to seek in books of history for the source of his song," but affirms, "that, in composing it, he has sought after that truth which never was and yet always is." He means, I believe, to give to his fictitious characters such emblems of our nature, that they may be taken as models, not of individuals, but of the whole species. The characters are not to be found either in history or in nature, though it is possible Buonaparte may have suggested Yngurd.

The era of the fable is 900 or 1000 years before the birth of Christ, and the scene is laid in the south of Norway. Of this country at that period we have no knowledge, and therefore the author was perfectly at liberty to give his dramatis personae any characteristics he pleased. All that readers or critics can require is, that they should be consistently kept up throughout, and be consistent with one another. The critic can only judge of those works of the imagination which are purely imaginary, and have no real types, as the author directs him. He has no other guide but the work itself.

Yngurd is the son of peasants; he raises himself by his valour to command the armies of Norway. He marries Irma, the daughter of the king, - and with the approbation of the States, he succeeds him on the throne. The king leaves a wife, named Brunhilde, behind

- 205 -

him, who, after his death, gives birth to Oscar. Irma spreads a report that Oscar is illegitimate, and he is excluded from the throne. His mother retires with him to the court of her brother Alf, king of Denmark. When Oscar is sixteen years old, his uncle invades Norway to place him on the throne. This is the period when the action commences. He is aided by a party who dislike the origin and severity of Yngurd. "He wants an ounce of royal blood," and he is always engaged in war, as necessary to support his power.

> -    Er will den Sieg,
> Erbraucht den Ruhm, weil's inmam Rechte felilt:
> Denn etwas will das Volk, woran sich's hält.[117]*

Through the defection of this party, Yngurd is on the point of losing a battle; and he who had been till then a hero, full of noble and eminent virtues, blinded by anxiety and ambition to maintain the crown, formally asks the aid of the devil.

> Weg, Weiber —Oeffne dich, der Erde Mark,
> Und lass mich schauen in der Hölle Glut !
> Herauf, ihr Geister, die ihr Böses thut
> Zum Zeitvertreib–den Bergmann in dem Schacht
> Am Rand des Abgrunds blind und schwindlich macht,
> Dass sein Gebein auf ehr'nem Grund zerschelle–
> Herauf! Eu'r Handwerk treibt an Tageshelle,
> Bethört der Dänen Siegestrunkne Haufen,
> Dass sie einander in die Schwerter laufen !
> Herauf, du Satan ! Was Brunhild" auch bot
> Für deinen Dienst, ich will sie überbieten.
> Was kann das Weib dir seyn ? Mit meinem Tod
> Stirbt ihre Wuth, und sie wird wieder fromm.
> Ich bin ein Mann, zu meinem Beistand komm,
> Und wie mich Gott verlassen in dcr Noth,
> Dass mich die Knechte knechtisch feig verriethen,
> Will ich dir treu seyn über's Grab hinaus!
> Ist es die Wollust, Satan, die dich kirrt;
> So komm fortan zu Anslo's Festgelagen!
> Willst du dem Unrecht einen Tempel miethen;
> Zieh' ein damit (die Hand auf der Brust) in diessgewölbte Haus!
> Ich bin ein König, der gefürchtet wird,
> Ein Wink von mir, und Norwegs Richter zagen,
> Und Unschuld wird vom Henkerbeil erschlagen.

---

[117] **Hodgskin's F/N:-** "He seeks victory. He needs fame, because his right is weak. The people will still have something by which to hold."

Lockt dich des Krieges Sündenreiche Noth,
Die Raub und Mord fell macht um täglich Brot;
Ich kann sie über eine Welt verhängen,
Von ihrem Boden Städt und Dörfer sengen,
Wie Haar vom Haupt–und muss ich endlich sterben;
So weckt mein Name, von der Jahre Lauf
Schneerein gewaschen, neue Helden auf,
Und stürst die späte Nachwelt ins Verderben.
D'rum, Satan, brich dem tollen Weib den Kauf,
Und lass dich für den Dienst des Yngurd werben![118]

Assistance is immediately granted him; he wins the battle; and Oscar falls into his hands . Oscar, from being a dreaming sort of enthusiastic child,

Der weich und weiss, wie das Gewand der Schwäne,
Sich kindlich schmieget an des landes Brust,
Welcher unbewusst
In's Herz sich schleicht, gleich einer Kindesthráne,[119] *

is converted, by his love to Asla, the daughter of Yngurd, to a hero. He claims his rights before the assembled nobility in a manner that alarms Yngurd, who is now given to the powers of darkness. Evil predominates in his mind over good, and he orders

---

[118] **Hodgskin's F/N:-** Away, women! Earth, open out your inmost part, and let me pry into the burning hell! Come here, ye spirits, who mischief work for pastime — who make the miner at the border of the precipice blind and giddy — that his bones are dashed on the iron rocks! Come here and do your deeds in open day; bewilder the victory-drunk Danish host, that they may fall by the swords of one another!
"Come here, Satan! I will outbid whatever Brunhilde has offered for thy services. What can that woman be to thee? Her wrath will die with me, and she will be again pious. I am a man—come to my support; and as God hath so left me in my need, that knaves have cowardly betrayed me, I'll be true to thee beyond the grave. Doth pleasure tempt thee, Satan? — come quick to Auslo feast. Wiltst thou hire a temple for unrighteousness? — dwell in this arched house, (laying his hand on his breast.) I am a king, and dreaded. A sign from me dismays the judges of Norway, and innocence will fall under the axe of the executioner. Doth war's distress, so rich in sin, that robbery and murder are bought for daily bread, delight thee? I can heap it on the world — can burn off towns and cities like hair from off the head. And must I die at last? My name, by time made clean as snow, will rouse up other heroes, and bring destruction on the after-world. Therefore, Satan, break thy bargain with the furious woman, and enter the service of Yngurd."
[119] **Hodgskin's F/N:-** "Which, soft and white like the garment of the swan, clings like an infant to the bosom of the land, — which glides unfelt into the heart like the tear of childhood."

his favourite attendant to murder Oscar. Macduff, a Scotchman, has not courage enough to perform it, but shuts Oscar up in a retired part of the castle, from whence he attempts to escape, and is dashed to pieces on the rocks. Asla jumps after him and is also killed ; and her mother dies with fear and grief. Oscar's death is attributed to Yngurd. The rebel party gathers strength and attacks him. He disperses them with his "lion's voice," kills their leader, but falls himself by the spear of some obscure warrior. As he dies, he presents the crown of Norway to Alf, who thus unites it with the crown of Denmark. Brunhilde had before gone mad from the effects of heating herself in battle, and from dreaming Oscar was murdered. In the course of the play, therefore, there are only five persons who die, or who are killed, and one goes mad.

This is tragic enough. It is enough to justify classing Yngurd with the other monstrous productions of the German theatre. There are other apparent faults in the piece. Asla is rather a lovely and a novel character-an enthusiastic, gentle, and dreaming maiden, warmly attached to her mother and her home till her sixteenth year, when she dreams

> Ein junger Ritter, glänzend wie der Tag,
> Zog her von Osten mit bewehrten Schaaren.
> Er zog vorüber, und mein Blick ihm nach,
> Ihm nach der Wunsch: Entrinne den Gefahren!
> Ein andres Heer von stahlbedeckten Leuten
> Zog her von Westen, dunkel wie die Nacht,
> Und fing sich an im Blachfeld auszubreiten,
> Und sich zu ordnen, wie zur blutgen Schlacht.
> Vernichte sie ! rief ich empor zum bauen
> Gewölb des Tags: Gieb Sieg des Ritters Speer –
> Da trieb mich's achtsam wieder hinzuschauen,
> Und ich erkannte–König Yngurds Heer.
> Und ich erkannt auf Schaumbedecktem Pferde
> Des Vaters Federstraus und Helm und Schild,
> Und wirbelnd hob der Staub sich von der Erde,
> Und Schlachtgewühl bedeckte das Gefild.
> Da war's, als fasst es mich mit rauhen Händen,
> Und wollte theilen die beklommne Brust;
> Doch immer nach dem Ritter sich zu wenden,
> Zwang meinen Blick ein schauerlich Gelust.
> Und siegreich sah ich seine Fahnen wallen,
> Und freudig rasch flog mir das Blut durch's Herz:
> Des Königs Banner sah ich niederfallen,
> Der Normann floh–ich fühlte keinen Schmerz.
> Doch plötzlich stand die Flucht. Ich hört ein Fluchen

Von Yngurds Stimme; sah ihn Löwengleich
Sich wenden, und den zarten Ritter suchen,
Und meine Wangen fühlt ich kalt und bleich.
Der steile Fels, von dessen Spitz' ich schaute —
Als sollt' ich nichterblicken, was geschäh —
Wuchs in die Wolken, dass mir schwindelnd graute:
Doch nieder zog mich's aus der stillen Höh.
Und tiefer stets, halb fallend halb getragen,
Sank ich herab–Oed' war das Kampfgefild
Der Ritter lag der Ritter lag erschlagen,
Zerschmettert! und weit von ihm lag sein Schild.
Und seitwärts sah ich, mach des Waldes Nächten,
Den König fliehn, sein Haar des Sturmes Spiel.
Das meine riss ich wild aus seinen Flechten,
Und rauft es mir, und stürzt' auf den, der fiel –
Und fluchte dem, der floh vom blut'gen Werke
Ich wusst' es wohl, dass es mein Water war –
Und dennoch –

IRMA (in hochster innerer Bewegnug.)
Oh, hor' auf! des Mannes Starke
Hält das nicht aus.[120]*

---

[120] **Hodgskin's F/N:-** ""A young knight, glorious as the day, came with an armed host from the east, and passed on. My gaze went after him, and after him the wish — escape from danger. Another army covered with steel, dark as night, came from the west, and began to range itself in the plain as if for bloody battle. Annihilate it, I cried above to the blue arch of day. Give victory to the spear of the knight. Then I was forced to look on it attentively, and I knew King Yngurd's army. And I knew, on a foam-covered steed, the helm, and the plume, and the shield of my father; and whirling rose the dust from the earth, and fighting crowds covered the fields. Then I felt as if seized by rude hands, and as if my anxious bosom were to be divided. Yet a terrible desire constrained me to look on the knight. And I saw his colours waving victorious, and quick and joyful flew the blood through my heart. I saw the banner of the king falling; the Norwegians flew; I felt no pain. Yet sudden stopped the flight. I heard the voice of Yngurd cursing; saw him turn him like a lion and seek the tender knight, and I felt my face cold and pale.

"The steep rock, from whose point I viewed, grew in the clouds – that I was giddy with terror - as if to hide from me what further happened: yet it brought me out of the still height. And, half falling, half carried, I sank to earth. The battle field was waste. There lay the knight: there lay he – slain – crushed; and far away there lay his shield.

"And, sidewards, I saw the king flee to the darkness of the forests – his hair the plaything of the storm. I tore mine from its bands; I plucked it out, and threw myself on him who fell; and I cursed him who flew from the bloody work. I knew well it was my father, and yet –

IRMA.

And this dream gives her the power to curse and hate both her father and mother, and to tell them "she could leave them in death." She says to her mother –

> Ich kann's nicht mehr gewähren;
> Was dich bestürzt, lockt mich, wie siisse Spiele.[121]

This is most perverse, unnatural, and immoral. The language in which all this is told is beautiful, but the whole sentiment could only have been conceived and put into words by a person who had always lived out of the reach of good example and sound remark. There are some other faults which are the result of dreaming; for it is only the dreams which the muses bring before the mind that are fit for poetry. Irma, Oscar, Brunhilde, Asla, all dream or prophesy through the piece. It is a fault, also, to make Yngurd fall at once from his high place and thoughts to despicable and deadly fears and deeds. It is only accounted for by the influence of Satan. Poor human nature, tortured by all its evil passions, is not bad enough for the purposes of the poet, and he gives it the devil as a helpmate. Yngurd's character is throughout noble and well sustained till the sudden fall.

> Erist des Himmels Flamme,
> Wermit ihm focht, der kennt die Furcht nicht mehr.
> Sein ist das Reich, erist geborner Herr,
> Entspranger gleich nicht königlichem Stamme.[122]

He surprises his nobility and gains them by a very noble address. – (p.42.) In like manner, he trusts himself in the camp of his enemy, and behaves equally well. "The peasant trusts when a prince promises." He is described as such by Oscar, and he makes a long prayer; but the moment before that battle begins, in which he implores assistance from the evil powers.

> "King of kings," he says, "ruler of the world, thy name is peace. War is the seed of hell. It is thy holy and perfect will that the guilty fall; therefore, in battle, I have never prayed for victory. What is right fulfil; but still the beating of the blood, father of courage. The will of princes is hard like metal; like gold, mixed with dross. There is an eternal

---

Oh, hold, hold! the strength of a man could not bear this.

[121] **Hodgskin's F/N:-** "I can no longer help it. What destroys you, charms me like a sweet game."

[122] **Hodgskin's F/N:-** He is the flame of heaven. Whoever has fought with him can never more know fear. His is the empire; he is born its master, although he sprung not from a royal line."

war betwixt the heart and the head. Melt the ore here.
(Laying his hand on his breast.) Make the soul loose from
its bonds. Destroy necessity, that I may be free to
choose."

Yet the author, soon after, fouls the mind of such a man, so
noble, so daring, so pious, too, with the crime of murder. With this
exception, Yngurd seems one of the most manly of the pure poetical
creations of the whole German drama.

This play is, by no means, without gentle sentiments and
feelings, some specimens of which I shall add. They principally
describe the character of Oscar and Asla. — Oscar says:

- Mich zogen diese Küsten
Mit unsichtbaren, sanften Banden an.
Wie Kinder triumen an der Mutter Brüsten,
Träumt' ich non Norweg, seit ich denken kann.—
Wieanders find' ich's Mit verworrnem Sinn
Betret' ich der ersehnten Heimath Boden,
Und kann der Ahndung nimmer mich entschlagen;
Dass ich in Norweg nicht willkommen bin.
Ich sah das Leben
So ungeheu'r im Preisse steigen, und so tief
Im Werthe fallen, dass dem Tod ich rief,
In seinen armen Freistatt mir zu geben.
Ich sah zerreissen aller Ordnung Bande,
Das Mitleid sterben in der Brust; zu Bären
Die Menschen werden um ein schmales Bret,
Und Söhne Vätern Kahn und Balken wehren.
Mir ist nicht wohl mehr, wo ein Athem weht
Von Menschenlipp', und Mensch seyn, dünkt mich Schande.
- Das Leben meiner Seele,
Das inn're Leben, zehrt mein Leben auf.
Nach aussen strebt in eurer Thatenwelt
Nach aussen stets das gierige Beginnen;
Was mir an Kraft ward, wendet sich nach innen,
Und unter Scalden nur bin ich ein Held.
In einem Reich von Bildern und von Tönen
Ringt Geist und Herz dem Grossen nach, und Schönen,
Und meine Thaten find–Gesang und Thränen.
Traut dem Gefühl; das mir im Busen schleicht:
Die schwache Pflanz aus spät gesätem Kern
Bringt nimmer Frucht auf diesem niedern Stern.
Wenn sie erschöpft sich hat in bunter Blüte,
Wenn ihre Kraft in Farben still verglühte,

Senkt sie das Haupt-vielleicht von selbst–vielleicht
Von rauher Hand, vom Hauch des Nords berühret.
D'rum bitt' ich euch, lasst alles, wie zuvor!
Bin ich ein König für das Volk des Nor,
Das mühsam Yngurds Löwenkraft regieret?
Wollt ihr den Riesen tödten, und ein Kind
In seine ungeheure Rüstung stecken?
Auf hohem Berg die Ceder niederstrecken,
Die kaum das Hauptbeugt im Gewitterwind,
Und eine Lilie pflanzen an die Stelle 2
Du, Mutter, hassest Yngurd."[123]

I dare not venture to quote any more. In its diction, in the vigour of the conceptions, and in the spirit of its characters — in its weaknesses, its sentimentality, and in what the Germans so expressively call "Schwärmery" — in the softness and gentleness of many of its expressions — yes, even in its length and in the vulgar horror of some of its phrases, such as "the mouth of death wide open stood as if he hungered" — Yngurd is a good specimen of the present dramatic literature of our neighbours. Mr. Müllner, its author, may be estimated as one of the most rising poets of Germany.

---

[123] **Hodgskin's F/N:-** "These coasts attracted me with soft and unseen power. I dreamt of Norway, ever since I can remember, as children dream on their mother's breast. How different do I find it ! Confused I tread the long-desired land of home, and cannot chase foreboding fears away, that here I am not welcome.

"I saw life rise so high in price, and fall so low in worth, I called on death to give me an asylum in his arms. I saw all the bonds of order broke — compassion dead within the breast. For a small plank men were become as bears, and sons kept boats and beams from fathers. I am no longer pleased where men do breathe; and to be a man seems shameful.

"My soul's power,--the inward spirit eats away my life. In your active world every desire tends to outward objects. Whatever power I have turns inward on myself, and only among Scalds am I a hero. In a world of pictures and of music strive my mind and heart for greatness and for beauty; and my deeds are songs and tears. Confide in what I feel. In this poor world the weak plant which springs from late sowed seed bears no fruit. When it has exhausted itself in variegated blossoms — wasted in silence its strength in colours — then bends its head, perhaps by its own power worn out — perhaps assailed by some rude hands, or the raw northern blast. Therefore do I pray that you will leave all things unchanged. Am I a king fit for the people of the North, whom Yngurd's lion power with trouble governed? Will you kill the giant, and place a child in his prodigious armour fell the cedar on the mountain top, which scarcely bowed its head in storms, and plant a lily in its stead? Thou hatest Yngurd, mother."

It is by no means consistent with the title of this work to discuss the merits or demerits of German literature. To do that properly would require me to read much more than I have read and would probably also demand a work at least half as large as the whole of this. But I may be permitted to remark, that German literature has been unjustly condemned in the gross from some few examples of such pieces as those I have already mentioned, and from all the different kinds of literature having been confounded together. At the same time, the lovers of novelty have despised the laws of taste and have praised this literature more than it deserved.

All literature may be divided into two parts, each of which, from having qualities different from the other, deserves to be separately considered. These are the literature of facts, and the literature of imagination. To the first belong such writings as philosophical, political, biographical, moral, and historical — to the other, dramas, novels, romances, &c. The former must be judged of by a standard different from the latter. It must strictly conform to truth; it must be an accurate and complete representation of *facts*. The other must conform to taste. The former reflects nature as a perfect mirror. The latter rather refracts and transmits her. It changes her correct and her lovely form, but it decks her with all the beauty of colours.

Taste is entirely artificial and is the result of cultivation; it depends on opinion and varies in every country. The literature of imagination, therefore, of each nation, which must conform to its taste, is different from that of every other nation; while their literatures of facts, though they have still some national differences, resemble one another. The works of Shakespeare and Racine have scarcely any resemblance, though they both bear the name of dramas; and the works of each are vastly admired by the nation in whose language they are written. The historical works of Voltaire and Hume, the philosophical writings of Locke and Condillac, of Degerando and Mr. Stewart, are all so much of the same family, that there is little other difference between them than the language.

When nations readily and freely communicate with each other, their respective literatures of facts may be so much more readily imitated than their literatures of imagination; and what is excellent in the former is so much easier seen, and so much more certain, than what is excellent in the latter, that the former will always resemble one another much more than the latter. The historical and philosophical literature of the Germans resembles the same species of literature of the other enlightened countries of Europe. Since the year 1770, the Germans have adopted, imitated, and improved the manner of writing history, which was introduced about that period;

and their historical literature now equals, and perhaps surpasses, in extent, in accuracy of research, and profundity of thought, that of any other people of Europe.

In one point it is superior. The extensive knowledge and the industry of the Germans allows them, in general, to acquire so great a mastery of the subject they treat, that they arrange it in a most accurate, minute, and comprehensive manner. Vivacity and profundity may be occasionally missed, but a misplaced remark is never made. The separate histories of the church, of philosophy, of languages, and of the arts, which are written in the German language, are considered to be unequalled for depth of research, and accuracy of arrangement. It is no exaggeration to say, that the historical literature of the Germans equals the historical literature of any other people.

Schlozer and Spittler may be considered as the fathers of German historical literature; and Herren, Luden, and Rotteck, are amongst the youngest and the worthiest of their sons. The two former were professors at Göttingen: Herren has been mentioned. Luden is professor of history at Jena, and Rotteck at Freyburg in Baden. From one of the works of Spittler I have had frequent occasion to quote; and he is also the author of a History of the Christian Church, and a History of Wirtemberg, both of which are very highly praised. He was a native of this latter country, but he lived, and wrote, and taught at Göttingen till he was called ack to Wirtemberg to fill the office of a minister of State.

At Göttingen he seems to have been the idol of his friends, who still speak of him with the greatest enthusiasm. His writings have the defect of being sometimes obscure from a laboured and artificial construction of his periods, and from his hinting at events rather than narrating them. But the manner in which he traces causes and effects, and philosophises in his history, is deserving admiration.

He spares no species of injustice, and he marked more accurately than any preceding German historian the effects of lawless power. He has one fault that is seldom found in German authors — a want of minuteness, or he writes so well that you feel disappointed he has left anything unsaid it was possible for him to say. As an historian he is much superior to Schiller. The histories of the thirty years' war, and of the separation of the Netherlands from Spain, will always rank the latter among the historians of his country, and as one of the greatest improvers of its language and literature. But these two compositions must rather be considered as splendid descriptions of some leading characters and events, than as regular histories of these two remarkable periods.

I might here give a short passage from a universal history by Mr. Rotteck, the latest writer I am acquainted with, to show the spirit of the present historical literature of the Germans; but, as it is opposed to some favourite religious opinions, and as I do not know exactly the limits of our libel laws, I must abstain from doing it. It is highly remarkable, as a specimen of the doctrines which are both generally believed and taught in Germany; and as a proof that freedom of discussion on matters of religion is carried further there than in our country. The work in which it is to be found was employed by the author in his lectures, and it is intended by him for the instruction of young men, and the amusement of those more advanced in life. When such passages are found in historical books, they are strong evidence of the general taste.

If they were put into the hands of young men in England, they would excite some disturbance. The author would probably be called an enemy of religion and would be clamorously assailed. He has, however, been promoted by his sovereign to a higher professorship since he published this work. He is not to be considered as a regular combatant on the subject of religion, but as merely expounding opinions which are generally received. If such sentiments as are to be found in this book appeared in our country, in a work expressly written to oppose the claims of the Jews to the honour of a particular inspiration, it would be thought we were making a progress in rational knowledge. But if they were found in our schoolbooks, and if they were taught in our universities, without occasioning persecution, we should be set down as totally emancipated from the intolerant dominion and principles of Jewish priests.

Of the philosophical literature of the Germans something has been already said. Apparently because it is less interesting to mankind, this species of literature has been far less improved by the Germans than their historical literature, and it yet retains many scholastic distinctions and incongruities. Its chief characteristics, so far as I am acquainted with it, are, a multitude of words, a great many artificial distinctions, and a great want of accurate thought. It is the worst part of the German literature of facts. The chief principles which the German philosophers have followed, namely, that philosophy has nothing to do with facts, and is above them; that it consists in what they are pleased to call pure reason, is the great cause why their philosophy is in general little more than words grammatically arranged. Their whole philosophy signifies and explains nothing.

It is obvious that the political literature of any people, if both the form and the matter of it be not borrowed from some other people, will take its colour from their political education. It is equally, obvious, from the situation of their country, that the political education of the Germans has hitherto been very bad; and, consequently, their political writings, except treatises on political economy, the matter of which they have borrowed from others, are in general shallow, metaphysical, and theoretical. The interest, however, which the subject excites, stimulates so many powerful minds to inquire into it, that the political literature of Germany is more rapidly improving than any other. In fact, the attention of most of the powerful minds in the whole country is now ardently and devotedly given to political literature, and we may expect greater advances to be made in it than in any other branch of literature.

The great faults of the German literature of imagination seem to be a great want of sublimity, and a burlesque, overstrained, and rather horrible imitation of this quality. There is a perpetual effort, on the part of their authors, to sustain the characters of their pieces at a pitch beyond nature. Suffering is made horrible. Their heroes are merely men who despise the common rules of life. They are more outrageous and extraordinary than sublime, more extravagant than virtuous or vicious. Such is Charles Moore, Don Carlos, and Marquis Posa. It seems as if the authors had thought all the usual sources of pleasure were exhausted, and that they must seek novelty, though at the expence of consistency and truth. They began to write when other nations had long written, and, as other authors had carefully avoided absurdity, it remained to be adopted as a novelty. Their works, which contain any sublimity, such as The Robbers, Cabal and Love, and the Don Carlos of Schiller, seem also to abound in an overstrained semblance. Faust, and Gotz of Berlichingen, Wallenstein, and Maria Stuart, ought to be exempted from this censure. The first is coolly and calmly devilish throughout. Gotz is an accurate picture of the manners of former times and is true to nature. Faust derives its great merit from a similar cause. It is an old woman's tale, all the circumstances of which are carefully preserved and put into elegant language. The great merit of the heaven-born genius is, that he perpetuates the errors of the nursery. It is less an imitation of nature than an imitation of some superstitions of which we have all heard, and in which most of us have been taught to believe.

The literature of imagination may refract but ought not to distort nature. It must present to us some familiar features, or we regard its works as monsters. The German muse has given birth to more "mooncalves and sooterkins than any of the sisterhood." Many of the writings of the Germans want rationality and good sense. How absurd is it in Goethe to give Faust the power of a devil to seduce a naturally weak woman. It is arming a giant with thunder to conquer a defenceless dwarf; it is like bringing artillery against a town which is ready to open its gates to a single soldier. In the same manner he has worked up a combination of events which is almost miraculous, to attach a wandering player (*Withelm Meister*) to a nobleman, *Lothario*; as if he had not given the poor being, from his creation, a sufficient stock of vanity to make a nod from such a man as a nobleman the very summit of his ambition. The charming absurdities, as they may be called, of his Egmont are still greater; and yet Goethe is thought by the Germans to be the very prince of observers of human nature. Many of them describe him as having pried into all the secrets of the human heart, particularly of the female heart; and to be so well acquainted with it as if the hearts of all mankind had been concocted into one and given to him for inspection. He is in general, particularly in the south of Germany, much more praised and admired than Schiller.

It has been already remarked, that German philosophers consider philosophy as above facts; the poets have adopted a similar principle with regard to poetry, but they have carried it to a more extravagant length. Their constant object is to describe what they call the ideal — *Ideale*; — they disdain matter of fact, and they run into absurdity from forsaking that nature which is the only sure guide. The ideal of every individual differs from the ideal of every other, but we call that true and beautiful which conforms to that ideal which is common to the greatest number of persons; and an individual who will follow his own motion of ideal beauty, without regard to the notions of other people, must often necessarily be thought by them to be absurd. This is the case with German authors.

Criticism has now somewhat corrected them; but they have hitherto sought in the clouds of their own imagination for a true representation of the earth. They have found there all sorts of strange forms, and they have spoken of them as having an actual existence.

German literature is also very prolix. Authors think they have never said enough, while they can say anything more. Nothing is ever hinted and left to the imagination of the reader. Every idea which they can discover in their dissections of the mind is laid as bare as "the anatomist scrapes a bone when he means to demonstrate its parts to his pupils." This is a tedious more than a glaring fault. Nearly every page of German writing partakes more or less of it. It abounds in their philosophy, their novels, their poetry, and is also visible in their historical writings. The complexity of their sentences may in a great measure be ascribed to their wish to leave nothing unsaid. Every period is lengthened by numerous qualifications and additional remarks, that are not of sufficient importance to form a period of themselves. Perhaps, however, prolixity is a fault which every person finds in a foreign literature. Strangers want so many of the associations which make up the entire charm of trifles, that they can rarely think those minutiae are of any value which to natives are neither uninteresting nor tedious. The task of reading any work is so different to a stranger and a native, and it is so great a labour to the former, that he necessarily wishes every useless word might be spared.

There are many beauties consistent with these prominent faults, though it is possible my notion of these may not accord with that entertained by many other people. When the Germans will be content with the lowly ambition of copying or of imitating nature, they seem to do it more correctly and more minutely, and perhaps more spiritedly, than any other people. I conceive the little poem by Schiller called *Die Glöcke*, and the *Herrman and Dorothea* by Goethe, to be striking examples of this beauty. The latter is a most faithful picture of manners, of the soft, kind, and quiet dispositions, which distinguish the Germans. And the former, though a more spirited poem, gives an equally faithful transcript of many of their everyday thoughts and pursuits.

Another great beauty of the German literature of the imagination, and the only one I shall further add, is, that it contains as great a quantity of light, elegant, gentle, and pleasurable feeling, as any literature I know. Garlands and flowers, and children on the breast, and clear soft days, and gentle requited love, without any of the bitter ingredients of the passion, and the whirling dance, and the friendly greeting, and waggons loaded with corn, the earth smiling with fruits, and acts of kindness, and soft music, the light-blue heaven, and pearling tears, are the images or the passions which constitute the great beauty of German imaginative literature.

*Werther* and the *Robbers*,[124] the pieces which have excited most attention out of Germany, seem to me to be rather the exceptions to the general character of this literature than to form it. They were

---

[124] **Editor's F/N:-** *Werther* refers to *The Sorrows of Young Werther* (*Die Leiden des jungen Werthers*), a novel by Johann Wolfgang von Goethe (1774).

*The Robbers* (*Die Räuber*), was the first play by Johann Christoph Friedrich von Schiller (1781).

probably as much admired for their singularity as from their according either with the character of the Germans or with the general spirit of their literature.

Most of the works of Wieland,[125] all the smaller poems of Schiller, many of those of Goethe, most of the works of Bürger[126], the idylls of Gessner,[127] the two tragedies of Müllner,[128] and many other works, contain, or rather abound with evidence of a gentle train of pleasurable, contented, good-hearted feeling, which is more a chief characteristic of German poetry, than of any other with which I am acquainted.

There seems to be nothing bounding in the joy, and nothing turbulent or boisterous in any of the native and true German literature. Everything in the land, and in its writings, seems calm, and still, and kind. I may quote, as a more special recent example of this beauty, a little poem published at Leipsic in 1818, called *Die Bezauberte Rose,* – The Enchanted Rose. – It possesses no merit as a tale; the sentiments are often absurd, but it is full of gentle and quiet pictures of happiness. The author, Ernst Schulze,[129] was a native of Celle, and, after having studied at Göttingen, died there, in 1817, at the age of 29. He was too early called away for the honour of his country, for his own reputation, and for the good of his countrymen.

I have limited this characteristic to native and true German literature, because it is not so conspicuous in its drama; and, though this is written in the German language, it is so obviously an overstrained imitation of the drama of other nations, rather than a transcript of their own feelings, that it hardly deserves the name of a true native literature.

---

[125] **Editor's F/N:-** Christoph Martin Wieland (1733–1813).

[126] **Editor's F/N:-** Gottfried August Bürger (1747-1794).

[127] **Editor's F/N:-** Salomon Gessner (1730-1788) was a Swiss painter and poet.

[128] **Editor's F/N:-** Adolf Müllner (1774–1829), [See previously F/N 106].

[129] **Editor's F/N:-** Ernst Conrad Friedrich Schulze (1789 –1817).

# Chapter XII.

## Influence of the Situation of The Germans on their Literature.

*Influence of their historical situation ; of their political situation ; of not participating in the naval enterprises of Europe; of their education. – Their opinion as to authorship. – Of the recent date of their literature. – Share the inhabitants of Hannover take in the general literature. – Periodical publications. – Göttingsche gelehrte Anzeigen. – Freedom of the press in Hannover.*

It has been already remarked, that the Germans have few ennobling historical recollections. They have been so divided into petty states, that they have never had a national existence. If they remember the prowess of their ancient knights, they feel it was the prowess of robbers, of which they are now ashamed. They have long fought more as mercenaries than for their country, and they therefore want all those glowing and ardent recollections which belong to men who have had a continued national and free existence. Proud historical recollections are some of the principal ingredients in a national sublimity of character, and the want of them has had a pernicious influence on the nation al character, and, through that, on the literature of the Germans.

Facts support this opinion. The present Saxons were more distinguished by the share they took in the Reformation than any other people of Germany. It was a victory and a triumph for them and gave an impulse to their minds which has almost ever since made their country the classic ground of Germany.

The victories of Frederic the Great did something of the same kind for Prussia. They gave the Prussians a feeling of superiority which has ever since remained. "The Prussian party,'" says Goethe, speaking of these victories, "gained a treasure for their literature which the other party wanted, and which no trouble could afterwards gain for them." Frederic first gave the Prussians a national existence and a national character. A feeling of superiority amongst individuals, and amongst nations, when not proceeding from sheer vanity, is a powerful ingredient in sublimity of character.

This feeling was acquired by the Saxons at the period of the Reformation, and by the Prussians in the days of their great king. It has ever belonged in some measure to the inhabitants of the free towns and has ever given them a greater name in the world, and greater talents, than are possessed by the rest of their countrymen.

When Spain, France, and England, had long been great united nations, the Germans remained in their ancient divided state. They lived under many petty tyrannical governments. This is, in fact, the great historical distinction between the Germans and the rest of the nations of Europe, and it has prevented them from attaining that eminence and that force of character to which, from their numbers, from their central situation, from the happy fertility of their country, and from their progress in civilization, they ought to rise.

To the want of ennobling historical recollections, and of a feeling of national importance, must be added the sad influence of a state of political servitude. Social regulations have always, in Germany, fixed the station of man in society, have left no opening for active talents, and have deprived individuals of those energies for wanting which the nation is conspicuous. Till the revival of their literature, which they themselves date from 1740, there was no means of rising to distinction or obtaining public honours. Their social regulations, their casts, guilds, and restrictions, have been fetters on their talents and genius so well as on their industry. The understanding and character of men are refined, strengthened, and corrected, by free, manly, and public discussion and competition. The Germans have never possessed these; and their character has proportionately suffered in strength, vigour, and acuteness.

They have been excluded, by their situation, from all participation in those naval enterprises which, from the time of Columbus to our last polar expedition, have inspired young minds with much ardour, and have given a bolder character, a greatness, and a glory, to the nations who have achieved them. Their influence on national character may be known from their effects on the Portuguese, and Spaniards, and Dutchmen. For a long period, the former were two of the most conspicuous nations of Europe; their naval discoveries and conquests brought them wealth and dignity, gave them pride and power, and saved them for many years from that utter degradation to which their miserable governments and superstitions have at length brought them. Naval expeditions have always been attended with dangers, distress, and sufferings, and the noble exertions of the individuals who have achieved them have spread a lustre, not only over themselves, but on all the people who bear the common name.

The Germans have had no participation in those adventurous exploits which have thus ennobled some of the other nations of Europe, and have given to their poetry, particularly to the poetry of Britain, many new and beautiful incidents and images. No German could ever have conceived or executed anything analogous to the *Shipwreck* of Falconer or the *Corsair* of Byron. They have never "danced in triumph o'er the waters wide," never felt:

"The exulting sense, the pulse's maddening play,
That glads the wanderer on that trackless way;"[130]

and the whole nation wants all those feelings which are connected with great and daring enterprise and wants a great and daring character.

Scholastic education, with a taste for music, and other elegant accomplishments, have long been general in Germany; and, although they amuse and charm us, it will be readily conceded that they rather take from than give strength of mind to the persons who make them their chief pursuit. They weaken and dilute the passions by constantly occupying them all. Those persons whose whole existence is employed in learning sciences and languages, and who live in a society where there is a constant demand for all the pleasures which these accomplishments supply, can rarely possess those lordly passions which constitute what is called force of character. When the sciences and languages are regarded as mere objects of curiosity, no deep feelings can ever be connected with them.

A love for freedom may serve as a sort of master-passion to bind a variety of knowledge into a beautiful whole; but the Germans have lived for ages without any such master passion, and their learning seems therefore to have been only a beautiful statue, which no ethereal fire has ever animated. I am far from supposing that the most extensive knowledge and education, which is not a monastic or a Spartan education, can ever impede the flow of the imagination, or render the literature of a people less beautiful. Such an education, if men have room to act, and are allowed to feel, will only add to the beauty of an imaginative literature. But if both feelings and actions are prescribed, an extensive education will invariably only teach them to value too highly the mechanical parts of science, such as classifying butterflies and weighing atoms. Such knowledge and pursuits as these may please adepts, but they have nothing to interest the mass of men, and those who are

---

[130] **Editor's F/N:-** These three last quoted lines are from Byron's *Corsair* (1814).

conversant with them are little likely to write what will please the world. The mightiest talents of Germany are employed in the trifles of science, or in the subtleties of laws, and such employments are well calculated to make acute and attentive observers of trifles, but not to make great and dignified men.

We learn from the life of Goethe, (Aus Meinem Leben,) that he learnt ancient and modern languages, dancing, fighting, music, riding, painting, engraving; in short, he studied almost everything that had any relation either to science or art, or that could tend to make an accomplished man. The same practice is common to most young men. The industry which I have described as distinguishing the students at the university, they carry into every part of their pursuits. They are in general anxious to acquire all sorts of knowledge, and seek, by every possible method, to become learned, or, in their favourite phrase, *Ausgebildet*. They have ausgebildete classes, ausgebildete men, and every young man who studies talks of his Ausbildung. This comprises a vast fund of accomplishments, which nothing but a youth void of every vivid and evil passion could enable them to acquire. They do acquire them, while they at the same time mix with the world, and, as far as my observations have extended, the individuals of the ausgebildete, or learned classes, appear to unite more accomplishments than most other Europeans.

These are to be considered as causes of some of the distinguishing characteristics both of the Germans and of their poetry. They are a calm, gentle, learned, and laborious people; but they are not a deep feeling and a noble people. Their morality is rather to enjoy than to suffer. Their religion teaches the same principle and has nothing in it either austere or solemn. Imaginative literature derives the greater part of its value from describing natural, general, and strong feelings. An individual, and consequently a nation, who does not possess strong feelings, who is ignorant of them and their effects, can never describe them accurately. He may versify very well, but he wants one of the excellencies of a poet. The French versify very well, but their poetry wants all those tempestuous flashes of the soul, that poignant grief, that penitence and bitterness of heart, which we conceive to be so essential to poetry. The knowledge and education of the Germans enables a vast number of them to make very pretty verses; but wanting natural sublimity of character, they rarely or never infuse it into their writings. Their efforts to be sublime appear to be one great cause of all those perversions of sentiment which have, within a few years, rather disgraced their literature. It is not, as I have heard, suggested that their imaginations are slow and not easily affected, that their authors have multiplied horrors, but because, having themselves no real sublimity of character, they have employed them as a means of producing a sublime effect.

One of the opinions of the Germans, which, indeed, they only share with many other people, is — that reality is not fit for poetry. Mr. Müllner tells his readers this in an address prefixed to Yngurd: "Die Wirklichkcit taugt selten zum Gedicht." It is only the dreams which the muses bring before the mind's eye which are fit, in the opinion of the poet, for the purpose of amusing and instructing mankind. This has undoubtedly had a great influence on the quantity of nonsense which has been written.

Another opinion, which is nearly peculiar to them, is — that literature is a matter of trade; and they learn the art of book-making as other people learn to make shoes or hats. They are manufacturers of good articles rather than writers from feeling or schtiment, or a conviction that they have something important to communicate. I have known more than one young man who resolved to be a tragic author. Kant, as a boy, resolved to be Kant the professor and philosopher; and Schlegel studies criticism and fine writing, that he may be a critic. This is an admirable principle for improving in knowledge. "You may always write," says Dr. Johnson, "if you will but go doggedly to it." Study may make critics philosophers and men of science. It may correct and reform genius; but too much of it tends to model men after pre-existing authors — to deprive genius of originality, and literature of warmth. Book makers by profession make very saleable good articles; but if they did not begin the trade from the impulse of genius, they seldom write anything pleasing or new.

This principle seems to have had an influence on German literature. It stimulates to acquire learning and to multiply books, without imparting anything new. The gentle dispositions of the Germans allow everything which is said in conversation to be heard with attention and politeness. They appear to think they may write just as they speak: and hence they send into the world a vast number of volumes, on subjects which are trifling and not amusing.

A new literature is not necessarily a faulty literature; but some of the errors of the German literature may undoubtedly be traced to the recent date of its origin. From wanting a literature there was also a want of a literary public. Those German works which are intended only for learned men, such as historical, philosophical, and philological works, are equally as well written as similar works in other languages; but the works destined for the great mass of the people, the common mental food of the society, participated in the dispositions and the failures of the society, and were often faulty because it wanted a correct taste. A new literature, when the people are also new, may be rude, but it will be energetic ; and it could only be the new literature of an old people that could be both rude and weak.

If the Germans would leave out theories, leave off imitating other people, and write after their own hearts, and according to the manner in which they observe life and nature, they would write the most gentle and pleasing poetry of any people in Europe. They are not a sublime people; and till some alterations in their political condition shall give them sublimity of character, they will essay in vain to write lofty and noble poetry.

Whatever may be the opinion entertained of German literature, it can hardly be denied that Hannover and the very northern part of Germany contribute a very fair proportion of the whole. The coteries and sonneteers of Dresden and Weimar would fain persuade the world that there is no poetical talents in "the cold and sandy north." They give the natives of the north the praise of being solid, deep thinkers, but deny them the vivacity of genius, and the fire of poetry. The Hannoverians are certainly not so lightly enthusiastic and easily moved; nor do they write so many trifles as their southern brethren. They do not constantly trill, like the Saxons, the same unmeaning tones on their harps, and imagine flowing hair, a flushed cheek, and disordered robes, to be mental enthusiasm.

You do not meet in Hannover, as in other parts of Germany, with a set of young men who are unwashed and unshaved; and who, though they never wrote anything beyond an occasional ode to procure them admittance to a literary society, imagine it is necessary to be negligent and dirty as an evidence of genius. Leibnitz, with all the great names that have been inscribed at Göttingen, are proofs of the powerful capacity for thought which belongs to the people of the north, and which is a merit that their southern countrymen most readily allow them.

When a large proportion of the resources of a country are monopolized by the sovereign, his patronage is necessary to the existence of learned men and of literature. But, from the sovereign residing out of the country, there has been no patronage of this kind in Hannover other than what has been bestowed on Göttingen. Courts are, in modern times, the nurseries of polite literature. Hannover has wanted a court and has not therefore shone in this branch so much as in some others.

Yet Iffland, the father of German comedy, was a Hannoverian. No names stand at present higher in the polite literature of Europe than those of the Schlegels, and they are natives of Hannover. Bürger was, I believe, born in Saxony, but a great part of his life was passed in Göttingen and its neighbourhood. A valley there, in which he loved to pass his time, still bears the name of Bürger Thal; and he must be considered as a poet of the north. I am unacquainted with any living poet of Hannover who is celebrated. A Mr. Blumenhagen[131] is sometimes spoken of as a writer of occasional verses. Ernest Schluze,[132] who has been mentioned as the author of two poems of some merit, was also born and educated in the dominions of Hannover.

It is probably owing to the want of patronage in Hannover that many clever natives of this country seek reputation and wealth in other parts of Ger many. The Schlegels and Mr. Thaer have been mentioned; and when, to their names, are added those of Mr. Luden, a celebrated professor of history in the university of Jena — of Prince Hardenberg — of General Benningsen — and of General Scharnhorst, who was killed while serving in the armies of Prussia at the battle of Leipsic — it will assuredly not be supposed that the Hannoverians are deficient in talents of any description.

There is not a single sculptor of the least eminence, and not one good gallery either of pictures or statues, in the whole of Hannover. Count Walmoden had a collection of pictures, but that is now dispersed. The only painter of the least reputation is a Mr. Ramberg, who was educated in England and in Rome at the expence of the sovereign. He is chiefly celebrated for the numerous and well executed devices with which he has enriched many of the almanacks, the Titanias, Uranias, and pocket-books of literature, which yearly issue from the presses of Germany. It is a curious circumstance of this painter, which has been remarked by several people, that he has never been able to paint a female who possessed the characteristics of modesty.

There is not a single good engraver in the kingdom. In these points Hannover differs much from the other parts of Germany. Berlin, Vienna, Dresden, Cassel, abound with sculptors, painters, and artists of all descriptions. There has been no demand for such persons in Hannover, and there are none, and never have been

---

[131] **Editor's F/N:-** Carl Heinrich Ernst Julius Blumenhagen (1789-1870) was a German poet and lawyer.

[132] **Editor's F/N:-** Gottlob Ernst Schulze (1761–1833) was a German philosopher. Arthur Schopenhauer was his illustrious student.

any. Should the Duke of Cambridge[133] continue to reside there, he will occasion a small demand; and then Hannover will, in these points as in others, equal the other countries of Germany. The taste of his Royal Highness is chiefly directed to music; and the orchestra of Hannover is not the worst of Germany, which boasts so many of the first musicians of Europe.

A large portion of the literature of Europe now consists of periodical publications. This is particularly the case in Germany, where novels, comedies, tragedies, histories, are all published as pocket-books, and as almanacks. The political periodical literature of the present time is perhaps, in point of effect, the most important of all literature. It would, therefore, be unpardonable to pass over that of Hannover in silence, though little or nothing can be said of it. It is necessary to record its non-existence. "Die gelehrte Anzeigen" of Göttingen, or Literary Notices, is the only periodical paper published in Hannover that deserves an encomium. It is a duodecimo, of which four numbers are published weekly. Each number contains either a half or a whole sheet of print. It is published by the members of the university. Heyne was the editor for more than 40 years, and Eichhorn succeeded him. It gives an account of such books only as are purchased for the university library. And, generally, the observations it contains are confined to the work noticed rather than to giving new and enlarged views.

I have given one or two extracts from it in the course of this work. The side of politics it generally takes is that of liberality and reason. The contributors are the professors; and the greatest part of the political articles of importance are written, I believe, by Professor Sartorious.[134] From such a man nothing can be expected but what is scientific and rational, well weighed and calmly delivered. It contains none of the floating half-formed opinions of the moment, which find their way into daily newspapers. It contains nothing which appeals to popular prejudices, or which can be considered as an index of popular opinion. All its political articles are more scientific than popular. It is the vehicle, also, for much of the

---

[133] **Editor's F/N:-** From 1816 to 1837, the Duke of Cambridge (1774-1850) was the 7th son of King George III and served as viceroy of Hanover on behalf of his elder brothers, George IV and then William IV. When his niece, Victoria, succeeded to the British throne in 1837, the 122-year union of Hanover and the United Kingdom ended as Hanover was under Salic Law, which forbade a women become Queen. The Duke of Cumberland (the 5th son of King George III) became the King of Hanover and the Duke of Cambridge returned to Britain.

[134] **Editor's F/N:-** Georg Friedrich Sartorius (1765–1828) was a German research historian, and economist.

discussion which takes place in Germany on the subject of legislation. In this point, and in philological remarks, it is surpassed by none of the numerous journals of Germany.

The town of Hannover does not boast a single journal that can be called exclusively political. The Advertiser is a sort of gazette belonging to the crown. There is a meagre chronicle of the theatre, and a sort of weekly paper which announces the comings and goings of illustrious persons. With Hamburg on one side, and Jena, Brunswick, Weimar, and Leipsic on the other, in which places some of the best political works of Germany are published, there is less occasion to print any in Hannover. It is, in this point, much behind. Its people appear hitherto never to have busied themselves with their dearest interests, though, at last, they begin to be political.

It is sometimes stated that the press is free in Hannover. This is entirely a mistake. It is totally free in no part of Germany, though it is subject to less restrictions in Weimar, Hamburg, and Bavaria, than in other parts. But even in these places books are suppressed at the whim of the governors, or by the representations of ambassadors. What a weak cause must that be which requires to be supported by forbidding human thought and speech to attack it!

A regulation, made in 1705, forbids any native of Hannover from printing any work, either in the land or out of the land, for the purpose of circulating it in the land, till it had been approved of by the censor. All works published at Göttingen must be submitted to the censorship of the members of the university. No printer is allowed to print a work unless it has been approved of by the censor, under penalty of losing the privilege of printing, and of being otherwise punished.

For works published out of Göttingen there are other censors. One who is charged with the inspection of all works of poetry and literature is dependent on the justice-chancery; another, to whom all political works must be submitted, is dependent on one of the departments of the ministry. The consistoriums take care that the doctrines of the church remain unassailed.

There is a control established over the press, which, when it is complete, is but another name for absolute dominion. This is, however, a nugatory power. For what is offensive to the government of one country is printed in another, and thus the separate governments of Germany have in some measure served to secure a free press to the whole of the country. Their jealousy of each other has allowed attacks on each which have ultimately weakened the power of all.[135]

# Chapter XIII.

## Private Life and Morals,

*Private life of a foreign people difficult to learn. – The religion of the Germans. – Toleration. – Examples of Catholic sovereigns with Protestant subjects. – Causes of tolerance. – Character and principles of Luther. – Church has no power. – Ceremony of confirmation. – Gentleness. – Instances of politeness. – Christmas presents. – Sociality. – Ceremonious ness. – Endearing epithets. – Free intercourse. – Commerce of the sexes. – Number of divorces. – Selection of wives. – Freedom of manners-Extensive education of women. – Public display of affections, – Manner of announcing deaths and marriages.*

Much has been already said, at various places in this work, on the manners and morals of the different classes of society in Germany; but, as something may yet be added, I shall here employ a whole chapter for the purpose. It is extremely difficult for a traveller to appreciate, from actual observation, the domestic manners of a foreign nation. He is seldom admitted to the privacy of family scenes; the natives are on their guard before him, and are generally clothed in some of those disguises, which they wear, like their apparel, more for fashion and shew than for comfort and convenience. He learns little or nothing of the amiability or rudeness of their domestic intercourse. He sees them at table, in the ball-room, in the saloon, when all the politeness, knowledge, and wit, which can be mustered, are brought on, rank and file, for the entertainment and accommodation of the company. Gallantry may lead to the chambers of the ladies, but that is an intercourse which spreads its own colours on every neighbouring object, and seldom allows a correct judgment to be formed of what is seen. A

---

[135] **Hodgskin's F/N:-** It must now be said this was the case. The conferences of Carlsbad have endeavoured to destroy the liberties of Germany and Europe. Without these conferences, and their subsequent measures of harshness, there would undoubtedly have been a great reform in the political institutions of Europe, now, unfortunately, we may expect, not reform, but revolution.

long residence in a foreign land makes the manners of the people familiar; and those slight differences of character, which distinguish one European nation from another, are them never remarked.

We are well acquainted with the manners of the people of Paris, and we have learnt them from the memoirs, letters, and novels, of the Parisians. I believe also, that any foreigner who has acquired a correct notion of our manners, has acquired it rather from our own writings than from his own actual observation. So far as I am acquainted with German literature, it contains but few works from which much information relative to their own morals and manners can be procured.

The follies or vices of courts, which are much the same all the world over, have been sketched in the comedies of Iffland.[136] Kotzebue[137] deals more with the people at large, but he has so caricatured them, that the likeness can seldom be discovered. The novels of La Fontaine,[138] though they lay claim to be representations of manners, are written with less regard to truth than to false and ridiculous effect.

Goethe's *Memoirs*, his *Herman and Dorothea*, his *Wilhelm Meister*, some of the smaller pieces of Schiller, and some of the poems of Bürger, may all teach something concerning German manners; but, in general, the Germans have few books written expressly for this purpose, and the traveller must be content with very moderate gleanings.

Much of the character of our countrymen is known from their public actions. But the Germans seem to do nothing more in public than teach and pray. Schools and churches are open to the stranger, but parliaments and courts of justice are closed. Unfortunately, also, the part of Germany which I had the most opportunity to become acquainted with, does not possess any of those celebrated men whose names are known all over Europe, and of whom the merest trifle is a matter of interest. The looks of such people seem regarded like amusing anecdotes. Hannover is in all things a humble town, to which even the presence of the Duke of Cambridge gave neither celebrity nor magnificence. On Saint George's day, when there was a review and a levee held, the

---

[136] **Editor's F/N:-** August Wilhelm Iffland (1759 –1814) was a German actor and author.
[137] **Editor's F/N:-** August Friedrich Ferdinand von Kotzebue (1761–1819) was a German playwright (of over 200 plays) and author.
[138] **Editor's F/N:-** August Heinrich Julius Lafontaine (1758–1831) was a very famous German novelist.

splendour was about equal to what we might expect at the house of a nobleman who commanded a corps of volunteers, and who did the honours of his sovereign's birthday to the military of some garrison town. Hannover has none of the scandal of a court. I am anxious, by these preliminary remarks, to caution the reader against expecting any of those amusing anecdotes which the title of the chapter might seem to promise, and to provide an excuse for not having it in my power to give any.

There seems to be no part of morals which is more deserving consideration than what is dictated by religion, and, though something has been said of the church government, it yet remains to describe the practices of religion. In Hannover the reigning religion is the Lutheran. In some other parts of Germany, the Catholic, or the Calvinistic modes of worship, are most prevalent. In no part are sectaries numerous, and the only conspicuous sects more than those mentioned, are the Herrenhuters and the Jews. It is said that there are in the whole kingdom 1,060,000 Lutherans, 160,000 Catholics, 90,000 Calvinists, 10,000 Jews, and 1000 Herrenhuters and Mennonites.

A particular instance of toleration, – the admission of Catholics to be members of the highest court of appeal in Hannover, – has been already mentioned, and Catholics may be generals or ministers of state. There is no law of exclusion. There is a pleasure in recording virtues, though they may not be our own, and the toleration which exists in Germany seems worthy of our imitation. No question is there made as to a man's faith. He may believe either of the numerous fables which are commonly believed that he pleases, and if he deliver his reasons in support of it, he is sure to be listened to with attention and candour. Both Catholic and Protestant professors teach at the same university, and in the schools children of every description of parents listen to the same moral lessons.

Men are not likely to persecute their school-fellows and their playmates, nor look with bitterness and anger on those with whom they have grown up to manhood, merely because they differ from them on some speculative point. In several parts of Germany, the Lutherans and the Calvinists have recently joined in one common mode of worship, and, in 1817, the Catholics lent the Protestants the ornaments of their churches, that they might more pompously celebrate the centenary of the Reformation. The only restrictions on opinion, of which I heard, were on political opinions, and almost the only persecutions were of the Jews and of the philosophers. Kant was threatened with the loss of his professorship on account of some of his opinions, and Fichte was subjected to some sort of trial at Weimar, in 1807, for a similar cause, and he is said to have died of chagrin in consequence.

The Jews are still subjected to odious distinctions in many parts of Germany. In Prussia they enjoy protection the same as the other citizens. In Hannover they are not allowed to hold land, and each Jewish family must pay the sovereign a certain sum of money for protection. There are some certain trades which none of them are allowed to practise, and no one must live in the old town of Hannover. The poorer classes of Germans hate and despise Jews, because they envy them their wealth. Excluded from all places of honour and trust, the Jews naturally sought wealth as a means of buying protection and respect. They have not been strictly scrupulous in the means of obtaining it, and their conduct now serves as an excuse for persecuting them. The poorer classes of the Germans believe the most absurd stories of the Jews; such as, that they possess the power to make people wither and die under the curse which they have uttered in secret, and that children are driven mad by the wrath of their parents.[139]

Toleration, in its most lovely form, seems to exist both in public and private life, to regulate the manners of the people, and to sway the councils of monarchs. We learn from history also, that this has long been the case, and we shall probably seek in vain for examples of tolerance in other European countries similar to what are found in Germany. When Louis XIV. of France was persecuting and banishing the Huguenots, John Frederick, the Duke of Kalenberg, and a friend of Louis, allowed his Protestant subjects to live in peace. This prince governed between the years 1665 and 1679; he was a zealous Catholic, surrounded by priests; he had the highest opinion of his own powers, frequently styling himself emperor in his own dominions; he was an active and intelligent prince. The greater part of his subjects were Protestants, yet he never ill-treated nor oppressed them, nor made any efforts to convert them to the Catholic faith.[140] When we compare his conduct to that of our James II. we immediately perceive either a superior penetration, or a want of that fiery zeal which drove our sovereign from his throne.

The members of the present royal family of Saxony, whose subjects are almost exclusively Protestants, have been Catholics for

---

[139] **Hodgskin's F/N:-** These unfortunate prejudices have lately been the cause for the Jews being insulted and oppressed.

[140] **Hodgskin's F/N:-** Spittler's *Geschichte*, Vol. II. History of the reign of this prince.

more than 100 years, that is, since 1697:[141]  yet they have never oppressed their Protestant subjects, have never attempted to gain converts, or to make Catholicism the religion of the land.  Although they differ in their religion from their subjects, they are probably as well beloved as any royal family of Europe.

As common religious ceremonies are sometimes called spiritual drams, the gay chapel of the sovereign at Dresden, with its fine Italian singers, and exquisite music, may be called the very Champagne of religion.  While the monarch, with his hands in a large white muff, was devoutly saying his prayers in the gallery, the lower part of this chapel was always filled with his Protestant subjects, who go there to take intoxicating draughts of the music and singing.  For those persons to whom amusement is necessary, or who seek enjoyment in religion, there can be no question that Catholicism has many more charms than any other, and those who saw only that part of it which is seen in the chapel of Dresden, might easily justify preferring it to every other.

As it may teach us that no danger can ensue to the Church of England, while its votaries are the majorities of the nation, from the

---

[141] **Hodgskin's F/N:-** I have lately read the Travels of Mr. Jorgenson, in Germany, who seems to wish to shew that faithlessness has long been characteristic of the sovereigns of Saxony.  If they are to be judged by their vacillations during the thirty years' war, and the wars of religion prior to that period, they must not be stigmatized more than the other sovereigns of Germany, for they seem all to have vacillated alike.  Mr. Jorgenson is wrong in the period at which he says the royal family of Saxony became Catholic, and this error may be taken as a specimen of the probable correctness of some facts which he has given, "though no historians have narrated them." It was Augustus, the Elector of Saxony and King of Poland, who changed, towards the end of the seventeenth century, from Protestantism to Catholicism.—(Putter, Vol. II. p. 353.)   But Mr. Jorgenson makes this Augustus the brother and successor of Maurice, who died in the year 1553, and who, consequently, lived near a century and a half prior to the Augustus who changed his religion.  I may also add, in order to justify the Saxons from some of Mr. Jorgenson's remarks, that, during the three months I remained in their country, I saw nothing but what was amiable, polite, and friendly.  If any difference could be discovered between them and the other Germans, they appeared more gentle, more kind, and softer. I know that this opinion of the Saxons accords with the opinions of many English travellers, and of many Germans.  If it were not for the influence of political prejudices, it would be difficult to understand how Mr. Jorgenson could single out the Saxons as the only exception to the good character he has in general so justly given to the Germans.  There can be no justification of telling untruths even of a tyrant and oppressor, but it is surely much worse to calumniate a whole people to justify the ambition and the imagined expediencies of political charlatans.

sovereign being a Catholic, and while we may learn, from the tolerance of Catholic sovereigns to their subjects, to be ashamed of our own intolerant laws against Catholics, I shall here mention two other instances of Catholic sovereigns with Protestant subjects. Indeed, in most of the reigning families of Germany, some of the members profess a faith different from the majority of the people. The sovereigns of Wirtemberg were Catholics from 1738 to 1793 – although, during that period, their subjects remained Protestants, and remained unpersecuted. Frederick, the Landgrave of Hesse Cassel, the ally of George II. and George III., changed from a Protestant to a Catholic; yet he was not banished from his throne, — nor did he persecute his Protestant subjects.[142]

More such instances might probably be found; and, compared with our own conduct, they seem to prove that Catholicism is not more intolerant than Protestantism. As another instance of the harmony which exists on the subject of religion between subjects and their sovereigns in Germany, I may mention the King of Prussia, who is a Calvinist, while the majority of his subjects are Lutherans; and he might be a Catholic if he pleased.[143]

The manner in which different principles, some of which are called irreligious, have long been discussed in Germany, is a matter of public notoriety: and it may unhesitatingly be affirmed, that tolerance is greater in Germany than in any other part of Europe. It has also been greater for many years and must have had a proportional influence. The Germans have known none of the angry passions of religious opposition and know nothing of the bitterness of persecution. One part of their society has not been the declared religious enemies of the other; and the whole, therefore, display features of mildness and of love.

Various causes have conspired to produce this effect. Luther and his friends appear to have been more animated with their good cause, and less with worldly ambition, than most reformers. They laid it down as a rule that, as their Master and his apostles had given no direction for the government of the church, and had prescribed no form of worship, so each community must be left, in these particulars, to its own discretion. They recommended the Scriptures as the best guide to the several sovereigns and the inhabitants of those free towns which embraced the Reformation; and they assisted in drawing up forms of prayer, and prescribing

---

[142] **Hodgskin's F/N:-** Hassel.
[143] **Hodgskin's F/N:-** Demian Handbuch, p. 123.

religious ceremonies, — but they left the church to be modelled, particularly in its temporalities, by the people themselves.[144]

Hence the government of the Lutheran church differs in almost every town and city in a variety of minute particulars, which helped to teach moderation to all. So long as the principle of not prescribing a form of church government, and of not fixing articles of faith and belief, was followed, there were no quarrels among the different sects of Protestants which grew out of the Reformation. But so soon as the Confession of Augsburgh had clearly prescribed the bounds of Lutheranism, there was a ground of exclusion for the Calvinists, and the two parties of Protestants became the enemies of each other. The Reformers did not adhere to their principle throughout; and while the Reformation, which they had themselves brought about, was a great change, they vainly attempted to fix their own rules forever on their children. Every improvement is a change, and nothing can be more absurd than to prevent improvement by those fixed regulations which proscribe every change. Till they had this fixed Confession, the Protestants of Germany went on rapidly improving; and though differences of opinion then existed sufficient at length to teach all parties moderation, it was long prevented by fixing as dogmas what ought to be for ever left to discussion.

There is one point in which the Lutheran church is almost everywhere the same. The clergy have little or no wealth, and they have no political power. Their salary is proportionate to their labours, and they have ceased to stir up the spirit of persecution, because no worldly wealth or power was to be gained by it. Ever since the Reformation, whatever religion the sovereigns might profess, they have always been superior to the priesthood. Wherever the church retained a power nearly equal to that of the magistracy, as in the Hanse Towns, there intolerance was, and is greater, than where it lost all its worldly dominion. Exclusive, therefore, of the poverty which an opulent priesthood entails on the industrious classes of a society, there is a powerful motive, in the persecution such a priesthood has always occasioned, why it ought not to be allowed to grow into existence.

The authors of Lutheranism were not sour, morose, and disappointed men — the enemies of natural pleasure, and the lovers of mystical dogmas.

---

[144] **Hodgskin's F/N:-** See Putter, Vol. I. p. 373–381; Spittler, Vol. I. p.137, where there is an example of the inhabitants of a very small town making regulations for their own church.

"As for the Lutherans," says Riesebeck,"[145] (and the observation is correct,) "they possess part of the humour of their founder, and, to a high degree of frugality, unite a great love of pleasure and jollity. An unnatural hatred of joy does not damp their wit and good temper. They have none of the savage slovenliness, the dark hypocrisy, and the ill-breeding, which distinguish the majority of other sects."[146]

The strong natural sense of Luther seems to have extended itself to most of the actions of his followers; and they did not fill their books with absurd and incomprehensible creeds. They lost their worldly grandeur, and nothing remained to excite envy ; and, as they did not impose "articles" and tests on the consciences of men, there was no motive for opposition and hatred. Hence few sects have grown up in Germany, and hence the people are mild and tolerant.[147]

---

[145] **Hodgskin's F/N:-** Letter 46.

[146] **Hodgskin's F/N:-** Luther seems to this day to be as much remembered as the apostle of good living as of religion. He is thus commemorated in song: —

D'rum stosset an,
Und singet dann :
Was Martin Luther spricht :  :  :

Chor: Wer nicht liebt Wein, Weib und Gesang
Der bleibt ein Narr sein Lebenlang,
Und Narren sind wir nicht.

"Then let us drink, and sing what Martin Luther said — Who does not love wine, women, and music, remains a fool all his life; and we are not fools."

[147] **Hodgskin's F/N:-** The clergy of Germany, to judge from the following sample among others of their conduct, appear to have had similar propensities with their brethren in all parts of the world. In some little town on the Rhine, on a particular feast-day, one of them preached a long and an eloquent sermon against intemperance, which he concluded by describing what intemperance was. It was passing those bounds which nature had prescribed. It was intemperance, he said, for some men who were quarrelsome in their cups ever to drink wine. There were others to whom a bottle was refreshment, but to whom two caused sickness. They were intemperate when they drank more than one. Some men enlivened a circle of friends, and were kind to their wives, even after they had drank four bottles; and it was not right in them to diminish their kindness by drinking less. There were others, more highly gifted servants of the Deity, who felt their hearts warm with gratitude to Him as the generous juice circulated in their blood, who were friendly with their families, generous to all men, and even nobly forgetful of injuries, when they had drank eight bottles. With them intemperance began at the ninth. But these, he said, are the peculiar favourites of God, to whom he has given the joys of the world as an

To these causes may be added the fact, that the Germans, more particularly the northern Germans, seem never to have been so degraded by Catholic superstition as some other of the nations of Europe. The reader may see this fact fully explained in Venturini, Vol. III. p. 36. The passage is too long to quote. The senses were less dazzled in Germany, and the understanding less deluded, than in Italy. Poverty had not allowed superstition to be arrayed in all its pomp; and Luther, according to this author, was successful because he had less delusion to combat.

An increase of knowledge has utterly changed the character of the Germans. They were dark, cruel, and unrelenting. They were persecutors and martyrs. They were bigots and ferocious murderers. Now, they are gentle, mild, and forgiving. When such a lovely change has taken place in some of their evil passions, it is only rational to extend the inference which may be drawn from this fact to the whole race, and to hope that all our evil propensities may be rendered harmless or extirpated by an increase of knowledge. By the progress of opinion, ferocity and bigotry have been changed to gentleness and tolerance; and there is no reason to despair that the lust of wealth, which is our present curse and crime, may not be so modified as to produce, at a future period, nothing but honest pains-taking industry and ingenuity.

On Sundays, some few people go once to church. They sing psalms, they hear prayers and a sermon, and are dismissed with a blessing. Sunday is rather a day of recreation than of prayer; and the dancing-houses are more crowded towards evening than the churches at mid-day. Church-going is not a matter of necessity in Germany, and, in truth, few people go to church. The inhabitants of the towns communicate seldom: those of the country flock in crowds to partake of the bread and wine.

Among the followers of Luther, confirmation seems to form an epoch in their lives, which, like their marriage, is never forgotten. In England, it reminds one of the story told by Dr. Franklin of saying grace over a whole barrel of beef. Our young people procure a certificate from any priest they please; they collect in numbers in a church and are blessed in dozens by the bishop  they remember the ceremony from the quantity of people, and probably because they then saw lawn sleeves[148] for the first time in their lives. In England it

---

evidence of the joys of hereafter; and all his congregation knew with what gratitude (bowing as he said it) he acknowledged himself to be one of these favourites.

[148] **Editor's F/N:-** "Lawn Sleeves" in this context is referring to the sleeves of Bishops' ceremonial gowns. "Lawn" is an archaic reference to *Fine*

seems to be a matter of indifference whether people are confirmed or not. In Hannover the law orders everybody to be confirmed; and no Lutheran there reaches his 18th year without paying the priest for dispensing to him, as the law says, "The great and wonderful advantages which come, even in this unmiraculous age, from laying on hands in public."

Previous to being confirmed, the children are instructed by the clergymen during several weeks; and even the young girls are publicly examined in the church, that they may testify their fitness to be admitted members of the congregation. This public examination, and the confirmation, are very trying, and seem to be thought very momentous by the children. They are collected in the body of the church, totally separated from the rest of the assembly.

Those whom I saw were dressed in black; the girls wore white shawls, and had flowers in their bosoms, and the little things trembled and cried through the whole two hours which the ceremony lasted. They were, for the whole of this time, the exclusive objects of attention. The clergyman prayed for them, he preached to them, he questioned them, and he called on them to testify their faith aloud. When they had done this, they were led to the altar, and allowed to communicate for the first time in their lives. The ceremony seemed impressive. The clergyman, the congregation, and the children, all wept. The latter, indeed, seemed to suffer much. It was a sort of tragedy, in which all were actors. "This painful solemnity," I was told, "made a more powerful impression;" and I was not a little surprised to learn, from several young women, that they remembered the day on which they were confirmed as one of the sweetest of their lives. After confirmation they go no more to school. At the end of the ceremony they receive the congratulation of their friends, and they are changed at once, as it were by magic, from boys and girls into men and women. These following consequences make this day of trembling and of tears a day of sweet recollections throughout life.

This ceremony is one of the many instances of the manner in which an ambitious priesthood established that dominion over other men which is now so fast decaying. There is a period of life at which instruction must cease, and at which the ambition of children must be gratified by a participation in the pursuits and employments of their parents. This period has been sanctified by a religious ceremony, that the power of giving or of withholding the pleasure might belong to the priests.

---

*Linen.*

Nothing, surely, is more natural than love; but they have persuaded us that even its joys are unholy if they are unsanctioned by them. A day of rest which every man should take when it is convenient to him, and which, when it is general, is to both man and animals a most beneficial institution, has been likewise claimed by the priests as a gift of religion, that they might build their power on our most innocent enjoyments. Our entrance into life, our rest from labour, the joys of love, and even our death, have all been turned by these gentlemen to the account of their firm, as if they were derived from them, and gave them a claim to our gratitude and obedience. If it were possible for the man to trace, through the whole of his life, every sensation which has ever entered into the composition of the sentiment of faith, or which now make up the consolations of religion, it would be a curious inquiry to ascertain how much of this sentiment and of these consolations were de rived from the sensual enjoyments with which all religious truths have been combined. The mince pies, songs, gambols, and friendly parties at Christmas — the fritters of Shrove Tuesday — the pudding-pies of Lent — the geese of Michaelmas — the fine clothes and amusements of Sunday — the pompous ceremonies of the church — and, above all, the manner in which faith is sung into the heart with sweet and solemn music, and in which it is taught to us in multitudes, when men catch enthusiasm from one another[149] — are probably some of the most powerful ingredients in what is called religious emotion. The very attempt to analyse it takes from it all its pleasure, and all its influence, except that which it derives from the truth combined with these sensual enjoyments.

The whole conduct of the Germans seems to me to partake of that gentle and tolerant character which also belongs to their religious practices. There is a quietness, placidness, and cheerfulness in their countenances, a readiness to oblige, and a true and estimable politeness, which can be much better felt and enjoyed than described. I should have thought either that my estimate of their character was wrong, or that I had been peculiarly fortunate in the individuals I had encountered, had I not recently seen my opinion confirmed by the author of *the Life of Haydn*.[150] In

---

[149] **Hodgskin's F/N:-** Schiller understood the effects of religion being taught to a multitude of people at once. When he said, "That nothing but the faith of all can strengthen faith, where thousands pray and honour, there the glow becomes a flame, and the winged soul soars in every heaven."
Denn nur der Glaube Aller stärkt den Glauben,
Wo Tausende anbeten und verehren,
Da wird die Glut zur Flamme, und beflügelt
Schwingt sich der Geist in alle Himmel auf.
Maria Stuart, 5 Act, 7 Scene.

numerous parts of his work, he displays his knowledge of "the native goodness of German hearts." There is nothing in this which is strongly expressive — nothing which he who runs may read. There is no contortion of countenance, and absurdity of conduct — no strength of phrase and vigour of step — but all is calm, quiet, and methodical. The following instances of politeness may be taken as specimens of their general conduct:-

I became acquainted in Hannover with a most respectable gentleman. In the course of our conversations I remarked, that, in consequence of the general secrecy observed on matters of government, it was difficult to acquire any accurate knowledge of them. In a few days afterwards, he invited me to visit him on purpose to introduce me to a gentleman holding a high situation under government. From both I repeatedly received marks of kindness and attention no unknown stranger can ever rationally expect. If I have any regret at the nature of my remarks on the Hannoverian government, it is only because I think they impose on me the necessity of not mentioning the names of these gentlemen. I should have been otherwise proud to record them as the names of men who knew and practised the most estimable politeness. By another gentleman, who was also a stranger to me, I was introduced to one of those public reading rooms, which are such agreeable places, both of amusement and instruction. I experienced repeatedly such instances of kindness, my wants and my wishes were often prevented by a politeness that seemed to delight in finding out what would be agreeable to me.

This is a part of the German character which necessarily escapes the notice of those travellers whose acquaintance with the people does not extend beyond the inhabitants of their hotels, and beyond a knowledge of some distinguished men. It is found in all classes and has left in my mind an indelible esteem for their private character. That part of hospitality, which consists in feasting strangers, seems rare. In truth, they do not abound in wealth, and are obliged, in general, to live so economically, that they have no power to waste much on strangers. But, among themselves, there is a better hospitality, which the foreigner learns when he becomes intimate with them, which makes them offer him a share of their family meals without ceremony, and which frequently invites him to partake of their evening amusements, of the morning dram, or of the refreshing coffee.

---

[150] **Editor's F/N:-** Hodgskin is presumably referring to the *Life of Haydn In a Series of Letters,* now known to have been written by Marie-Henri Beyle, which was published in English by John Murray in 1817.

I have already frequently mentioned the delight they seem to have in cultivating and adorning their gardens; and it seems to be done less from ostentation than from real love to the amusement. The taste for flowers is carried into their houses, and roses or hyacinths adorn all their windows. As spring approached, husbands and wives, parents and children, rich and poor, were seen every evening cultivating a thousand little spots lying in the neighbourhood of Hannover. This taste is nearly universal and serves at once to adorn the land and tranquillise the passions.

The reciprocal presents they make at Christmas, and on birthdays, seem also proofs of a gentleness and amiability of character. Such presents are made in other countries. *Les etrennes* of the French are, however, the gifts of vanity and gallantry, and are little more than baits for sensuality. The Christmas boxes of England have degenerated to mere fees of office, not always willingly given; but *Das Weihnachts Geschenk* of the Germans is the offspring of friendship or love and is made by all classes. Towards Christmas, fairs are held in the towns, in order that all persons may provide themselves with what they mean to give. There is not a wife in the whole country who does not lay by some of her pennies to purchase a present for her husband. There is not a husband who does not pilfer his till, or curtail his pleasures, that he may give something to his wife. There is not a maiden nor a youth who is so unlucky as not to have some friends with whom gifts are exchanged at this season. The rich buy luxuries and ornaments – the poor necessaries. The prince and the noble decorate their rooms with evergreens, that they may make the presents they give to their children and servants more acceptable. Boys receive skates, or guns, or new clothes – girls, albums, work-baskets, and necessaries. The wife buys her husband a coat, and she receives a new gown, or some article of furniture. Whoever is not so dreadfully poor at Christmas as to have no friends, and nothing to give, is then happy; for he has something over which he exults, which is a secret for some persons, and a subject of conversation with others. The nature of the present is carefully concealed from those who are to receive it till the moment it is given, though it is always something for which the person receiving it has expressed a desire.

Between Berlin and Leipsic, I had for a short time a female companion, who had sufficient reason to complain of her situation. She had three children, and though both her husband and she were always ready to do any kind of work, they could barely obtain a subsistence. Their united labours procured them about 1s.6d. per day. She complained of nothing so much, however, as that she had received no Christmas gift. She had never before known the season to pass without receiving something, and never, she said, "were times so hard?" These are quiet offices of kindness, and sources of attachment and affection, which a mere traveller can rarely observe, and which, if he saw them occasionally, he might imagine were displayed for some purposes of deceit and ostentation, if he had not inquired and found them universal.

The presents which are given on birth and name days are like Christmas presents, and are given by parents, children, and friends. They are an interchange of visible signs of love and serve to bind all the parties together by acts of kindness. In *Die silberne Hochzeit*, one of the best of the comedies of Kotzebue, is a very good description of the eagerness with which a whole family of children tried to make themselves acceptable to their parents by the presents they made them on their wedding day. There is perhaps a little more outward sh0w in such acts than suits our character, but there seems also to be a light tenderness and cheerful affection that are almost unknown to us.

With all this gentleness, however, of the polished classes, there is yet a sort of rudeness and cruelty amongst the lower classes of the people. The murders which have been mentioned in the Chapter on Criminal Laws is one proof of this, and another, and more important one, because more general, is, that both masters and mistresses yet occasionally permit themselves personally to chastise both male and female servants. Some instances came under my observation, and I have heard of several more. The relation betwixt, masters and servants is so perfectly derived from the barbarous feudal laws, that the charity of feeling which is so common in other parts of their conduct, seems not yet to have extended to this. An equality of political condition has many advantages; and it prevents the opposite vices of servility and pride, of meanness and arrogance, of hatred and cruelty. There can be no doubt that this unfavourable trait of character in the Germans has been occasioned by their want of political equality.

It is well known that music is most extensively cultivated in Germany; that there is scarcely a young man or woman, of decent family and education, who does not both play and sing scientifically; but perhaps it is not so well known that the words are as musical as the people, and these have borrowed some part of their taste for harmony from the songsters of the forests. Never did I hear so many nightingales as sang every evening in the vicinity of Hannover. Other places are equally blessed with them, and all the woods resound with notes of harmony which respond to the voice of the people.

To an extensive cultivation of music, and an extensive education, the Germans add a great love for society, and such a gentle stream of pleasure flows through their life, that they have no time left to brood over anger, or to nourish disdain. In every town there are some public rooms constantly open, where society, amusements, and books, are always to be had, and no sooner is ennui felt than relief is sought in some place of this kind.

They pass much time in society, and smoke, and game, and converse a great deal, and they seem to be easily made happy by trifles. They have no Birmingham festival once a-year, but music is their hourly relaxation. They have neither routes nor squeezes, and yet they are constantly in society; they look on it as a source of enjoyment, and not of ostentation. Everything seems to interest them.

A new game of chess, a newly-discovered insect or plant, or an event on which the fate of mankind depends, seemed to be equally regarded, and to excite an equal degree of warmth. Passion seldom mixes in their conversation, disputes never. Even when the uproar at Göttingen excited universal remark, the party-spirit was only visible in a somewhat greater warmth of phrase. Their conversation is light and agreeable, but not important. A people who are constantly occupied with trifles cannot speak of matters of importance. When men regard sucking tobacco smoke through a wooden tube as one of the greatest earthly enjoyments, they may also possess a love for light and agreeable amusements, but they will hardly combine with these any special admiration for what is noble and grand. And, accordingly, though I always found something to amuse me in the conversation of the Germans, I rarely observed anything in it to admire, or received from it any valuable information.

German pride, says the author of the *Life of Haydn*, is ridiculous only in the printed accounts of their ceremonies; the air of kindness which accompanies the reality, gives a pleasing colour to everything.[151] We are apt to imagine them a stiff and ceremonious people, when we learn that there is no man, from his excellency a cabinet-minister to a door-waiter, who is not addressed in conversation by his title of office.

Women also receive the titles of their husbands and must never be addressed without this mark of dignity. *Die gnädige Frau Ministerinn* – My Lady Minister, – Mrs Secretary – as the wife of a copying-clerk is called, and Madame Shoemaker, all have their titles

---

[151] **Hodgskin's F/N:-** Page 197.

bandied to them whenever they are spoken to by equals or inferiors. In point of phrase, they certainly surpass the ceremony of the Parisian water-carriers, but, like them, they accompany their ceremony with much good will.

By the bye, the politeness of those men of pails does far more honour to the peasantry of France, who go in crowds yearly to Paris to fill this honourable office, than to the Parisians themselves, who are too much lost in selfishness to know anything of true politeness. With a ceremonious mode of address, however, there is a freedom and a familiarity of communication. The stiff disdainful pronoun, the third of the singular, with which great people were accustomed to speak to tradesmen and servants, is going out of fashion.

Strangers are readily associated with, and indeed sought after, and no introduction is wanted to make the most agreeable acquaintance. Taverns are frequented by the learned and the great, and you may become acquainted with some of the first men of the country at a table d'hote. Parents and children address each other freely and without reserve. Pleasing epithets are in common use. A husband, a wife, a relation, or friend, is seldom spoken to without the epithet My dear, or Beloved.

A stranger or acquaintance is soon called My dear, or My best friend. The Deity is rarely spoken of without some term of love. Such epithets, according to the laws of association, serve to produce in the minds of those who use them those gentle affections for which they stand. The people are made by them kinder to each other, and the Deity is stripped of half those terrors with which he has been clothed by an ambitious priesthood. Terms of endearment are, however, too often used without discrimination, and the affections are somewhat weakened by being spread alike over worthless and valuable objects.

I once called on a magistrate, and unthinkingly asked if Mr.___ was at home. Mr.___, the consistorial councillor, is not at home, was the stately reply of the servant. I resolved afterwards not to forget any person's title. This gentleman received me, however, without any ceremony whatever, and executed the little business I had with him with great dispatch. I have entered apartments, both as a stranger and as an acquaintance, when they were yet littered with the night-dress and breakfast apparatus, and when the persons were in their morning-gowns and slippers.

I had, on another occasion, to ask a magistrate for permission to see the workhouse of Hannover, and, while he regretted that other occupations prevented him accompanying me, he continued to regale himself with his pipe, and, very deliberately resting the bowl on the far side of his desk, he smoked on as he wrote me the permission.

The rulers of Germany, or their ministers, may have busied themselves, and have wrangled whether they should sit at feasts in arm-chairs or chairs without arms, but such follies have either not descended to the people, or are now entirely banished. There was a time when nobles and persons not noble never breathed the air of the same room, but as masters and servants; – when public places, such, for example, as the *Aue Garten* at Vienna, could be entered only by those persons who were enrolled in the College of Heralds. To this day an inscription remains at Herrenhausen, a seat of the King's close to Hannover, telling the citizens they are at liberty to sit on the benches round the large fountain, when the said benches are not required by strangers and people of distinction. The pride of the aristocracy may have excluded citizens from its parties, though this is not always the case, and never extends beyond their private circles.

In all public places, the mixture of all ranks, whatever may be their political names and privileges, is perfect. Persons of any one class are not to be distinguished, either in their manners or their dress, from those of any other, and this mixture compensates to the citizen for much of the nominal superiority of the noble. At the subscription reading-room in Hannover, before mentioned, the museum, which was frequented by several nobles, there appeared to be no other qualification required in the members, then that they were gentlemen, and of irreproachable character.

In this society the Lord-Chamberlain, the President of the Justice-Chancery, the Director of the High-School, the Inspector of the Seminary, pastors, advocates, army officers, amtmen, surgeons, all familiarly associated with each other. The nobles have a particular club, into which none but nobles are admitted; but in most of the towns of any importance there is a society like this, of which all gentlemen may be members. At public concerts, the best seats are sometimes kept for ladies, but the nobles at the same time stand, and speak, and mix with grocers, confectioners, and tinmen.

The nobles still keep political offices in their own hands; but that broad distinction of men into casts, of which we have heard so much, no longer exists. It may be doubted if the aristocracy of wealth, whose signs are so easily distinguished, be not now more punctual in its separation into castes than the aristocracy of birth. Certainly, if an individual of one caste glides into another caste, he only effects it by assuming the external marks of the caste into which he intrudes.  The distinctions of wealth are broader and more precise than those of birth, and, with all our democratic institutions and boasting, ours is the country of Europe in which there is the greatest inequality, and the most marked distinctions *between* men.[152]

A ceremonious manner of writing, somewhat similar to that of speaking, is also common to the Germans.  They pay a vast deal of attention to give each other all sorts of pleasing and meritorious titles; such as well-born, or high-born, or high and well born, with all the possible distinctions of birth.  A polite and friendly invitation to visit a club or society addresses the stranger as a highly-prized, most estimable, and honourable gentleman.  Our language has scarcely any corresponding terms to those of *Hochfürstliche*, *Allerdurchlauchtigste*, *Grossmächtigsle*, *Allergnädigste*, &c. &c. which are used in addressing the mighty sovereigns of 20,000 men, and of £5,000 revenue *per annum*.

*Divorces sued out in the Consistorium at Hannover by Inhabitants of the Counties of*

| In the Years | Kalenberg and Göttingin. | | Grubenhagen | | Lüneberg | | Hoya | |
|---|---|---|---|---|---|---|---|---|
| | Full di-vorce | Sepa-ration | Full di-vorce | Sepa-ration | Full di-vorce | Sepa-ration | Full di-vorce | Sepa-ration |
| 1790 | 11 | 2 | 2 | | 5 | 2 | 1 | |
| 1791 | 11 | 12 | 3 | 2 | 14 | 9 | 1 | |
| 1792 | 27 | 12 | 3 | 1 | 22 | 18 | 8 | 4 |
| 1793 | 18 | 10 | | 1 | 18 | 15 | 2 | 1 |
| 1794 | 15 | 14 | 1 | | 14 | 16 | 2 | 1 |

The numbers are couples.  The first columns contain those who are wholly divorced; the second those who have a separate maintenance.  The list is taken from Jacobi and Kant's *Annals of Brunswick Lüneburg*.  From the same work I learn that the number of applications for divorce, in the quarter of the year beginning

---

[152] **Hodgskin's F/N:-** Since this was written, I read, in a military journal, a sort of correspondence between a colonel of the army and a respectable tradesman, in which the former, prouder of the tinsel with which another man decorated him when he was made a soldier, than of the dignity which his Creator bestowed on him when he was made man, refused to sit at table with the latter, because he "would not level all the distinctions of society."  The German nobles may call bauers and journeymen tradesmen ill names, but it is believed no instance of such aristocratical disdain of one decent man for another can be met with in that country.

Easter 1793, was 54. In the last quarter of the same year the number was 48. In the quarter beginning Easter in the year 1795, the number of applications was 53. I have met no later records of this kind, in consequence of this work not being further carried on. There is some reason, however, to believe, that the numbers have not since then decreased.

I have given this list of divorces, though rather old, as a sort of document relative to the domestic morality of the people. I should suppose, considering the number of people, that the number of divorces is great. Compared with our own country, they can only be considered as an evidence of the less expence of a divorce in Germany than in Britain; and, probably, that the marriage tie is somewhat less strictly regarded, where the sanction both of government and of religion must be added to that of nature, than it is with us, who need only the sanction of religion. There it has been doubly fortified; both the priest and the king must confirm the impulse of nature and the affections of the heart, or their gratification remains unholy.

The quantity of divorces is perhaps not an accurate criterion for judging of the character of the intercourse of the sexes, for who can tell how many intrigues never end in divorce? Individual experience is also of no use. It may be so much the measure of the individual's power to please as of frailty. It can also be rarely had recourse to, for there is no worse traitor than he who exposes to public scorn the face that was hid in his own bosom. The opinion of the Germans, so far as it has been gathered from the writings of their authors, from their conversation, and from the manner in which people guilty of *faux pas* are treated in society, appears to be by no means favourable to the encouragement of chastity.

Marriage is generally a contract for an establishment in which affection has no share, and in which fidelity is not one of the stipulations. At the age of thirty, when the round of libertinism has been beaten, if a man have any property, he thinks it right to secure an heir to it, and looks about for the most convenient wife, according to his circumstances. He asks her of her parents; her heart has no share in the choice. She is bestowed as a present. She is thus taught to undervalue all she has to give, and she is ever afterwards ready to bestow it on whoever may have a better claim, by pleasing herself. It is the men of Germany who have degraded the women by making a property of them, and they have no right to complain.

There is hardly any part of Germany in which public women, except those of the very lowest description, can be distinguished from other women, till darkness permits a more open display of the signs of their avocations.  Their trade does not seem necessarily connected, as in our country, with numerous other vices.  Public opinion does not banish them into corners, nor doom them to bear any conspicuous marks of guilt, and they have no occasion to assume a hardened impudence or have recourse to drunkenness to stifle shame.  The distinction between public women and other females seemed stronger in Hannover than in most other parts of Germany.

They are there few, and in general distinguished by a flaming vulgarity of dress and rouged faces.  For concealed dissoluteness it is like other places.  At one end of the Kalenberg Street there always sat rather a nice-looking girl selling fruit and cakes.  This was the visible means she had of getting a livelihood, what she presented to the police as her occupations, and to her neighbours as her character.  Her invisible occupations, her hidden sale, were something different.  She was seen, towards evening, accompanied by a child, walking in the different streets, giving signs to whoever, she thought likely to attend to them.  It is a notorious fact, that, among the higher classes, a want of reputation does not exclude women from society.  This is also true of the middling classes.  At balls I have seen young women who were described as of very doubtful reputation, and, in a private circle of the middling classes, in which were mothers and daughters of unblemished fame, a lady and her daughter were pointed out to me, the former of which was notoriously kept by a man not her husband, who was at the same time said to be the lover of her daughter.  His appearance was almost a security for any lady's reputation.  It was natural to ask how he could succeed.  He was rich, and the women here, as in other places, can give themselves up to dotage and ugliness for fine clothes, gay ornaments, and the miserable gratification of their vanity.

> "Maidens, like moths, are ever caught by glare,
> And Mammon wins his way where seraphs might despair."[153]

From such a fact, and from the facts that parents talk of such things before their daughters, as mere matter of amusement, without reprobating them, much more may be inferred of the state of morals than from any accurate enumeration of divorces, or from any single anecdotes of intrigue.  No person would have dared to venture into such a society with a torn coat or a dirty gown.  These ladies and their paramour would not have intruded in a morning-

---

[153] **Editor's F/N:- These** two lines are from Canto I, Stanza 9 of Byron's poem *Childe Harold's Pilgrimage* (1812).

dress, but they come clothed in all the deformities of vice; and when these are not reprobated, there is a great chance they will be practised. When the chaste and the unchaste are equally admitted into every society, and are equally honoured and respected, there are no other motives for chastity than what may be derived from bodily temperament.

There are some virtues possessed by the women of the north of Germany which must be here remembered, that it may not be thought they are worse than they are. From the good education which is common to all classes, you find females in the middling ranks of life, who have read, in the original language, and justly appreciated, most of our celebrated works. Walter Scott, Miss Edgeworth, and Lord Byron are known to them without the help of translations. There are few English ladies who can say as much of those works of Goethe and Schiller, of which they, however, speak very fluently. It is not uncommon to meet, among the females of the middling classes, many who not only know and practise music, but who are also acquainted with both the language and literature of France and England. Many of them are also good housewives, the managers of the kitchen and the seamstresses of the family. The education of the higher classes is equally attended to, though they necessarily follow the fashion, by seeking, in amusement and dissipation, that forgetfulness of care which other people find in their necessary employments.

It is probably owing to their excellent education that the ladies, finding amusement in literature, have not yet reached that extreme point of civilization at which nothing is regarded as of any value but sumptuous dresses and superb furniture. A love for ostentation is rapidly increasing in Germany, but it does not seem to have reached so far as to suppress in the heart every other affection. They have not yet arrived at the most glorious practical conclusion, that man is nothing to his house, and that he may be sacrificed, provided it glitters with polished ornaments and shining furniture. Finding amusement in their books and music, it does not seem to be necessary to their bliss to condemn a large number of immortal beings to degradation, that their rooms may be resplendent and be admired.

The Germans have a method of hawking their affections in public, which robs them of much of their sanctity and holiness. There is a mawkish display of love between persons of different sexes that is rather indelicate and disgusting. In both public and private rooms, when other persons have been present, I have seen husbands kiss and fondle their wives, and young men bestow those caresses which are better reserved for secrecy. This probably gives them a reputation for unchastity which they do not deserve.

The manner in which baptisms, marriages, and deaths are announced, seems to partake of this character of publicity. Such events are officially notified by the parties themselves. A man informs the public and his friends, through the medium of a newspaper, "that his wife yesterday added to his happiness by presenting him with a boy, who remains, with his mother, in perfect health." – "We hereby," says a newly-married couple, "inform our friends that our marriage was consummated on the 29th day of last month." A widow advertises;

> "that the death of my beloved husband, Daniel Leibgot Rau, from apoplexy, on the 28th of October, has inflicted great sorrow on me and on my young daughter. I make this heart-rending death hereby known to my friends, and I beg their silent pity. I continue the occupations of my husband and solicit all those who honoured him with their custom to continue the same favour to me. His last poem, on the Centenary of the Reformation, that was printing at his death, is now to be had of me. – 12th of November 1817."

The regulations of the police, also, have some influence on this part of the character of the people. They oblige every man to notice every alteration in his family to it. When a child is born to him, or one dies, or he brings home a wife, or discards a mistress, he must give official notice of the alteration in the number of his family to the police.

This seems to be treating men something like beasts, in whom their rulers have a property. Our best affections are degraded to a level with a partnership in trade, or a common mercantile speculation. To gratify the impertinent curiosity of the magistrate or his nonsensical regulations, neither the griefs nor the joys of the heart are allowed to be secret and sacred. They must all be open to his inspection and registered in his book. The art, or science, or craft, or knavery, whichever it may be, of government, considers man as a sort of machine, that can be wound up, and made to point with its index to some events the magistrate wishes to be acquainted with.

# Chapter XIV.

## Alteration of Morals.

*Are the morals of the Germans deteriorated? –
Influence of the immorality of sovereigns. – Murder
of Count Königsmark – Former state of sexual
intercourse. – State of morals according to
Riesebeck. – German morals improved. – Source of
the opinion that they have deteriorated.*

It is very generally asserted, that the French Revolution, and the irruption of the French armies into Germany, have done a serious injury to the morals of the Germans. The same effect has been said to have been produced in other countries; and nearly all the existing immorality of Europe is now charged, by certain classes of society, on that single event. From the instances which have been already mentioned of improvements in Germany, as to punishments, as to toleration, as to education, as to the situation of the peasants, and as to the intercourse between the different classes of society, it appears doubtful if the fact of a deterioration of morals amongst the Germans be, on the whole, true. The assertion is, however, one of so much importance, that it deserves further consideration.

In respect of public opinion, the Germans have most rapidly improved since that period. It is only since then that there has been either a public or public opinion in Germany. This latter is the great means of modifying our passions, and directing our pursuits; and, in proportion as it is correct, so the virtues of any people will be great. To suppose that, when a whole nation take part in examining and making laws, it will not be better regulated than when laws are made by one person only, is to suppose that the wisdom of the whole race is not equal to the wisdom of the smallest of its parts. The many causes which, under the name of Government, have an influence on the morality of a nation, make it a matter of certainty that every nation will be virtuous in proportion as it is rationally governed. Since public opinion has grown powerful in Germany, its various governments have improved, and they who make the sweeping assertion, that the morals of the people are corrupted, must keep all the influence of this powerful cause entirely out of view.

Forty years ago, the sovereigns of Germany sold their people for soldiers to any person who would buy them. It is yet barely possible that the inhabitants of Hannover may be compelled to fight in the cause of Britain; but so strongly is the opinion of the Germans now set against the sovereigns selling them like slaves, that they will never again be subjected to anything so infamous.  Neither the inhabitants of Brunswick nor of Cassel will, in future, be sent to subdue the freemen of America, that the debts of one sovereign may be paid with the price of their blood, and a palace built for the other.  That the Germans have thought with shame on this part of their situation, and have thought of it, resolved to bear it no longer, is evident from a thousand passages in modern authors.  I shall quote one whose authority is greater than the newspapers of the day, in which the subject has been often alluded to.

> "Amidst the tears and complaints of parents, relations, and sweethearts, the hired soldiers left their paternal homes to reduce a people who were called rebels to obedience. The lamentations of their wives and children only increased as their absence was longer, till many of the former found consolation in the arms of another man. Many a soldier on his return found his wife an adulteress, his children neglected and sunk in vice, his little property in the hands of usurers, and his name a prey to calumny. Many quitted their homes with hope, but all returned sorrowful.  It was said they were sacrificed for the good of their country, but it received no benefit from an expedition that, even in the annals of war, was covered with shame. These sufferings, also, are past, and will never return. Never again will German blood be shed in foreign countries, as it has been, for the interest of English merchants."[154]

We learn, from the same author, that the government of Brunswick, towards the year 1767, placed some kind of receptacles, like the lions' mouths at Venice, on all public places, for the purpose of receiving secret denunciations.  This is a sort of bribery to vice which the governments of Germany will not now dare publicly to adopt.   They may keep their police-spies, they may receive information in secret, and reward the bringer, but they will not again publicly invite men to be traitors to one another.

Prior to the French Revolution, the Germans were notorious for rudeness and incivility.  Baron Riesebeck, for example, speaks of the brutal conduct of Austrian soldiers to passengers on the Danube.  I travelled the same route; and, though we were often

---

[154] **Hodgskin's F/N:-** Venturini, Vol. IV. p. 583.

obliged to stop, I never saw anything like incivility. Yet I had some companions who sometimes rather invited it by their own presumption. Two or three instances of amicable politeness have been mentioned; and, during my whole stay in Germany, I never experienced rudeness or incivility but once, and it was partly occasioned by my own conduct.

Some few years ago, excessive drinking, and, indeed, drunkenness, were very common in the north of Germany. I hardly ever saw a drunken man, and never one drunken woman. The people have changed the beer they used to drink for spirits, but drunkenness is much less frequent than formerly.

We learn from Dr. Burney's *Travels*[155] (p.331-332, Vol. I.) what the amusements of the people of Vienna were prior to the French Revolution. The barbarous diversions which are there described are now changed for round-abouts, swings, feats of horsemanship, and conjuring: and brutality does not now extend beyond a bull-bait.

The principal point of complaint, however, is the attachment of women to luxury and finery, and the looseness of their morals. I know not what sort of consciences our countrywomen must have if the first of these actions of which the Germans are accused be a crime; for they are far surpassed by our more luxurious ladies. I am also at a loss to tell what criminality there is in wearing silk more than woollen, or in using mahogany chairs instead of fir-planks for seats. There seems to be no scale yet invented by which the respective atrocities of coloured woods and satins are accurately marked; and therefore, I cannot decide on the criminality of the Germans in this point.

> There is, however, a great alteration in their manners and morals. "Here in our country," says the historian,[156] "throughout the whole of the sixteenth century, the household of our prince was regulated like an ordinary house. His wife and daughters took the whole under their care, knew how to make excellent soup, were not afraid of the kitchen-smoke, – and sometimes, as the wife of Julius the Duke of Wolfenbüttel, they even made the medicines for the court dispensary. The daughters were obliged to spin and sew; and, on pain of punishment, they dared not read love romances. They were called misses, ("*Jung fern*,") or, at most, ladies, ("*Fraulein*,") and their noble

---

[155] **Editor's F/N:-** Dr. Charles Burney's *Continental Travels*, 1770-1772.
[156] **Editor's F/N:-** Presumably Venturini, as he is elsewhere referred to as "the historian" see subsequent footnote (154).

companions were called maids of honour. Nobody in those days would like to be called lady of the bed-chamber, (*Kammer-Jungfer*, or *Kammer Fraulein*.) That was a disgraceful name. It was too well known what took place with ladies in bed chambers."

"The mothers of our sovereigns," (he speaks of our own royal family,) "carefully attended themselves to the piety, cleanliness, and conduct of their children. The girls were obliged to say grace at meals; and even Erich II. after he was sovereign, was obliged to do this. The princess was called housewife (*Hausfrau*) and landlady, (*Wirthin*.) She slept with her husband in one bed, and everything had its proper name."

Since then a great alteration has taken place in the manners, both of the sovereigns and of the people. We find the first traces and causes of this in sending the young men to see the world, who carried back to Germany the outward polish of the despotic French court, and its inward corruptions. The princess was obliged to leave the bed of her husband, unless she would share it with his mistress. He had adopted the French practice of keeping one. It was this importation of foreign manners, by the sovereigns of the country, and their pernicious example, which gradually led to the corruption of the people. Love or gallantry allowed some women to rule over many of the countries of Germany; and the more sober part of the community imitated the vices of their rulers, and contemned the housewife conduct, which they saw despised by them.

It is not a very pleasing thing to rake up the tales of scandal which have been told of the sovereigns of Germany for the last two centuries; but it is right to remind the reader of them, and of the possible influence which they may have had on the manners of the people. It is impossible to overlook the fact, that many of the vices of Europe are caused by the reverence of its inhabitants for its sovereigns. When they, and their flatterers, and partizans, are constantly calumniating nature and the race of mankind, in order to justify, by our immoralities and vices, their claim to our more implicit submission, it is right, when it can be done with justice, to retort these calumnies on their heads; and to show, if it be possible, that many of our vices are the result of our reverence for them, and that, whatever they have of virtue, they derive from the influence of the public over them.

At the latter end of the seventeenth century, Ernest Augustus, the father of George I., and George I. himself before the death of his father, both kept mistresses, who were sisters. Both had wives at the same time living, and both publicly neglected them. The wife of George I., irritated by this neglect, entered into some sort of intrigue with the Count of Königsmark: it was discovered – she was confined for life – and the Count was executed in a manner that the historian calls murderous; and George, shortly afterwards, consoled himself in the arms of another mistress.[157]  Such was the altered conduct of the sovereigns; and this was undoubtedly one cause for the alteration in the conduct and morality of the people.

Other sovereigns of Germany were not better.  The celebrated Augustus of Saxony, at the same period, kept a large seraglio, and lived in open incest with his daughter, who boasted of sharing her happiest moments with her own brother.  The electors of Bavaria hung the portraits of their mistresses in the halls of their palace for the admiration of strangers.[158]

The morals of the sixteenth century were probably better than the morals at the beginning of the French Revolution; but that event has rather improved than deteriorated them.  It frightened sovereigns and made them pay attention to their conduct.  It taught them that they do not reign by any divine right, but by the sufferance of the people; and they must take care not to outrage their feelings if they wish to retain their situations.  No sovereign of Germany will now dare to behave as Augustus of Saxony did; and if anyone should execute a man in the dark, as Ernest Augustus had Count Königsmark executed, he would be most certainly execrated as a monster.  The personal crimes of Buonaparte were not half so flagrant as those of these sovereigns; and, owing to the improved morality of the world, they hurled him from his throne, and banished him from society.

There are many circumstances which prove that the commerce of the sexes was not very moral in Germany prior to the French Revolution, and that the chastity of the females was not very great. It has long been customary there for fathers or brothers to select husbands for their daughters or sisters.  This custom remains to this day.  The husbands are selected by other people, and naturally the ladies select their lovers themselves.  Acting on such a principle vitiates the engagement of marriage from its outset.  For an attachment to be permanent and moral, it must begin in inclination, and be confirmed by habit and constant intercourse.

---

[157] **Hodgskin's F/N:-** For the whole of this beautiful specimen of monarchical morality, see Venturini, Vol. III. p.621; Vol. IV. p.59-63.
[158] **Hodgskin's F/N:-** Riesebeck's *Travels,* Letter 8th.

To substitute for these the mere ceremony of marriage, and to expect to ensure fidelity by unmeaning forms, is something like expecting to supply the place of appetite and digestion by the grace before dinner. Wherever any foreign and artificial sanction is substituted for the affections of the heart, there the morality of the sexual intercourse is assuredly not great.

The manner in which Frederick the Great of Prussia prostituted his subjects to one another, when he thought it would procure him tall grenadiers, is notoriously known. At present, also, the sanction of the magistrate is substituted for the natural reasons for marrying: and all that ought to be holy in affection is made to give way to his views of political economy or state-craft.

Another class of men, whose actions have had a great influence on society, is the clergy. Since the Reformation in Germany, since they lost their power and wealth, their conduct has been exemplary. In the fourteenth century, they are described as keeping mistresses with their natural children in their houses; and then the whole of the convents were considered as so many brothels. To send a woman to a convent was synonymous to making her a prostitute.[159]

To show what morals formerly were, I may quote some other passages from the same historian and from Spittler. In the same century the art of wooing and winning was unknown, and the laws were not directed against the passion which was mutually gratified; but against violence and rape, which were then frequent.[160] Women were then stolen like cattle, and the embraces, even of noble ladies, were bestowed as a reward for dexterity. At the famous groel-feast at Brunswick, the best marksman was rewarded with a handsome woman.[161]

Prostitutes were publicly licensed. What should we think of *licensing*[162] assassins? And one may, with as much propriety, be licensed as another. Some public ladies of that day dwelt in the Red Convent, in the Wall Street, at Brunswick; and the common

---

[159] **Hodgskin's F/N:-** Venturini, Vol. III. p.414,415.

[160] **Hodgskin's F/N:-** Spittler, Vol. I. p.58.

[161] **Hodgskin's F/N:-** Venturini.

[162] **Hodgskin's F/N:-** To lay a tax on any occupation, makes it legal to the mind of the person who pursues it, as well as to the community. And, in France, where prostitutes are taxed, it is not uncommon for these unhappy beings publicly to defend their trade by saying they have paid the tax. Surely the governments of the world have to answer for the greatest part of the immorality of nations.

executioner levied the tax which they paid for the exercise of their trade.[163]

At every former period, the same complaints were made of luxury which are made at present; and it and the growing prosperity of the people seem to have attained their height just before the thirty years' war. That checked both prosperity and luxury; for at that period the power of the monarchs became fully established, and liberty was gradually destroyed. The morals of the Germans in those days, which are called chivalrous, appear to have been no better than the morals of the rest of Europe. That age has only been praised, because the violence of passion was taken for the energy of virtue, or the glare of putrefaction for the animation of life.

That the state of morals was not very pure in Germany immediately prior to the French Revolution, may be argued from the sort of morality which is displayed in German literature. Marriage is seldom regarded in it as sacred; nor are the utmost excesses of the passion of love ever treated as criminal. Some young men may be occasionally found in every society who coquet with their own affections, and with the affections of females; but when they confess to the public, in manhood, having done so in youth – when they confess this without offering any apology – when it can no longer gratify their vanity – and when they speak of it as a sort of joke – it is clear they must feel and know that it accords with the manners of the public to which they address themselves. Goethe has done this in his memoirs;[164] and he there confesses, without any shame as a man, that, as a boy, he should have been proud if he could have proved that he was the bastard descendant of a nobleman, though it was only to be attained by the adultery of one of his female ancestors.

An equally discreditable story is told of Bürger. His own wife was unfaithful to him, and he is said to have lived in adultery with her sister, and to have afterwards married her. It might have been expected that he would have been desirous to let the world forget the whole adventure; but he has taken care to excite its attention to it by his *Hohe Lied von der Einzigen*.[165] And he has, in that, endeavoured to console her by calling the reproaches thrown on her conduct "vulgar blasphemy." It is a tolerable measure of the virtue of the people, that this conduct subjected Bürger to their reproaches, though they were not severe enough to prevent him

---

[163] **Hodgskin's F/N:-** Venturini, Vol. II, p.194,195.

[164] **Hodgskin's F/N:-** Aus meinem Leben, Vol. I. p. 160-170, 151.

[165] **Editor's F/N:-** Translates as *High song of the only one.*

endeavouring to change them to a matter of triumph. They rather laughed at than scorned him. They reproached, but did not reject, him; and he continued to live in the same society as before.

Individual sentiments, extracted from comedies of other works, may frequently be considered as caricatures; but they are very generally founded in some facts. Schiller, in his *Kabal und Liebe*, makes one of the chief officers of a German court say to his secretary,

> "What consequence is it to you whether you receive your ducat fresh from the mint, or from a banker's? Console yourself by the example of the nobility; with or without knowledge, there is seldom a marriage concluded amongst us without at least half-a-dozen of the guests or attendants being able to judge exactly of the paradise of the bridegroom."

Though such sentiments may not be strictly true, they make the following anecdotes and assertions probable.

When Joseph II. was recommended to set apart a place for courtesans, to which they should be confined, he replied he had nothing to do but draw a cordon round the whole city of Vienna; for he believed it did not contain one honest woman. In Baron Riesebeck's *Travels*, Letter 8th, the reader may see a confirmation of this opinion of Joseph's. The passage is too long to quote; but I am persuaded, bad as the morals of that city may be at present, they are not worse now than they were then. The same author says the canons of Augsburgh purchased the daughters of the citizens by dozens every year.[166]

Noblemen procured their own female relations as mistresses for monarchs, that they might rule in their counsels.[167] Of this there are numerous examples. In Bavaria, he says, "Every noble kept his mistress; the rest of the people indulged in promiscuous love; and the whole country was the greatest brothel of Europe."[168]

This sort of vice still thrusts itself on the notice of the traveller, but it is certainly now less than it was as described by the Baron.

> "If the females of Salzburgh," he says, "are disposed to make a lover happy, neither the shame of an illegitimate

---

[166] **Hodgskin's F/N:-** Letter 6.
[167] **Hodgskin's F/N:-** Letter 10,
[168] **Hodgskin's F/N:-** Letter 11.

birth, nor the fear of being obliged to maintain a child, is of any consequence to them. Custom sets them above the first, and they disregard the other. A peasant seldom forsakes his girl, particularly after having two or three children by her, if he can marry her."[169]

In truth, it has long been customary in Germany not to look on children born out of marriage (*Kinder der Liebe*) in an opprobrious manner. The very name (*children of love*) is something very different from bastards. A *Bey Schläferinn*, or woman who sleeps with a man without the ceremony of marriage, and though the connection is only to last for a convenient season, is never regarded in any other light than as an amiable pleasure.

Again, Riesebeck says, "He found, at every place, in his voyage down the Danube, women waiting at the inns, who seemed ready for more services than one." On this point, there seems no alteration. He describes the manners of Cologne as most licentious, and concludes thus:–

"The evening services of the monks are like the evening walks in the suburbs of Vienna; and every ale-house round the place teems with adultery and fornication. If you happen to go into them of a holiday, you will commonly find the visitors in such a state of drunkenness as exactly reminds you of the old Germans and Scythians." [170]

These remarks apply principally to the south of Germany; and, as this author nowhere mentions the character of the females of the north, but, in his 44th Letter, where he praises the Saxon women, and, in his 55th Letter, where he insinuates something not very chaste of the inhabitants of the neighbourhood of Hamburg, it would not be right to extend his remarks to the people of the north of Germany. But, from the conduct of the sovereigns, – from the facts quoted of a former period, – from the general character of the writings of Germany, – from the list of divorces which has been given, and from the number of natural children born at a former period, – there is reason to conclude the morals of the people of the north were not much better than those of the south.

The second point of accusation, namely, a fondness for prodigality and luxury, may also be traced to sovereigns having adopted splendour and extravagance to distinguish them from the rest of the society. It is the imitation of their corrupting example

---

[169] **Hodgskin's F/N:-** Letter 15.
[170] **Hodgskin's F/N:-** Riesebeck, Letter 67.

which has created all which is wrong in these desires. They exist in a still more reprehensible degree among people who have always treated French principles with the greatest disdain, and whom French armies have never visited but as prisoners; but who have always been governed, like the Germans, by monarchs who thought splendour necessary to their trade. The wasteful extravagance of princes exciting imitation is a constant, existing, and proximate cause for their subjects to be wasteful and extravagant; and it is most absurd to charge such conduct on the presence of the French armies.

So far as I know, the taste for finery and luxury is never condemned but in the poorer people. In the rich, particularly when it is directed to statues, paintings, and music, it is much honoured. The taste itself prompts the poorer classes to industry and ingenuity. Corrected by general opinion, it leads only to an increase of comfort and enjoyment; and it only corrupts men when the extravagance of princes is made the rule of society.

Germany has always been overrun with soldiers, and there is no reason to believe that a revolutionary Frenchman could commit more violence, or set a worse example, than the Uhlans, Croats, Hungarians, and Germans, who have, from time immemorial, devastated and plundered Germany. There can be no doubt that war and large armies, supported by the industry of other men, and corrupting the morals of women for want of better occupation, are very great causes for vice. But these are causes which have always existed in Germany. The princes have always kept large armies, and Germans have always made war on Germans. The French Revolution, and the overwhelming power of France, have, for the first time, made the Germans unite as a power; and wars amongst themselves will excite so much horror in future, that they will ultimately cease altogether. If it were for a moment allowed that the presence of the French armies had corrupted the females, what sort of virtue can be ascribed to them when they thus gave themselves up to the invaders and oppressors of their country? Had they not previously been corrupt in principle, the French, gay and gallant as they are, would have found a different reception.

On the whole, therefore, it appears that the Germans are improving in morality, and improving very rapidly. There is, at the same time, an abundance of proofs that they were improving before the French Revolution. That event gave a fresh impulse to their minds, but was, at the same time, connected with many impediments to improvement. It was followed by long and destructive wars. But the lovers of legitimacy have the sin of these wars to answer for as much as the lowers of revolution. The monarchs were rather more guilty than the people.

The very great improvements which the Germans have made, are, in some measure, the causes why some of them are of opinion that their morals are corrupted. The improvements are changes, and, as men generally assume their own habits and manners as the criterion of perfection, there are very few who do not regard every change as a deviation from right. The wealth and increased importance which the poorer classes have acquired in Germany, have enabled them to vie in comfort and prodigality with those who formerly considered themselves as their superiors.

Philosophy regards the increase of the poorer classes in knowledge, and the greatest possible approximation to equality in society, as the surest means of promoting the happiness of all. But those persons who have been accustomed to despise all the pleasures of a free interchange of sentiment, and knowledge, and services, between equals, and to place all their happiness in having their wants provided for by unremunerated and trembling slaves, – who look on a great portion of mankind as destined to toil for their benefit, regard every alteration in society which tends to elevate the poorer classes to an equality with them, as fraught with evil, and they name every such alteration a departure from morality.

Such persons describe the present artificial distinctions of society as necessary to the happiness of all, and they not only spurn at every enjoyment which is inconsistent with their habitual worship of the idol their forefathers set up, but they sacrifice mankind to their idolatry. Artificial distinctions between men are diminishing in Germany, and all those persons whose importance was chiefly derived from these distinctions, cry aloud in the world that the society is corrupted. Their power and superiority rest on no merits of their own, but on the unreasonable submission of other men, and, prompted by a base selfishness, they name every diminution of this submission immorality and vice. According to their view, morality consists in quietly submitting to misery if it be inflicted according to law, and every attempt which men make to escape from this legitimately inflicted misery is stigmatized as immoral.

The French Revolution is one of the most conspicuous series of events of modern times, and it is contaminated with many great atrocities; but some of the principles which were loudly published in a moment of freedom, gave an impulse to a spirit of inquiry and a desire for liberty which before existed, that bid fair ultimately to put an end to every species of bad government. Those atrocities may be chiefly ascribed to the corrupting influence of that wretched government, and that miserable superstition which had long substituted in France their own despicable mummeries for the natural reasons why men should be moral. As these mummeries were founded in error, they necessarily came to be despised, and those who had built their power on them were the first and the chief victims of the delusions they had so long upheld.

The partizans of legitimate misrule, and the lovers of the artificial distinctions of society, fixed their attention only on the atrocities, and they sought the support of the virtuous part of mankind, by stoutly affirming that all these atrocities were occasioned by a mere attempt to get rid of their systems. They have everywhere affirmed that the world was growing immoral, and that this immorality was all occasioned by the French Revolution, – as if drunkenness, fornication, and thieving, were first known within a quarter of a century. The horrors of that Revolution have been made the defence of present errors and are to be the bugbear of future generations. Wherever men seek to improve the laws of their country, they are held up, like a gorgon's head, to terrify them from alteration.

The Germans, like other people, have acquiesced in the assertions of those who have affirmed that the destruction of their own power is ruin to the happiness of society, because all men are willing to believe that every evil they suffer is caused by some extraordinary event rather than by their own conduct. To suppose that evil is caused by those social regulations which men prize as the highest effort of human wisdom, would imply that they were both deluded and guilty in submitting to them. And they therefore seek a cause for their misery in some single event, in some change of government in a distant country, or in the influence of the stars, rather than confess, even to themselves, that it is occasioned by their own unworthy submission to systems which have substituted the will of one man, the decrees of a few men, or the ceremonies of priests, for the natural and unchangeable reasons why one line of conduct should be preferred to another. So far as these systems could effect it, they have made some of the worst of our species the patterns of imitation, and the criterions of virtue. And their long continuance, not a momentary attempt to abolish them, must be considered as the true cause for much of the vice and misery which have long existed in the world.

The morals of a nation cannot be suddenly changed or destroyed by any single event. It requires time to make any considerable alteration in them. Nothing is more certain than opinions and habits of action descend from parents to children, subject only to little improvements. No miraculous change ever has, or ever can take place, in the conduct of a whole nation, and he who at tributes the immorality of any people to a single event, not only rejects the evidence of a regular government in the moral world, which every day brings before him, but also all the evidence of history.

The moral laws of nature are as regular and unalterable as her physical laws. He who has so beautifully constructed our bodies, has not left our conduct, on which our happiness depends, to be regulated by chance. The power which governs the world is not a sanguinary tyrant, who delights, by momentary and unexpected storms, to blight the best hopes of mankind. Regular laws are established in the moral world, and we have a capacity to discover them, and so to regulate our conduct by them, that we may diminish or destroy every species of evil. Patience disarms pain of its sting, foresight prevents calamity, and knowledge, as it advances, seems so to direct our passions, that they all work together for good. It was no momentary change in the government of France which made the mob of Paris into monsters. They were as much delighted when they shouted with joy at Lally's execution as when they exalted on their pikes the head of the Princess Lamballe. It was not the sudden irruption of the French armies into Germany, nor was it the wars which followed the French Revolution, which occasioned any corruptions which may exist in the morals of the Germans. Such as they are so they have been, with some gradual improvements, for ages past. And whatever there is in them of evil must be attributed to some long-existing cause, such as their governments, and not to any momentary and single event.

The few general remarks which my residence in Germany taught me to make are now concluded, and I shall terminate the work with an account of my journey to Frankfort.

# Chapter XV.

## Cassel and Frankfort,

*Cassel; situation. – Wilhelms Höhe, date of its improvements; paid for by the blood of the Hessians. – The Museum – Examples of the absurdities of learning. – Difference between Cassel and Hannover. – Fritzlar. – A tar on travellers. – Marburg – Giessen – Wetzlar. – Frankfort. – Fair. – Musicians.*

Cassel is only a few hours' walk from Münden,[171] and I arrived there at noon on September 3rd, 1818. It had rained extremely hard during the night, and the morning had the fresh cold feel of Autumn. Towards mid-day the weather became warm, and the palaces of Cassel, as I approached it, gleamed glorious in the sun. The outspread plain at the extremity of which it is situated was yet bright with newly-reaped corn fields. The Fulda, clear and bright with several tributary rivulets, was flowing at its foot, and the dark wood covered hills in the back-ground, made its buildings whiter and more glancing. The plain was thickly studded with villages and single houses, and the peasant, proud of a rich crop, was carrying home the last produce of his field.

Few towns, indeed, are more beautifully situated than Cassel. It lies at the eastern foot of some commanding, well-wooded, and beautiful hills, and overlooks a fertile well cultivated plain. Nothing, however, commanded my attention so much as the palace, situated on a hill above the town, and, not knowing what it was, I inquired of a peasant. "That," he said, "was the Wilhelms Höhe." – "But the building at the very top of the hill? – What is that which is seen from so far?" – "Oh, that is the Great Christ." I then knew it was the celebrated copy of the Farnesian Hercules, which the Landgraf Charles caused to be erected in the beginning of the last century.

The peasantry, however, have given their prince credit for a reverence for their own religion rather than for the mythology of the

---

[171] **Hodgskin's F/N:-** See Vol. I. p. 336.
**[Editor's F/N:-** This page makes no reference to Münden. It would seem that page 364 in the original edition was the correct page – this equates to page 204 in these *Collected Works* version.]

ancient world. They have transformed the son of Jupiter into their own Saviour, and they venerate the piety, as they record, with marks of wonder, the power of their sovereign.

After seeking, in Cassel, during the early part of the day, for any political or statistical works relative to Hesse Cassel, none of which I could find, except a Court Calendar, I strolled alone to the Wilhelms Höhe. This is the place which every stranger is most desirous to see. On Mondays, Wednesdays, and Fridays, all the fountains, cascades, and other rattles of this monarch's bauble, are made to spout and tumble for the amusement of the infant, or, as the Germans more pompously call it, the great public – *des grosseren Publicum*.

It is only on one of these days that this royal plaything can be seen to advantage, and then it is visited by many parties, who come to Cassel for no other purpose than to see and admire it. There is nothing in the north of Germany more praised than it. It is thought to do honour to the taste and genius of the whole country. Every German appears to be enraptured with it, and when I sometimes attempted to laugh at the trifles they frequently described, I was assured I should change my opinion when I saw them. Perhaps I should, had I visited it in company with many other persons, and had I had a Cicerone[172] to marshal my thoughts into the common order. But I was alone, and rather prejudiced against the place, because I knew the price of many of its beauties had been paid with the blood of the Hessians.

It certainly is one of the handsomest palaces of Germany. Its situation, about three miles from Cassel, at a considerable elevation on the same hill at the foot of which the town itself stands and commanding a view of it and of all the surrounding country, is noble and grand. By it the hill, which is covered with fine woods, begins to rise more abruptly. It was made a charming spot by nature, and needed nothing from the labour of man but a few scattered flowers and tasteful bushes, and winding walks, easy of ascent, to have rendered it a fit place either for the residence of a prince, for the retirement of a philosopher, for the haunts of a poet, or for the exercise and health of the population of the neighbouring city.

I enjoyed the situation and the delightful evening when I visited it, but I looked on its numerous ornaments as the follies of a vitiated

---

[172] **Editor's F/N:-** Cicerone was an old term for a guide, one who conducts visitors and sightseers to museums, galleries, etc., and explains matters of archaeological, antiquarian, historic or artistic interest. Nowadays the term is used for a line of guidebook performing a similar purpose.

taste, and I was more displeased than amused by them  The sovereign and his architects, measuring the taste of mankind by their own taste, have converted this noble hill into a larger museum of monstrosities, and the attention of the people who go there is constantly turned from the admiration of nature to worship the petty wonders of mimic and useless art.  Some places are levelled into gardens, and others are hollowed into ponds; cascades tumble from artificial rocks, and fountains spout up in a wilder ness; old castles, newly built, to imitate ruins, in which all the arms and ornaments of the days of chivalry are collected to make up a goodly show, tower on the heights; and grottos of yesterday, to imitate the eternal caverns of the world, have been dug under every brow.

Homer's hell, all on fire, with Pluto and Proserpine, and the grim judges, with Cerberus threatened by Hercules, all as large as life, and as natural as they were ever seen in a penny show, ornament one spot.  Not far from it are the Fates and the Furies, with Orpheus and Eurydice, and all the gods, goddesses, thieves, and jades of the ancient mythology.  Giants are buried under rocks, and spout scorn and defiance against the heavens; water is made to turn organs, blow flutes, and sound trumpets, and to give forth all the sweet sounds which are supposed to be heard in Elysium.

The grotto of Neptune, in imitation of that of Tivoli, and Virgil's tomb; a Chinese village and a Swiss cow-house; the Devil's Bridge from St. Gothard's, and aqueducts from Rome; superb palaces, and numerous hermitages, are all crowded on this spot.  In short, there is nothing, either of fancy or of reality, either of ancient or modern art and poetry, of which some counterpart, or some imitation, does not deform this beautiful hill.  Taste looks at these disfigurements of nature with disdain, good sense deplores such a waste of labour for so perfectly childish an object, and philosophy execrates the whole, because it influences a trifling people to admire a magnificence that is purchased with their own degradation.

Most of these playthings were made by sovereigns who lent their armies to Great Britain.  They were, in fact, paid for by the bones and the blood of those Hessians who were sold by their *fathers*, – for so the sovereigns call themselves, – as soldiers, to put down freedom in America. It is left to nice casuists to determine, whether there be more guilt in buying or in selling men; but surely nothing but an utter forgetfulness of the fact, could save any man from the reproaches of his own conscience, who could look on this blood-bought splendour with any feeling but horror.  Yet men do look on it with rapture, and our modern Iscariots are prevented from hanging themselves, because they find a world to flatter, to imitate, and to worship them. But it is perhaps wrong thus to speak of the great; for he who ridicules their splendour, though it be bought by oppression, and their amusements, though they are childish and absurd, is known to weaken the claim they make to the respect of mankind, and he rebels against that authority to do mischief which they are said to derive from God. Such, however, were some of my reflections as I strolled through the beautiful gardens, and I felt no gratitude to the prince for any pleasure I enjoyed.

Some of the ornaments of the Wilhelms Höhe, particularly the water-works, were made in the beginning of the last century, but the new palace and the new old castle were built, and many of the other wonders were made, by the present sovereign, who began to reign in the year 1785. He inherited a large treasure from his father, the Landgraf *Frederic*, although he had always been a prince who loved pomp. But the historian accounts for his leaving this behind him by saying, "he had kept a large army on foot, the greater part of which was in the pay of Great Britain." The palace contains a number of pictures, most of which are the work of Tischbein; some few are by Böttner.

The new-town of Cassel, ornamented by the palaces of the sovereign and of his son, is well built. The streets are wide and well paved, and the Elector is about to make it still more magnificent by rebuilding the ancient residence of the Landgräves. The orangery, the park, and the walks, are all very fine, but Frederic's Square and Bellevue are the handsomest parts of the town. In the former stands a colossal statue, fifteen feet high, of the Landgraf Frederic, erected to his honour by the states of the country. It was the last work of a sculptor called the famous Nahl, and it is recorded, as something extraordinary, that for this work he received 1000 R. Thalers, about £160 Sterling. At one side of this square stands a superb palace built by Frederic. He was the father of the present Elector and reigned between the years 1760 and 1785; he was the great beautifier of Cassel; he loved magnificence and was a patron of the arts; he founded an academy for them, and an agricultural society, and he built the palace just mentioned, which is now named Frederic's Museum.

It contains a library, galleries of pictures, statues, urns, and antiques, collections of curious workmanship in ivory, of minerals, and insects, of medals, of mathematical and optical instruments, of old arms and armour, of figures in wax, *particularly all the family of Hesse Cassel, dressed in the very clothes they wore while living,* – of musical instruments, and, in short, there is an immense building full of all sorts of curiosities. Indeed, a museum means a collection of things that are of themselves of no value. They are full of the baubles of nature, or the remains of antiquity; they are of great use to idle men, by enabling them to pass their time without doing mischief, and they afford the rich a manner of disposing of their wealth somewhat less pernicious than gambling or debauchery. A few hours might be passed in them with pleasure, if doing so did not tend to encourage people to form them, and if they, too, were not a part of that splendour or dissipation in the rulers of nations, which the subjects are impoverished and oppressed to support.

On several occasions I have mentioned the taste for trifles and absurdities which yet so much distinguishes scientific Germans, that their country is sometimes called a madhouse of natural philosophers. This unhappy propensity has undoubtedly been invigorated by the honours bestowed on such pursuits by the numerous sovereigns of Germany.

At Cassel I was informed of a physician of Heidelberg, who, in the madness of scientific, or rather witchcraft experiments, prescribed human brains to be taken inwardly as a cure for violent fevers, and he had worked something like a wonder on his patients, probably by affecting their imagination. Another celebrated man had recently adapted the entrails of cats as a specific for all disorders. And a public newspaper, while it announced the death of the child of a celebrated physician, also announced his intention of preserving it in his anatomical museum, along with some more of the issue of his loins who had before died. I give these anecdotes as forming the best illustration I know of the effects on the human mind of the patronage of scientific trifles.

Cassel possesses a great number of pictures, both in the Academy and in the Gallery of the reigning sovereign. Many of them are works of famous Italian and Dutch masters. The works of Tischbein are seen in various parts of the city. It was here the celebrated painters of this name, for there were two, lived and flourished. Cassel is ranked, by connoisseurs, as fourth in the list of the cities of Germany which ought to be visited. Vienna is first, then Berlin, Dresden, Cassel. Travellers, therefore, who have not grown weary of seeing wonders and sights, would do well to visit the palaces and curiosities of those fathers of their people, the Landgraves and Electors of Hesse Cassel.

With fine palaces in a land without commerce there may be much poverty and many beggars, and I saw more of the latter in Cassel than I had seem for some time. They are not shy in demanding alms. When I had given one a Hessian albus, about a penny, to buy potatoes, as he explained it, he asked me for another, "that he might buy fat to them." He was an old soldier, left to beg or starve. I met two or three such instances, and one old man said he had served in America.

The character of the Hessian people among the Germans is, that they are rather stupid and heavy, but very loyal and faithful. No stranger must breathe a word against their prince; and, with such devotion, they, of course, think the splendour of Cassel cheaply purchased with their own blood. Loyalty of subjects says nothing for the character of sovereigns. Men may be degraded to honour mortals who inflict misery and death on them. The inhabitants of Morocco are undoubtedly very loyal.

This disposition of the Hessian people accounts, however, for the joy which was exhibited by all classes as the Elector re-entered his dominions in the year 1813. He has since been involved in disputes and has grown unpopular. He has forfeited love, though he is not yet hated. He seems to have forgotten that, in 20 years, another generation is walking the earth, who differ from their fathers. He returned too rashly to his former plans of government.

Every part of the country to which regulations could reach, even to the ancient uniform of the soldiers, pig-tails and all, was to be restored to the precise same state as it was in the year 1798. This, of course, excited some murmurs; – even the military were offended at being exposed to the laughter of the rest of their fellow-citizens and of Germany.

The students of Göttingen, who make frequent excursions to Cassel, helped to ridicule the whole. To do honour, they said, to the Elector, they visited Cassel in a large body; and everyone wore a tail that reached to the ground. The citizens chuckled – the soldiers were offended – and the Elector himself, though he could not openly be angry, sent a message to Göttingen requesting the young men might be kept in better order.

The splendour of Cassel made me more sensible of the difference occasioned by the sovereign living in or out of the country. Hannover, whose sovereigns have long been more powerful than the landgraves of Hesse, has no sort of magnificence. Cassel has a great deal. The sovereign of the one draws as large a revenue from his country as the sovereign of the other, but the electors of Hannover have resided out of the country for more than a century, while the landgraves of Hesse have lived at home. This is probably the point on which the natives of .Hannover have suffered most by their sovereign being king of Great Britain.

I do not believe much of their wealth has been imported into Britain; and I am sure there are no traces of the wealth of Britain in Hannover, but the Hannoverians have wanted all the advantages which the residence of a sovereign brings. His revenues have been divided amongst numerous nobles, who have spent them in trifles, and have left no memorial, either of usefulness or magnificence. The sovereigns of Hannover have, however, nourished one of the best universities of Germany; and probably the encouragement which they have given to learning by the establishment at Göttingen would not have been bestowed had not their taste for magnificence been gratified at the expence of another nation. The Hannoverians may have lost something by wanting the splendour of a capital, but the dignity of their sovereign has been a means of increasing their attachment to him; and, like the Hessians, they also are distinguished for their loyalty.

It is by no means a revolutionary practice, that sovereigns should keep mistresses while their wives are yet living. This is an immorality of the old school, which is still practised by the Elector of Hesse Cassel, probably from his reverence for former customs. Three ladies have been distinguished as having enjoyed his embraces. He has still one. In this point, his son follows his example. In one part of a square is the palace where the wife of the young prince in another is a house which is the residence of his mistress. The elector openly lives with his mistress, but the son only openly visits his, as if he were ashamed of following too closely the example of the father. Sovereigns deserve to have tales of scandal told of them by their flatterers; and they would not be here mentioned, were it not that their example has a vast deal of influence on the morality of the world; the guilt of corrupting it attaches much less to the Jacobins than to them.

Between Cassel and Frankfort, which it cost me three days to reach, the country for the whole distance is fertile and agreeably diversified. It is well peopled, and there is a considerable traffic, but the roads are by no means good. The inns are large, but dirty and ill-provided. Some traces of prosperity were visible, but more of poverty and want. At Fritzlar, which is a Catholic town, I was rather incommoded by intrusive begging boys. There had formerly been a large convent of Ursulines here, which was recently destroyed, – though a few pious nuns still remain, who employ themselves educating girls. A considerable number come from the neighbouring villages to learn fine needle-work. The former revenues of the convent will now swell the revenues of the prince; and the people, on whose industry they are a tax, will derive no benefit from the change. The evident poverty and beggary of this little town, while it is situated in a pleasant fertile country, was undoubtedly owing, in a great measure, to the convent and the Catholicism.

Some students, who came from Göttingen, and were going to Nassau, were my companions for some time. They were quite boastful of what they had done at Göttingen and seemed to think they could accomplish whatever they pleased. They sang as we marched; and though they had been so reduced by their pranks, that one of them was actually without shoes, and they had but little money to pay their travelling expences, they were merry companions. The Germans understand, in general, the art of self-denial very little; and these young men, as they encountered any person by the road, adopting the phrase of relationship, (*Vetter,* cousin,) borrowed tobacco, or stopped the traveller till he had given them a light. Their quarters at night did not precisely suit me; and I left them to enjoy their thick milk covered with grated bread and sugar for supper, and their straw to sleep on; and, by walking some distance further, I procured a good bed, a cleaner inn, and better food.

The sovereign of Cassel levies a tax on people passing through his dominions, by making them pay for their passports. The fee, which was two pence, was exacted at Marburg. There is a university here. It is the only one belonging to Cassel but is not very celebrated at present. The whole population of the town does not exceed 6,000 souls.

The town of Giessen, where there is another university, and which is very little more populous than Marbourg, is situated about 20 miles from it. It is in the territories of Hesse Darmstadt, and on the high road. Not far from Giessen, but out of the high road, lies the town of Wetzlar, which was formerly celebrated as the seat of the Cammergericht, one of the highest tribunals of Germany under the old constitution of the empire, and one of the means by which the subjects of every part of it were protected from arbitrary injustice. Like the other tribunals of Germany, the judges belonging to it were divided into two banks – a bank of nobles, and a bank of jurists; and it exercised a considerable degree of power over the minor princes of the empire. It was one of the means by which the jurisconsults established their extensive dominion in Germany.

It lasts to this day. They are, and have long been, as councillors and as judges much more the rulers of Germany than the nobles. Their fetters bind even the princes. Wetzlar is also celebrated as the place where Goethe composed the *Sorrows of Werther,* and where he placed the scene of this romance. This circumstance, with the fountain of Charlotte and the tomb of Werther, both of which exist as described by the poet, may still induce travellers to visit it; but its political importance was destroyed with the ancient constitution of the empire. And there is now no tribunal but the public press, to which complaints can be carried of the sovereigns of Germany.

The whole of the country through which I pass ed to arrive at Frankfort abounds in fruit. Apples, pears, and plums are preserved and dried on an extensive scale and form a considerable article of commerce. The road-sides were planted with fruit trees, which seemed common property; for everybody plucked and eat their produce. When the traveller is oppressed with heat and dust, no labour appears so benevolent as that which thus supplies him both with shelter and refreshment.

Even in places where the trees were enclosed, their branches hung so often temptingly in the road, that it was impossible to refrain from plucking the fruit; and the gardeners and labourers seemed not to envy the traveller the trifling theft. As I saw some bare-footed women travellers doing this, I could not avoid thinking, if mother Eve had been a German soldier's wife, travelling on a dusty road, on a hot day, there would have been some excuse for her breaking the command by which she doomed her posterity to sin and misery. But, living in the midst of sweets, of fragrant flowers, and refreshing streams, and not condemned to labour, she could only have done it from that disposition to disobey arbitrary commands, which, whether she bequeathed it to her descendants or not, is now evidently universal. The luxuries of fruit and fine weather made a walk, otherwise solitary, extremely pleasant.

There was a fair in Frankfort when I reach ed it, and every inn was so full that it was with great difficulty I procured a lodging. This is a city which has been so recently described by other travellers, that I shall say nothing of it. I was surprised by the whirl and the bustle in its streets, and by the immense quantity of itinerant musicians whom the fair had brought together.

There was not a street in which three or four parties or bands were not playing; not a day passed in which the inn was not visited during dinner by several companies, and there was no inn in which their strains were not heard at various hours of the day. I once formed a devout wish that music might be more spread amongst our people – that it might be taught to them in their daily schools, and in large assemblies of children.

Frankfort led me to modify this wish. If such an improvement should be the result of the sovereign patronising music; if it should not grow from the people feeling the want themselves; if they should be schooled into it; and, above all, if it should precede political knowledge, and political improvement, as it has done in Italy and Germany; it will only render a vast number of our people like so many Italians and Germans—beggarly and wandering musicians. It may be wished that our countrymen may become more musical; but they should think only of music as an amusement, not as an employment, and they should spurn it, while it can be regarded as a means of making them content with the misery inflicted by bad governments.

Frankfort differs from Cassel as much as Cassel does from Hannover in its splendour; but, in Frankfort, it is spread over a great part of the city. It is not confined to a palace or a hill but adorns the gardens and houses of numerous wealthy merchants and beautifies both the town and the environs. The suburbs are ornamented with fine walks; and the taste for flowers and gardens which distinguishes the other parts of Germany is very conspicuous in Frankfort.

From Frankfort I floated down the Rhine into Holland, where I remained some weeks; and then returned to England, where I arrived in November, after an absence of more than three years.

# APPENDIXES.

# APPENDIX.

## No. I.

*An Account of Births, Confirmations, Marriages, and Deaths, in the whole German Dominions of his Majesty our August Lord, from the 1st of January 1817, to the 1st of January 1818.*

| Names of the Provinces | BIRTHS | | | | | | | | Sum total |
|---|---|---|---|---|---|---|---|---|---|
| | In Marriage | | Out of Marriage | | Dead-born | | Total | | |
| | Boys | Girls | Boys | Girls | Boys | Girls | Boys | Girls | |
| Kalenburg and Göttingen | 3,390 | 3,219 | 398 | 373 | 169 | 151 | 3,957 | 3,743 | 7,700 |
| Plesse | 83 | 79 | 7 | 2 | 5 | 3 | 95 | 84 | 179 |
| Grubenhagen | 1,008 | 923 | 104 | 104 | 50 | 35 | 1,162 | 1,062 | 2,224 |
| Eichsfeld | 339 | 339 | 13 | 14 | 4 | 7 | 356 | 360 | 716 |
| Lüneburg | 3,958 | 3,668 | 255 | 244 | 186 | 128 | 4,399 | 4,040 | 8,439 |
| Lauenburg, remains | 157 | 148 | 19 | 12 | 7 | 10 | 183 | 170 | 353 |
| Bremen and Verden | 3,265 | 3,025 | 217 | 196 | 165 | 112 | 3,647 | 3,333 | 6980 |
| Land Hadeln | 242 | 206 | 24 | 28 | 9 | 11 | 275 | 245 | 520 |
| Hoya | 1,594 | 1,508 | 138 | 101 | 68 | 46 | 1,800 | 1,655 | 3,455 |
| The Amts Uchte, Auburg, Freudenberg | 175 | 161 | 11 | 15 | 9 | 5 | 195 | 181 | 376 |
| Diepholz | 249 | 258 | 14 | 12 | 12 | 16 | 275 | 286 | 561 |
| Hohnstein | 108 | 85 | 6 | 7 | 4 | 2 | 118 | 94 | 212 |
| Spiegelberg | 38 | 34 | 2 | _ | 1 | | 41 | 34 | 75 |
| Osnabrück | 2,218 | 2,012 | 111 | 92 | 90 | 78 | 2,419 | 2,182 | 4,601 |
| Lingen | 300 | 265 | 8 | 7 | 6 | 2 | 314 | 274 | 588 |
| Meppen | 629 | 612 | 7 | 11 | 20 | 12 | 656 | 635 | 1,291 |
| Emsbühren | 65 | 49 | 1 | 1 | _ | 1 | 66 | 51 | 117 |
| Bentheim | 326 | 281 | 7 | 3 | 13 | 8 | 346 | 292 | 638 |
| Hildesheim | 1,815 | 1,722 | 199 | 204 | 82 | 52 | 2,096 | 1,978 | 4,074 |
| City of Goslar | 71 | 87 | 15 | 11 | 3 | 2 | 89 | 100 | 189 |
| East Friesland | 2,174 | 2,149 | 44 | 47 | 94 | 94 | 2,312 | ,2290 | 4,602 |
| | 22,204 | 20,830 | 1,600 | 1,484 | 997 | 775 | 24,801 | 23,089 | 47,890 |
| | 43,034 | | 3,084 | | 1,772 | | | | |

| | |
|---|---|
| Subtract the Dead-born | 1,772 |
| Remain births | 46,118 |
| Subtract the deaths | 32,004 |
| More births than Deaths | 14,114 |

## An Account of Births, Confirmations, Marriages, and Deaths, in the whole German Dominions of his Majesty our August Lord, from the 1st of January 1817, to the 1st of January 1818. Cont.

| Births | Confirmations | | | | Marriages | | Deaths. | | | |
|---|---|---|---|---|---|---|---|---|---|---|
| Compared with year before | Boys | Girls | Sum. | Compared with year before | No. Of | Compared with year before | Males | Females | Sum. | Compared with year before |
| -263 | 2,612 | 2,539 | 5,151 | -635 | 2,266 | -45 | 2,822 | 2,870 | 5,692 | +443 |
| +17 | 61 | 45 | 106 | -24 | 64 | +10 | 59 | 56 | 115 | -4 |
| -177 | 678 | 721 | 1,399 | -163 | 510 | -90 | 811 | 750 | 1,561 | -238 |
| -152 | 204 | 192 | 396 | -7 | 208 | -10 | 316 | 311 | 627 | -16 |
| -107 | 2,888 | 2,884 | 5,772 | +171 | 2,412 | +4 | 2,764 | 2,430 | 5,194 | -231 |
| +1 | 110 | 117 | 227 | +13 | 75 | -11 | 104 | 107 | 211 | +2 |
| -110 | 2,327 | 2,193 | 4,520 | +106 | 1,700 | -74 | 2,335 | 2,132 | 4,467 | +12 |
| +11 | 161 | 151 | 312 | +19 | 144 | 23 | 190 | 173 | 363 | +19 |
| +87 | 1,189 | 1,120 | 2,309 | +101 | 874 | -65 | 1,052 | 1,004 | 2,056 | -57 |
| -30 | 139 | 112 | 251 | -9 | 87 | -19 | 126 | 114 | 240 | +11 |
| -47 | 179 | 183 | 362 | -40 | 130 | +5 | 152 | 137 | 289 | -53 |
| -36 | 81 | 66 | 147 | -10 | 56 | -2 | 66 | 48 | 114 | -37 |
| -11 | 26 | 27 | 53 | +12 | 21 | -5 | 30 | 29 | 59 | -11 |
| -976 | 1,523 | 1,428 | 2,951 | -483 | 1,187 | -110 | 1,641 | 1,665 | 3,306 | -45 |
| -15 | 257 | 204 | 461 | +21 | 170 | +39 | 234 | 218 | 452 | +40 |
| -116 | 474 | 478 | 952 | +952 | 334 | +55 | 400 | 399 | 799 | -92 |
| -65 | 45 | 27 | 72 | +72 | 26 | -28 | 53 | 48 | 101 | +1 |
| -140 | 267 | 258 | 525 | -59 | 228 | +16 | 320 | 270 | 590 | +61 |
| -463 | 1,349 | 1,309 | 2,658 | +89 | 1,162 | -64 | 1,535 | 1,525 | 3,060 | +49 |
| +35 | 75 | 56 | 131 | -9 | 50 | -4 | 42 | 66 | 108 | -34 |
| +190 | 1,191 | 1,260 | 2,451 | +304 | 1,111 | -550 | 1,358 | 1,242 | 2,600 | -67 |
| -2,367 | 15,836 | 15,370 | 31,206 | +421 | 12,815 | -971 | 16,410 | 15,594 | 32,004 | -249 |

As such tables as these are thought by statistical writers to be of importance, I shall here add an account of the number of births and deaths in Oldenburg. It is taken from the Royal Almanack for the duchy.[173]

|  | Number of | | |
| --- | --- | --- | --- |
|  | Marriages | Births | Deaths |
| 1815 | 1437 | 5711 | 3518 |
| 1816 | 1256 | 5605 | 3763 |

In the latter year the number of male infants born was 2005, of female 2700; 173 were still births; 173 were born out of marriage; 132 before the proper time. Of the 3768 deaths were:-

|  | Males | Females |
| --- | --- | --- |
| under 5 years of age | 782 | 639 |
| 10 | 72 | 67 |
| 20 | 104 | 88 |
| 30 | 96 | 111 |
| 40 | 122 | 131 |
| 50 | 115 | 132 |
| Over 50 | 173 | 163 |
| 60 | 173 | 205 |
| 70 | 175 | 186 |
| 80 | 83 | 88 |
| 90 | 18 | 22 |
| 100 | 2 | 3 |
| Total | 1925 | 1838 |

---

[173] **Editor's F/N:-** It may appear that even in 1816, 5 people leaved past a hundred and 5.8% (216) live past eighty, we can calculate (from this table) that the average life span of those 3763 that died in 1816 was 32.2 (for the1838 females it was 34 years; for the 1925 males it was 30.4).

Perhaps the largest influence on the average lifespan was the rate of infant mortality at 37.9% below the age of 5 and nearly 42% below 10.

The average lifespan of those that died in 1816 who had lived past 10, was 53.

# APPENDIX.
# No. II.

## Persons composing the States of Hannover.

### *Representatives of the Provinces of Grubenhagen and Kalenberg.*

#### CLERGY.

Dr. Salfeld, Abbot of Loccum, Consistorial Director, &c.; —a representative by virtue of his office.

Dr. Nieper, Court Councillor, Cabinet Councillor, and holding several other offices under government; elected by the corporation of St Boniface in the town of Hameln.

Mr. Blumenbach, Councillor of Government, member of the provincial government of Hannover, &c, ; elected by the corporation of Wunstorf.

Mr. Eichhorn, Superintendent of Road-making, a servant of the crown; elected by the corporation of St Alexander, at Eimbeck.

Dr. Rehberg, Secretary of the Finance Department, &c. elected by the Corporation of St Beatrice at Eimbeck.

#### NOBILITY.

Lord Chamberlain, Von Lenthe, Land Councillor von Münchausen; Captain of the Palace, Baron von Knigge; Land Drost, Captain von Stietencron; Land Drost von Grote; General von Wangenheim; Councillor von Hammerstein; Councillor von Zesterfleth; Ober Schenck von Platen. The nobility of these provinces are divided into nine districts, each district sending one member.

#### TOWNS.

Mr. Lichtenberg, Councillor of Justice; elected by the town of Göttingen. --

Mr. Meissner, Syndicus and Councillor; elected by the town of Hannover.

Mr. Ebert, Syndicus and Councillor; elected by the town of Nordheim.

Mr. Stolzheise, Merchant; elected by the town of Hameln.

Mr. Ernst, Bürgermeister; elected by the town of Eimbeck.

Mr. Jenisch, Collector of Taxes; elected by the town of Osterode.

Mr. Zwicker, Bürgermeister of Hannover, and holding several offices under government; elected by the town of Münden.

Mr. Domeier, Bürgermeister; elected by the town of Münden.

Mr. Meyer, Court Councillor; elected by the town of Moringen.

## Representatives of the Province of Lüneburg.

### CLERGY.

Vacant; elected by the Abbot of St Michael's.

Mr. Kneisen, Commissary of the Army; elected by the Corporation of Bardewic.

Dr. Sextro, Court Chaplain, Consistorial Councillor; elected by the Corporation of Ramelsloh.

### NOBILITY.

Count Schulenburg Wolfsburg;[174] Land Councillor von Meding, Land Councillor von Plato, Mr. von Weyhe, Mr. von Campe, a Councillor of War; Lieutenant-Colonel von Knesebeck; Major von Schrader; Land Councillor von Bülow: Mr. von Hodenberg; elected by the nobility, as described Vol. I. p. 423.[175]

### TOWNS.

Dr. Krukenberg, Bürgermeister, Chief of the Police, Commissary at War; elected by the town of Lüneburg.

Mr. Hartman, one of the Crown Members of the committee for the regulation of taxes; elected by the town of Uelzen.

Mr. Vogell, Bürgermeister; elected by the town of Celle.

Dr. Hoppenstedt, Consistorial Councillor; elected by the town of Haarburg.

Land Drost von Hodenberg; elected by the town of Burgdorf.

Mr. Thorwirth, Bürgermeister; elected by the town of Lüchow.

Mr. Heiliger, Court Councillor; elected by the town of Walsrode.

---

[174] **Hodgskin's F/N:-** This gentleman was afterwards appointed by the Prince Regent as guardian of the Duke of Brunswick, minister of Brunswick. He is since dead.

[175] **Editor's F/N:-** P.237 in the *Collected Works* edition.

The small portion of Lauenburg which remains in the possession of Hannover sends one member, Lieutenant-Colonel von der Decken, son, I believe, of the minister of the same name.

## Representatives of the Provinces of Bremen and Verden,

### CLERGY.

Mr. von Zesterfleth, President of the Nobility of these provinces, and Director of the Corporation of Neuenwalde; by virtue of his office.

### NOBILITY.

Mr. von der Decken, President of the Provincial Government of Friesland; Mr. von der Decken, Councillor of Justice; Mr. von der Beck; Mr. von Schulte, Domanial Councillor; Lieutenant-Colonel von Holleufer ; Land Drost von Schulte; Land Councillor von Möller; elected by the nobility.

### TOWNS.

Mr. Kobbe, Burgermeister, Land Councillor, Auditor of the Garrison; elected by the town of Stade.

Mr. von Hammerstein, a Cabinet Councillor, and member of the War Council; elected by the town of Buxtehude.

Land Councillor, Münchmeyer; elected by the town of Verden.

Willemer, Consultant; elected by the inhabitants of the marsh lands.

Dr. Götze, Bürgermeister; Land Hadeln.

## Representatives of the Provinces of Hoya and Diepholz.

### NOBILITY.

Mr. von Voss, Chief Hunting Master; Land Councillor von Pape, also Vice Consistorial Director; Mr. von Hintiber, Director of the Royal Post; elected by the nobility. Mr. von Ramdohr; Major von Arenstorff; Mr. Albers, Merchant; elected by the possessors of free property.

### Towns.

Mr. Falke, Court Councillor, member of the College of Justice, &c.; elected by the town of Nienburg.

Mr. Greve, Commissary for Domains; elected by the town of Hoya.

Mr. Storckman, Bürgermeister; elected by the town of Diepholz.

## HARZ.

Mr. von Meding, Cabinet Councillor, Chief of the Mines, represents the district of the Harz, constituents not known.

## *Representatives of the Province of Osnabrück.*

### CLERGY.

Count von Meerveldt; elected by the corporation of St. John's.

### NOBILITY.

Mr. von Bar, President of the Provincial Government; Mr. von Bar, Gentleman of the Bed-chamber; Baron von Schele, Member of the Provincial Government; Count Münster, Chief Forest-Master; Major General von Wincke ; elected by the nobility.

### TOWNS.

Dr. Kemper, Syndicus; elected by the town of Osnabrück.

Mr. Buch, Councillor of Justice; elected by the town of Quackenbrück.

Mr. Warnecke, Collector of Taxes; elected by the town of Melle.

## *Representatives of the Province of Hildesheim.*

### NOBILITY.

Mr. von Reden, Court Chamberlain; Land Drost, Count von Wrisberg; Mr. von Wrede, Chamberlain; Mr. von Dassel, Forest-Master; Count von Wrisberg, Gentleman of the Bed-chamber; elected by the nobility.

### TOWNS.

Mr. Lünzel, Town Judge; elected by the town of Hildesheim. Mr. Gudewill, Bürgermeister; elected by the town of Alfield.

## Representatives of the Province of Friesland.

NOBILITY.

Count von Wedel; Count von Kniphausen; elected by the nobility.

TOWNS.

Mr. Schepeler, Councillor of Justice; elected by the town of Aurich.

Mr. Tholen, Merchant; elected by the town of Embden.

Mr. Kettler, Administrator of Taxes and Revenue; elected by the town of Norden.

Mr. Thedinger, Agriculturist; Mr. Petersen, Bürgermeister; Mr. von Briesen, Agriculturist; Mr. von Mammen, Merchant; elected by the possessors of free property.

*Representatives of other Places.*

Mr. von Martels; elected by the nobility of Meppen.

Heyl, Councillor of Justice; elected by the town of Meppen.

Vacant; elected by the nobility of Lingen.

Mr. Thesing, Assessor of Justice; elected by the town of Lingen.

Mr. Schlüter, Town Judge; elected by the town of Goslar.

Mr. Arenhold, Secretary to the Ministry; elected by the town of Duderstadt.

Mr. Wilhelmi; elected by the town of Hohenstein.

Vacant; elected by the nobility of Bentheim.

Mr. Weber, a Judge ; elected by the town of Nordhorn.

# APPENDIX.

## No. III.

*REGULATIONS for the Meeting of the General States at Hannover, the 15th December 1814.*

FIRST SECTION. — *Of the Deputies to the General Assembly.*

*1st,* The deputies sent to the General Assembly must give in their powers to the ministry, and, if they are found good, it will certify this to the assembly.

*2nd,* Every person authorized by such a legitimation has the right to give a vote in his own person, but he cannot give a power to vote for him to any other member of the assembly.

Section Second. — *Of the President, General Syndicus, and General Secretary.*

*1st,* The election of a President, General Syndicus, and General Secretary, is to be made by means of a ballot. A positive majority of votes must be given, and when such a majority is not obtained by the first scrutiny, it is to be repeated in such a manner (till the necessary number of votes are given to one person) that votes must be given to those only who have before received them : he who has received the fewest is on every renewal of the scrutiny to be no more voted for.

*2nd,* After the opening of the assembly by a royal commissioner, the election of a president is to be its first business. In this election the deputies sent, in consequence of their offices, (the Abbot of Loccum, the Abbot of St. Michael's, Lüneburg, and the President of the Nobility of Bremen,) collect the votes of all the deputies, which are to be given in closed billets, and join their own with them. They enumerate them, and the numbers are to be written in the register of the assembly.

*3rd,* When the election is made, the king's commissioner is informed of it, and the elected president makes the following oath to him:

"You shall swear an oath before God, and by his holy word, that, in the office of president, to which you have been elected by the other representatives, you will keep the good of the whole kingdom in view – that you will, without partiality, preserve order in the sittings of the assembly; and that you will promulgate the resolutions made by the majority of the deputies. So help you God and his holy word."

4th, After the president is elected he causes a general syndicus and a general secretary to be chosen.

5th, The general syndicus makes the following oath before the president:

"You shall swear an oath before God, and by his holy word, that you will, in the office of general syndicus, to which you have been elected by the other representatives, keep the good of the whole kingdom in view; and that you will rightly preserve order in the committees of the assembly; and that you will also conscientiously compose, with the best of your discernment and knowledge, the resolutions it may be your duty to propose. So help you God and his holy word."

6th, The general secretary makes the following oath before the president:

"You must swear an oath before God, and by his holy word, that you will truly and honestly perform the duties of general secretary, to which office you have been elected by the other deputies; – that you will carefully collect and enumerate the votes, and pronounce in all cases, and write the register according to truth;-that you will compose conscientiously, and according to the best of your discernment and knowledge, the resolutions and other records of the assembly; and that you will keep its archives in proper order and preservation. So help you God and his holy word.

7th, The business of the president is the following:

(*a*) To announce the sittings of the assembly, to open and to close them.

(*b*) To preserve order in the deliberations.

(*c*) To observe, and to follow correctly those forms of procedure that are hereby prescribed.

(*d*) To write out and to bring forward the questions the assembly have to decide.

(*e*) To cause the votes to be enumerated, and to formally pronounce the resolutions agreed to.

8th, The following is the business of the general syndicus:

(*a*) In the meetings of the assembly, wherein the motions are prepared for a formal decision by a preliminary discussion, he takes the president's chair, preserves order in the deliberations, and when these are closed, reports to the assembly in its formal sitting the result of the preliminary discussion.

(*b*) He lays those propositions before the assembly, the examination and preparation of which have been confided to him by it.

9*th*, The following is the business of the general secretary :

(*a*) To keep the register of the proceedings of the assembly.

(*b*) To enumerate the votes by a division on any questions.

(*c*) To write out the resolutions of the assembly, and to notify and represent the same to the government and to the ministry.

(*d*) To keep the archives of the assembly under his inspection.

THIRD SECTION. — *Of the Sittings and Meetings of the General Assembly of the States.*

1*st*, The sittings and meetings of the general assembly of the states are of two sorts:

(*a*) Sittings for conclusive deliberations, and to form resolutions.

(*b*) Meetings for preliminary deliberations on certain objects.

2*nd*, A formal sitting cannot be opened when at least fifty-one members are not present. And no resolution can be made when this number of members are not present.

3*rd*, In the formal sitting the president directs the proceedings, but takes, however, during the deliberations, no other part in them than to put, in a precise manner, the propositions on which the assembly are to vote, by *Yes* or *No*, without giving or recommending his own opinion. The general syndicus sits among the deputies.

4*th*, Every member is allowed, on the questions being put, to propose amendments. When the amendment is negatived, the whole assembly must decide on the form of the question.

5*th*, When any question is brought forward, every member of the meeting may explain his opinion, but no one must speak more than once on the same question, and in the same formal sitting.

6*th*, When, at the conclusion of a debate, a resolution is agreed on, the secretary enumerates the votes, which are given aloud, according to the manner in which the deputies may chance to sit. He enumerates last the vote of the president and his own. He remarks every voter and inscribes the list of the names in the register.

7*th*, On motions regarding matters of importance, the assembly forms itself into a general committee to discuss them preliminarily. It requires, at least, thirty-one members to be present to form such a committee.

8*th*, The general syndicus takes the chair of the president in such a committee, and preserves order, but takes no other part in the discussion.

$9^{th}$, In such a committee the president takes his place among the deputies and may take part in all the deliberations.

$10^{th}$, When motions are to be considered which the general syndicus may have made in his character of deputy, the president takes his place, and presides at the discussion.

$11^{th}$, Whoever wishes to speak stands up in his place, and directs his discourse to that person who occupies the chair. When more than one deputy stand up at once, the president declares which of the two he has first heard, and the others must wait till his speech is ended.

The person who speaks is not to be interrupted; it is, however, allowed to correct misstated facts by means of a few words.

$12^{th}$, Both in the formal sittings, and in the preparatory committee, the president is always to be attentive that whoever speaks does not digress from the subject under deliberation. The president also, for the time, has a right to remind any speaker who, from extending his speech too far, appears likely to be troublesome, that it is better to be short.

$13^{th}$, Personal reflections are in both meetings forbidden. When any deputy may use such, the president calls him to order. If he believes this not to be correct he may refer the matter to the decision of the assembly.

$14^{th}$, The president in the formal sitting, and the general syndicus in the committee, uses a bell to command silence and preserve order.

$15^{th}$, When a deputy so far forgets himself as not to pay attention to the president, the assembly itself will adopt the proper means to bring him to order.

$16^{th}$, When, either in a formal sitting or in a committee, so violent a movement takes place that the president or general syndicus cannot again restore order, he adjourns the assembly for the day.


FOURTH SECTION. — *Manner of treating the Subjects brought under Deliberation.*

$1^{st}$, The propositions which are presented to the states by the king, or in his name by the ministry, shall immediately, and before all other propositions, be laid before the whole assembly, and, one after the other, be brought under deliberation by the president.

$2^{nd}$, Every deputy has also the right to make propositions.

$3^{rd}$, Whoever brings forward a motion that, after being deliberated upon, has to go to the royal ministry, must compose it in writing; and, after receiving permission from the president, who must not refuse it when it will not disturb the order of deliberation, he must lay it before the general secretary, that it may be inscribed in the register, and then declares the sense of his motion to the president, who waits to see if any other member stands up and supports it. When the motion is seconded, the person who brought it forward has a right to name a day on which to bring forward his motion, for decision. When he does not do this the president appoints a day for this purpose.

4th, On the appointed day it is decided if the motion shall be rejected or brought under closer consideration. If the last is voted the assembly can immediately form itself into a committee to discuss it preliminarily. The president resigns the chair to the general syndicus and takes it again when the assembly again forms itself into a formal sitting.

5th, All this may take place on one and the same day, or on several days, as seems good to the assembly.

6th, Every member may propose amendments to the motions made by others, in which case the amendments are first decided on, so that the motion, in an amended form, or when the amendments are rejected, in its original form is last decided on.

7th, To make a formal resolution that is to be laid before the royal ministry for them to give orders concerning, it is necessary that the subject should be deliberated on, at least, once in a committee, and read three times on three different days in formal sittings, and by every sitting it may be either rejected or be postponed for further consideration.

8th, When a resolution is made by the majority, at three different sittings, held on three different days, it is then noticed to the executive. In this notice, the three days must be particularly mentioned on which the resolution was agreed to.

9th, When the assembly thinks proper, it may refer the preliminary examination of a motion to a committee of its members. Every deputy can move for a committee for a preliminary examination and propose the number of members to compose it.

10th, The motion for such a committee cannot be immediately decided, but it must be twice repeated on different days, in order that the assembly may more closely weigh and decide on the conditions of the motion.

11th, When such a committee is allowed, and the number of members fixed, each member gives in a list of those to whom he gives his vote to form such a committee, and those members who thus receive the most votes form the committee.

12th, Every committee commences its business by choosing a president, whose duty it is to preserve order in the proceedings on that subject for which they were named, and to report their proceedings to the general assembly.

FIFTH SECTION. — *The Adjournment and Prorogation of the Sittings of the General States.*

*1st*, When the general assembly find it good to confide the preliminary discussions on particular subjects to special committees, whose examinations require a certain time, it may then adjourn the formal meetings, either by a motion from the president or from any other member, to a particular day; to which adjournment, however, when it is for more than fourteen days, or for an uncertain time, the approbation of the king's ministry is necessary. When, in the resolution made on this subject, the day is appointed on which the assembly is again to meet, the committee of remaining deputies can hold no formal sitting, nor make any resolution till then. During such an adjournment, every member not of the committee is at liberty to absent himself, to return, however, against the appointed day.

When the General Assembly of the States find it good to adjourn themselves, with the approbation of the king's ministers, for an uncertain time, they can only be again assembled by an invitation directed to every and each member, and by a publication in the Hannover Anzeiger, at least ten days before the time appointed for the new meeting. The president can send such an invitation, in consequence of the request of the remaining committee, or by directions from the government.

*2nd*, The crown retains the power to close the assembly, and it reserves also to itself the power of adjourning the sittings at pleasure: and so soon as either is ordered, and the assembly have made known their resolutions, no more deliberations can take place. It remains with the crown to decide if the present assembly of the states shall be again assembled, and at what time, and also with what modifications, it may again be called together as the permanent representative corps of all classes. Proper representations respectfully made on the necessary modifications, either called for or uncalled for, will be accepted.


SIXTH SECTION — *Indemnification of the Expences of the Deputies.*

As it cannot be expected that the deputies of the whole country should bear the expences of the office they have taken on themselves, they will be allowed an indemnification for what they may estimate their travelling expences, both in coming and returning, and also for their support during the sittings of the assembly, which will be in the following proportions.

*1st*, For the deputies dwelling out of Hannover,

From the opening to the close of the states, so long as they remain on this account in Hannover, lodging and diet money daily, four Reichs-Thalers.

$2^{nd}$, For those deputies who live in Hannover,

For each sitting, and each general preliminary committee that they attend, also for every committee's sitting that they are elected to attend, diet money daily, two Reichs-Thalers.

$3^{rd}$, During the time that the general assembly of the states have adjourned themselves, those members only who are appointed members of committees that are to sit during the adjournment receive any payment.

$4^{th}$, The assembly will determine as to the further remuneration of the general secretary, and general syndicus.

The foregoing regulations shall be in force till the states find from experience that some part of them should be added or changed. The change may be effected by a motion made for that purpose

# APPENDIX.

# No. IV.

*List of the Public Lectures given in one year at Göttingen, for the half year beginning in April 1818.*

### GENERAL KNOWLEDGE.

General information on the manner of living in German Universities.

### THEOLOGY.

A History of the most remarkable changes in Theology since the time of Leibnitz to the present.

Explanation of the Bible, of Job, of Isaiah, of the Psalms, and of the Pentateuch. Each of these explanations is given by a different person, making on the whole Four Lectures.

An Historical and Critical Introduction in the Writings of the New Testament.

Explanations of the New Testament. The Letters of Paul, the Books of John, the Acts of the Apostles, are all explained by different people.

An Historical and Comparative Explanation of the most eminent Systems of Christian Theology.

Dogmatic, and the History of Dogmas.

Moral Theology.

The Antiquities of the Old and New Testament.

The first half of the History of the Church.

The later History of the Church.

The Church History of Great Britain.

Homelitick, or the art of Sermon-making, Preaching, and Catechising, are all taught; and there is an examination for theological subjects.

### JURISPRUDENCE.

The Literary History of Jurisprudence, particularly the Roman.

A Law encyclopaedia, to teach method and the sources of the law.

An Encyclopaedia of the whole of the present Jurisprudence, and of Roman Jurisprudence as it now exists.

National Law of Europe.

Public Law of the Middle Ages.
Public Law of the Confederate States of Germany.
Political and Civil Laws of Hannover.
Natural Criminal Law, with its relation to the most eminent Law Codes of Ancient and Modern People.
Criminal Law and Criminal Process.
The History of the Roman Jurisprudence.
The Institutions of Roman Jurisprudence at present.
Pandects.
Rights of Persons, according to the most eminent existing Laws of Germany.
Law of Heritage.
The knowledge of bringing an Action and of Answering.
The Elements of Practice.
The Ecclesiastical Law.
The same for Theologians.
The Feudal Law.
Civil Laws of Germany.
Criminal Process, united with Criminal Law.
Theory of Common Processes.
Theory of the Civil Process in Hannover.
Practical Instruction.
General Examinations and Repetitions.


## HEALING ART.

The History of Medicine.
An Encyclopaedia and Classification of the Healing Art.
Osteologie and Syndesmologie.
An Examination on Anatomy and Physiology.
Physiology.
The Operations of Medicines.
The Operation of Surgical Means of Cure.
Pharmacy.
General Pathologie and Therapie.
Doctrine of Generation.
Special or particular Pathologie.
Special Therapie.
The Pathology of the Organs of Respiration, and Digestion of the Skin and of the Urinary Organs.
Venereal Diseases.
Diseases of the Eyes and Ears.
The first half of Surgery.
A Practical Introduction to Operative Surgery.
The Operations necessary in Diseases of the Eyes.
Practical Instructions in the art of Dressing Wounds, &c.

Midwifery.

Medical Jurisprudence.

Medical, Surgical, and Clinical Practice.

Clinical Practice in the Hospital.

On the Sickness of Horses, and Infections among Domestic Animals.

Veterinary Medicine.

Medical Jurisprudence as it regards Animals.

Practical Lessons in Veterinary Medicine.

## PHILOSOPHY.

General History of Philosophy.

Logic, and encyclopaedia of Philosophy.

General Introduction to Philosophy and Logic.

Psychology.

Psychology, description and scientific Explanation of the facts of Consciousness.

Principles of the Science of Education.

Metaphysics, and the Philosophy of Religion.

General practical Philosophy and Ethics.

General Political Science.

Finances.

Practical Lessons on general Political Science.

## MATHEMATICAL SCIENCES.

Pure Mathematics.

Practical Arithmetic.

Political Arithmetic.

Introduction to Practical Geometry.

Practical Geometry, with Land-measuring, Garden Planning, &c. &c.

Plan-drawing and Sketching useful to Miners.

The Knowledge of the Stars.

Differential and Integral Calculus.

Theoretical Astronomy.

Science of the Inequalities of the Motion of the Planets.

Practical Astronomy.

Knowledge of the Stars.

To determine Latitudes and Longitudes of Places.

Architecture, higher orders.

An Introduction to Town and Country Building.

Building of Bridges.

Accuracy of Building Calculations.

Military Sketching.

## Natural Sciences.

Natural History.

General Botany, Domestic Botany.

Botany as it regards Forests, and as it regards Medicine, are all different courses of instruction.

Pure Botany as it regards Systematizing.

Geognosy.

Mineralogical Systematizing explained.

Mineralogy.

Experimental Natural Philosophy.

The most particular Phenomena of the Atmosphere.

Mechanical Geography,

Theoretical Chemistry, with explanatory experiments.

The first part of the Introduction to Chemical Analysis.

Practical Chemistry.

## HISTORICAL SCIENCES.

General Knowledge of Countries and People.

Diplomacy.

Ancient History.

History of Modern Europe and its Colonies.

General History, since the beginning of the French Revolution.

History of the Reformation.

History of Germany.

History of the War of the Insurrection in the Tyrol, in the year 1809.

Statistics of the European and North American States.

General History of Literature.

An Introduction into the History of the Language and Literature of the Semitisch People.

The History of the Language and Literature of the East.

## FINE ARTS.

On German Style.

A Critical and Historical Sketch of the History of French Literature.

History of Fine Arts.

On some particular statues, such as the Laocoon, &c.

Art of Drawing with Perspective.

History of the Arts of Greece.

## EASTERN AND OTHER LANGUAGES.

The Hebrew Grammar.

The beginning of the Syriac.

Philological Encyclopaedia.

On the Metre of the Greek and Roman Poets.

On the Language, and some Poets, of the Greeks, divided, however, into three parts.

On the Latin Language, and on some Roman Poets, divided, however, into four parts.

An Introduction to understand and judge the elder German Poets.

The French Language.

The English Language.

The Italian Language.

# APPENDIX.

## No. V.

*Measures, Weights, and Monies mentioned in this Work.*

An Hannoverian morgen of land contains 24,844 Paris square feet. An English acre contains 38,343 Paris square feet, consequently, an English acre contains 13,499 square feet more than a morgen, or the morgen is nearly one-third less. The same term morgen is in use in various parts of Germany but does not always contain the same number of square feet, which is a source of much trouble and inaccuracy.

A himpt contains 1558 cubic inches, a bushel 1801 of the same inches, consequently, a himpt is nearly one-fifth less than a bushel.

A Hannoverian pound contains 10,127 Dutch assen, an English pound, 9434 of the same assen, consequently, a Hannoverian pound is nearly one-thirteenth part greater than an English pound.

A pistole, or George d'or, which is the gold money in circulation, is worth at par about 16s. 8d. It is also worth five thalers, cassen money of Hannover; each cassen thaler is therefore worth at par 3s.4d. Conventions, or reichs money, bears the proportion of 10 to 9 to the money of Hannover; consequently, the conventions or reichs thalers, which are most usually in circulation, are each of them worth only 3s. Each thaler contains 24 good grosschen, or 36 marien grosschen; consequently, the cassen good grosschens are each worth somewhat more than 1½d. a marien grosschen more than 1d. A conventions good grosschen is 1½d, and a marien grosschen 1d. Each good grosschen contains 12 pfennige, each marien grosschen 8. A florin contains 16 good grosschen, and is worth about 2s.

### Prices in Cassen Money.

In the year 1787, Beef per lb. 1st kind, 3 marien grosschen, 2 pfennige, 2nd kind, 2 mg. 6 pf.; Veal, 1st kind, 4 mg., 2nd kind, 3 mg. 4 pf.; Pork, 1st kind, 2 mg. 6 pf.; Mutton, 1st kind, 2 mg. 4 pf, 2nd kind, 2 mg. 2 pf.

Wheat per himpt 1 thaler 6 mg. 4;pf.; Rye 36 mg.; Oats 12 mg.; Barley 20 mg.

In the year 1818, Beef per lb., 1st kind, 4 mg., 2nd kind, 3 mg. 4 pf.; Veal, 1st kind, 3 mg. 4 pf, 2nd kind, 2 mg. 4 pf.; Pork, 1st kind, 4 mg.: Mutton, 1st kind, 4 mg. 4 pf. 2nd kind, 4 mg.

Wheat per himpt, 1<sup>st</sup> kind, 1 thaler 13 mg.6 pf, 2<sup>nd</sup> kind, 1 thaler 13 mg, ; Rye, 1<sup>st</sup> kind, I thaler 7 mg, 2<sup>nd</sup> kind, 1 thaler 4 mg. ; Oats, 1<sup>st</sup> kind, 18 mg. 3 pf.; Barley, 1<sup>st</sup> kind, 32 mg., 2<sup>nd</sup> kind, 31 mg. 4 pf.

## Wages in 1818.

Agricultural labourers, men from 6d. to 10d. per day; women from 4d. to 6d. Artisans, such as Smiths, Carpenters, Shoemakers, Tailors, &c. from 1s, to 2s. per day, the latter was, however, paid for extraordinary work.

END OF VOLUME SECOND.

# INDEX.

The items indexed below are those taken from the index at the end of his original second volume of his *Travels in the North of Germany* that are pertinent to this current edition.

# Additional Appendexes

Appendixes additional to those in Hodgskin's original 1820 edition.

A.1. Notes on Hodgskin's Business Cycles Concept

A.2. Reviews of *Travels in the North of Germany*

# Appendix A.1.

## Notes on Hodgskin's Business Cycles Concept

## By Dr. Fred Day

This appendix is intended to further Hodgskin's comments on page 170 which presents what were to become Hodgskin's notion of Business Cycles, that finds latter expression within the Austrian Business Cycle Theory.

To remind ourselves, these are the relevant comments:

> Through every department of industry, wherever an artificial stimulus, that is, a stimulus greater that the natural demand, has been applied to encourage the production of any commodity whatever, the effect has always been, that a greater quantity of talents and of skill have been directed to its production than could at length find a proper profit or reward. The artificial stimulus is either withdrawn, or it is insufficient, and the people who have been induced by it to employ themselves in a particular way, are sure to fall into poverty and distress. The same fact is true of many of the manufactories of Britain, to which a larger portion of the skill of the nation has been directed than would have been but for the frequent unwise encouragements of the Legislature, and the manufacturers are now involved in distress. (Hodgskin,vol.IV, p.170. [1820, vol.II, p.286-7])

Hodgskin's ideas on the nature of business cycles were thinly scattered through his writings. Another early example (after this work) can be found in a letter published on 12th Feb. 1826 in the *Trades' Newspaper - Effects of Repealing the Corn Laws*. These early conjectures were conceived around the idea that capitalists, being over-stimulated by government actions and encouragements, periodically overtraded or inappropriately invested. This over-stimulation resulted from non-economic or political circumstances; i.e. it was exogenous in character.

This can be seen in Hodgskin's letter which defended bankers but laid the blame with the government for the depression that followed the short-lived boom of late 1825.

A more efficient and certain cause can be found in ... the speculation of the capitalist and the master manufacturer, which were founded in the hopes of advantages that have never been realised ... I attribute [this] ... to the speeches and writings of the ministerial part of the Government, ... they have flattered the cupidity and stimulated the enterprise of our manufacturers and merchants, by talking of the increased market they were to find for their commodities. The latter eagerly hastened to supply the imaginary market. ... These speculations turned out not profitable – they became bankrupt, and distress among the workmen ... has been the consequence. (Hodgskin, The *Trades' Newspaper,* 12th Feb. 1826)

In *Natural and Artificial Right of Property Contrasted* the subject of business cycles was broached again with reference to the legal right of property and the businessmen's unreliable expectations.

When we look at the commercial history of our country and see the false hopes of our merchants and manufacturers leading to periodical commercial convulsions, we are compelled to conclude, that they have not the same source as the regular and harmonious external world. ... Starts of national prosperity, followed by bankruptcy and ruin, have the same source then as fraud and forgery. To our legal right of property, we are indebted for those gleams of false wealth and real panic, which, within the last fifty years, have so frequently shook, to its centre, the whole trading world. (Hodgskin, 1832, p.155-6)

Hodgskin's interest does not appear resurrected again until his review of McCulloch's *Treatise on the Circumstances which Determine the Rate of Wages* that showed that he conceived that the cyclical booms could involve an increase in consumption without an appropriate increase in capital:

It has always been the argument, of the Economist, that in those years [1842-46] capital was much misapplied and wasted; and hence the revulsion of 1847-8. There was something else, therefore, besides the quantity of capital which determined the employment and the wages of labour between 1842 and 1846, and that something every person knows, was a delusive and *false hope* in capitalists, or those who could obtain credit, which gave a wonderful extension to employment without any corresponding increase in capital. The quantity of capital was the ultimate test, indeed, of the validity of credit; it proved the credit to have been fallacious – the hopes to have been a delusion;  but in the meantime, the people were employed, the wages paid and consumed; (Hodgskin, *E.,* 27th Dec. 1851, p.1440)

The *Economist*'s position was generally that the "delusive and *false hope* in capitalists" stemmed from the government's exaggerated assertions and exogenous support regarding the expansion of railways, as such this interference had economically negative consequences.

Whilst it would be unrealistic to assert that Hodgskin possessed anything like a fully worked out theory of business cycles, the above passages illustrate that he was well aware of the problem. However, rather than lay the blame on changes to population or simple bad luck, he sought an economic answer primarily with government actions as the root cause of the difficulties.

The problems associated with business cycles were caused by factors outside the "regular and harmonious" conditions of an unfettered market, which would otherwise have progressed or grown in a manner favourable to mankind's economic needs.  As such these outside influences were exogenous to the economic ideal of a pure market economy.

# Appendix A.2.

## A Survey of some Reviews of
### *Travels in the North of Germany*

## By Dr. Fred Day

The reviews of Hodgskin's *Travels* were not, it must be admitted, all favourable. An example of such a negative reception can be found in the review of Hodgskin's *Travels in Germany* within Blackwood's Edinburgh Magazine for February 1820. The following passages reveal an almost venomous the

> "But we cannot help regretting extremely, that the demand, which certainly exists amongst us for such a book, should have been answered by nobody of more competent attainments and capacity than this Thomas Hodgskin, Esquire.

> We know not on what feasible pretence such a person as this can be encouraged, by the most partial of his friends, to lay his travelling journal before the public, more particularly in so elaborate and expensive a form. Destitute, as his style of language alone sufficiently testifies him to be, of all elegant education, and no less manifestly a stranger to elegant society, either foreign or domestic – profoundly ignorant of history, both ancient and modern – possessing merely a sort of common-place imperfect smattering of the doctrines of political economy, and a plentiful measure of vulgar assurance, Mr Hodgskin walks forth to survey the condition of the great kingdoms of Christendom; and he returns in a few months to pronounce his opinion concerning them which could scarcely have been pardoned in an Englishman of fifty times his acquirements, after a residence of many laborious years in countries everywhere so different from his own." (p.536)

Such was their antagonism that they provided him with what retrospectively could be understood as a very apposite moniker, although being born in Chatham rather than London was not his by birth, but rather by inclination:

"He is a literary Esquire of the same class with some political Esquires, whose names have gained greater celebrity than he is ever likely to reach; in other words, he is a radical traveller and Cockney philosopher" (ibid, p.537)

A far more favourable, but short notice, appeared in The Globe newspaper for June 5th 1821:[176]

Besides an interesting Account of the Author's Travels, this book contains a variety of important information relative to the Schools and Universities, and to the political Constitution of Germany, not usually found in Works of this description of the mere exterior of the country; from his acquaintance with the German language he was enabled to mix freely with the people, and to appreciate the spirit and tendency, as well as to describe the outward form of their institutions. (*The Globe*, 5th June 1821, p.1)[177]

Another review of Hodgskin's work appeared more than three years after its original publication in 1823, and is reproduced below:

Review of *Travels* in the *Monthly Review*[178] for August 1823. (Vol. CI, p.367-372)

ART. IV. Travels in the North of Germany, describing the present State of the Social and Political Institutions, the Agriculture, Manufactures, Commerce, Education, Arts, and Manners in that Country; particularly in the Kingdom of Hannover. By Thomas Hodgskin, Esq. 2 Vols. 8vo. pp. 1007. II. 4s. Boards. Hurst and Co.

In our preceding report of the work of Mr. Jacob, we took occasion to notice the advantage to a traveller of visiting a country for the second time, and of being thus enabled to mark the changes that had occurred in the intervening period. This advantage was not possessed by Mr. Hodgskin, who is not an "elder in years," and who now comes for the first time before the

---

[176] **Editor's F/N:-** A formal notice of the publication of Hodgskin's *Travels* had first appeared in The Globe on 27th January 1820 (p.1).

[177] **Editor's F/N:-** This exact text was reprinted in *The Morning Post* on 14th June 1821 (p.2).

[178] **Editor's F/N:-** Although the spelling in this article is what we would nowadays conceive as American English (rather than British) the *Monthly Review* was printed in London by A. and R. Spottiswoode, of New-Street-Square.

public in the capacity of a writer:[179] – but, on the other hand, his progress bore all the marks of the activity of vigorous health; for he had traversed, with the leisure and minute observation of a pedestrian, a part of France, Italy, and Swisserland, before he entered on the country described in these volumes; and he prolonged his stay in Germany, with the double view of acquiring the language and collecting statistical information. The first part of the work relates his tour and personal adventures; while the second and larger portion conveys the result of his observations and reflections. These embrace a variety of topics; – the territorial aspect, the political constitution, and the financial resources of the different states, the condition of agriculture and manufactures, and, finally, the education, private life, and morals of the people.

Though the views of Mr. H. were more particularly directed to Hanover, many of his observations are applicable to the centre and the north of Germany generally; a region with which our commercial connection is not great, and whither our countrymen, who visit the Continent in the capacity of travellers, repair less frequently than to the Rhine, Swisserland, or Italy. – Bohemia, the first state mentioned by Mr. H., is naturally fertile, but backward in point of civillization and comfort, to a degree that an Englishman who has not visited the Continent can hardly deem possible. Most of the travellers in that kingdom, whether mechanics or petty dealers, are pedestrians; and, as they are too poor to pay for beds, the innkeepers are in the habit of providing nothing but straw for their repose. This is strewed in the public room of the inn, which at night is lighted by a three-cornered lamp suspended from the ceiling, and is similar to those primitive contrivances for the distribution of light which are seen in old pictures; and the motley group thus rendered visible presents an appearance which reminds a traveller at one time of a company of pilgrims, at other times of banditti.

The towns in Bohemia are much on a par with the inns; containing, in general, a square or market-place, with a townhouse on one side, and in the middle a gilt cross, or column composed of three smaller columns twisted together, as an emblem of the Trinity. From these scenes of poverty, so similar to those which we witness in Ireland, the traveller experiences a pleasant relief on reaching Saxony. Its capital, Dresden, can indeed boast of few buildings of note: but it is, on the whole, a pleasant and even elegant town. One great part of its attraction

---

[179] **Editor's F/N:-** Not actually true as Hodgskin's first work was his Essay on Naval Discipline (1813).

consists in the beauty of its situation, the Elbe flowing here so smoothly as to resemble a lake more than a river; and the gentle hills, which rise in the north and south, placing the city in a long oval vale. The walks, the public gardens, and the well-cultivated environs, have all a pleasing effect; while the mountains of Bohemia, seen at a distance, add a grander feature to the scene.

Leipzic, the second town in Saxony, is not only inferior in beauty, but is inconveniently situated for trade, being without water-communication; and the roads leading to it are in general very indifferent. To what cause, then, is its commercial activity to be ascribed? To its central situation; and to the progressive effect of an old standing regulation, that all merchandise passing within sixty miles of the town should be carried through it, in order that the Leipzic merchants might have the first offer of purchase. Warehouses being once built, and capital fixed on the spot, this town acquired business, and continued the resort of merchants when the conveniences of its situation were surpassed by those of other places.

From Saxony Mr. H. travelled northward into the Prussian dominions; the scattered position of which led Voltaire to describe them, above half a century ago, as stretching along the map of Germany in a narrow line "like a pair of garters." Since those days, their length has considerably increased: but of their statistics a summary may be given in a few words. Their territorial extent (80,000 square miles) is equal to that of England and Scotland (distinct from Ireland), but the population is not above 10,000,000, and the revenue is somewhat under £7,000,000. As to the capital, several of the cities of Europe contain more fine buildings than Berlin, but few exhibit so many collected within a small compass. The palace, the arsenal, (a very handsome edifice,) the library, the University, the Catholic church, the Opera-house, several elegant private houses, and a fine street, Unter den Linden, planted with rows of trees, (and at the end of which stands the beautiful Brandenburgh gate,) may all be seen from one spot, and by a slight change in the posture of the spectator. The population of Berlin is on the increase, and is likely to amount in a few years to 200,000; an augmentation to be ascribed to the influx of those whom Mr. S. Gray calls "immigrants," or in other words to settlers from the country; since, unlike the majority of towns in England, the number of deaths is such as to exceed by more than 1,000 the annual births. Mortality takes place, as in Paris and other continental cities, chiefly among children.

Potsdam is a well-built place, with streets at right angles, and containing not less than eight royal residences: in addition to which it has a building for a truly Prussian object, viz. a hall of great dimensions for the purpose of exercising soldiers in rainy weather. Here is also what Mr. Hodgskin terms a "magnificent canal," which extends the water-communication from the Elbe to Berlin. – Wittemberg, the cradle of the Reformation, is, we are sorry to add, in a decaying state, although favorably situated on the Elbe. Its once celebrated University, the scene of the labors of Luther and Melanchthon, has been lately suppressed. This circumstance leads us to make a few remarks on the present mode of conducting:

*Education in Germany.* – Of the different Universities in Germany, Göttingen is the best endowed, although the total annual fund for the stipends of the professors, the repair of buildings, and the purchase of books, does not exceed £11,000 per annum. Here are no colleges of massy structure, no common tables, and few public halls: but the students lodge and board where they please, and generally receive instruction by lecture at the houses of their respective professors. The rule of most governments in Germany renders a course of study during three years, at an University, a necessary preliminary to official employment. The young lawyer attends lectures on jurisprudence; the medical and theological students follow the classes connected with their respective professions; and other branches, such as statistics, geography, and general history, may or may not be cultivated, at the option of the pupil.

Of the income of the professors, a part arises from fees and a part from a fixed salary; and although articles of provision and clothing are not above a third cheaper in Germany than in England, the difference of expence is much greater in consequence of the plainer habits of the people. One of the prominent characteristics of these public lessons is their minuteness; the manner of the professor being more like that of a school-master repeating a string of petty details to his hearers, than that of a philosophic teacher giving hints to be adopted and expanded by his pupils. The popular professors hold three or four classes daily, and the fee in each class is nearly a guinea per head for the course: each lecture lasts an hour; and the delivery of the professor, slow and inanimate as it generally is, has at least the merit of distinctness.

Historical writing has become an object of attention in Germany during the last half century, or rather since the year 1760; when the improving examples of Voltaire, Hume, and Robertson, began to introduce a better taste into such compositions. It is more common in Germany than elsewhere to divide and subdivide historical labor according to the subject; and to give separate narratives of ecclesiastical affairs, of a particular war, or of the progress of learning and the arts. Elegance and animation are seldom the characteristics of the authors of that country: but in careful and long continued research they are not often surpassed. In political affairs, the Germans, having as yet had so limited an experience, are little more than theorists. One general characteristic of their books, as of their lectures, is prolixity; arising from a belief on the part of the authors that they have never said enough while they can say anything more; – *dum quid restaret dicendum.* Every page, we might almost say every para graph of German composition partakes more or less of this feature; whether the work be a poem, a novel, an historical narrative, or a philosophic treatise.

Academical studies can, of course, occupy but a small portion of the public attention; and, as politics possess little attraction in the absence of representative assemblies, the Germans have given a different direction to their favorite pursuit. Music is the grand object of interest, the point to which the talents of the community at large are directed; and hence the number of eminent composers whose names are familiar to us in this country, and the still greater number of teachers who seek a livelihood in Holland and the adjacent parts of France.

*State of productive Industry: Manufactures.* – Woollens are made in Germany to a considerable extent, as far at least as they are requisite for home-consumption. Export is little contemplated; and we may remark, generally, that in many parts of this country, or in the smaller towns of France, the inhabitants transact business by a kind of barter, endeavoring to supply their own wants, but having very little money for the purchase of foreign articles. The staple manufacture of the north of Germany is linen; the value of which, according: to the quantity annually made in Silesia, amounted twenty years ago to nearly £2,000,000 sterling: but it has since experienced considerable diminution in consequence chiefly of the augmented consumption of cotton. The manufacture of the latter is on the increase; but, while linen was made in detached cottages, and by families who gave half their time to the labors of the field, cotton requires an assemblage of persons in a town or factory; so that the individuals employed are different, and an increase of work in the one does not directly counterbalance a diminution of it in the other.

*Wages,* – Manufacturers being in general paid by the piece, the amount of their earnings fluctuates with the state of trade. In the case of mechanics, wages are nearly on a level with their rate in France, viz. from is. 4d. to 1s. 8d. per day, without victuals, or any additional allowance. In many parts, it is common for journeymen to board in the house of their employers; in which case their wages vary from £5 to £10 per annum, a humble allowance when compared to the rate of wages in England; but there is also a considerable difference in the efficiency of the individual. It has long been remarked of our neighbours the Dutch, that bodily exertion was little practised by those whose circumstances enabled them to avoid it: but the Germans are commonly regarded as a more active race; with what truth we leave our readers to judge from the following paragraph:

"In the course of the day I met a great many carriages and waggons going to Leipsic, and all the travellers, wrapped up in two or three great-coats, with their faces buried in caps and handkerchiefs, remained sitting in a sort of stupid indifference, just preserving animation enough to keep their tobacco burning, and their pipes from falling out of their mouths. Not one of them attempted to walk, though they might all have walked faster than their carriages, and might have kept themselves comfortably warm; but bodily exertion of all kinds is most certainly avoided by the richer classes of the Germans. This indolence may be partly accounted for thus: their sleeping-rooms are generally heated, and the feather-beds, which are used as covers, always kept me – though, whenever it was practicable, I stripped myself to my shirt – in a constant state of profuse perspiration. The Germans, in addition to covering themselves with these beds, very generally sleep in night-dresses of flannel. In fact, they take nothing off but their upper garments, which are not unfrequently exchanged for some sort of jacket or gown. The beds and the rooms together make a sort of sweating bath, more enfeebling, probably, than a frequent use of warm bathing. The effects on myself were always refreshing, but weakening; they did away stiffness and fatigue, but sleep did not give me strength; and it is probable that the effects are the same on the Germans, and even much more powerful. The body is kept in a state of languid health, but all that freshness and vigour of limb which belongs to youth and a hardy people are destroyed. The Germans have no need of exertion, which we find so necessary to promote perspiration, and therefore they have no wish for it, and do not take it. The character of men is the result of all they feel ; and this state of the bodies of the Germans is undoubtedly a cause for some part of their character – for the placidness, stillness, and want of energy, which distinguish them the other nations of Europe. It does not hinder them from thinking, writing, and compiling, day after day, week after week; in fact, it permits them to do all these more than any other people can, for they can do them constantly, and with little fear of injury to their health; but it deprives them of the need and of the wish for active exertion.'[180]

We pass over that part of Mr. H.'s volume which relates to objects of secondary interest, – such as his notice of towns and districts in Hanover, – and must give our remaining space to a few remarks on the general character of his composition; which discovers in various passages the inaccuracy of an unpractised writer. Thus, in point of language we have occasionally such strange phrases as (vol. i. p.47.) "a large quantity of men;" and with regard to the matter of the book a similar charge is in some measure applicable. In his statistical notices, Mr. H. has followed chiefly the work of Hassel, a German geographer, of no mean repute; but he has not bestowed the requisite care on the reduction of foreign measures into English. We were accordingly not a little surprized to find (vol. i. p.19.) the extent of Saxony limited to 1,352 square miles, which does not exceed the average size of an English county, when an inspection of the map exhibits an extent of fully 7,000 square miles, a surface nearly equal to that of Wales.[181] Errors like these form serious deductions from the value of the book, especially when aided by the limited interest of the subject. It is however *de bon augure* as to the author's future productions at a more mature age, for it is marked throughout by a decided disposition to impartiality, and a wish to direct the attention of the reader to objects of serious interest.

Halévy summarised Hodgskin's *Travels* thus:

In his accounts of his travels he found roomfor all the anecdotes demamded by his publisher to make the work amusing. To a public, which for twenty years had almost

---

[180] **Editor's F/N:-** This paragraph ran from page 58 to 60, in the original volume 1 (p.44-45 in this edition)

[181] **Editor's F/N:-** This comment is a bit unfair as the original book does contain an Errata that notes that the on the original page 19 "The number of square miles requires to be multiplied by 4."

forgotten the existence of continental civilisation, he gave an abundance of interesting and novel infomation about North Germany and, in particular, about Hanover with its English king. But, above all, his description and information were accompanied by a sort of running commentary, consisting of a considered criticism of the ideas of government and law. (Halevy, 1956, p.43)

David Stack's summary rather concentrated upon its limitations:

[B]y Hodgskin's own admission the *Travels* suffered from the same stylistic weaknesses that had plagued his earlier works. The first volume was "rather slovenly", and both volumes suffered from "many inaccuracies of style", and an "inelegance of expression". (Stack, 1998, p.62)

As well as the criticisms within some of its reviews:

The reviews of the *Travels*, which appeared in the *Scotsman*, *Literary Gazette*, and *Blackwood's Magazine*, all pick up on this. Their varying degrees of admonishment reflected their differing attitudes to Hodgskin's politics. McCulloch in *The Scotsman*, and [Francis] Place in the *Literary Gazette*, were generally sympathetic. In *Blackwood's*, the Edinburgh advocate and Tory James Lockhart was less enamoured, describing Hodgskin as a "radical traveller and Cockney philosophizer". [182] All three complained of Hodgskin's "rage for philosophising", but only Lockhart noted that the imperative which underlay it was an opposition to all forms of government and systems of law. It was not Hodgskin's intention just to finf fault with German governments. Rather, his "wicked" object was "to abuse and vilify, in the lump, all governments whatever that do or did exist upon the surface of the earth. (ibid, p.63)

The Scotsman's review is, as Stack admits, quite sympathetic, to the degree that it does recommend his work to the reader:

We cannot conclude without again recommending Mr HODGSKIN's book to the notice of our readers. Mr H. has spent three years in his tour; and the circumstance of his having performed oi on foot, and to his intimate acquaintance with the German language, has enabled him

---

[182] **Editor's F/N:-** The original text is "philosopher" rather than "philosophizer". .

to communicate much curious information on subjects of the highest importance, but which are very generally neglected by tourists *en voiture*. Had Mr H. paid more attention to style, and been less infected with the prevailing rage for philosophizing, his book would have been as amusing as it is solid and instructive. But, when the matter is good, the manner is of less importance. It was not so much a well well written, as a fair and accurate account of the institutions, and of the social condition of the people of the North of Germany, that was wanted; and this, we do not hesitate to say, Mr HODGSKIN has supplied. (*The Scotsman*, 12th February 1820, p.50)